SCHOLASTIC YEARBOOK

2025

Illustrations

CHARBAK DIPTA AND PRIYA KURIYAN

SCHOLASTIC
New York Toronto London Auckland
Sydney New Delhi Hong Kong

Editors: Prerna Mathur, Ashley Kumar, and Samayee Gupte

Published by Scholastic India Pvt. Ltd.
A subsidiary of Scholastic Inc., New York, 10012 (USA).
Publishers since 1920, with international operations in Canada, Australia, New Zealand, the United Kingdom, India, and Hong Kong.

For information regarding permission, write to:
Scholastic India Pvt. Ltd.
A-27, Ground Floor, Sigma Centre
Infocity-1, Sector 34, Gurgaon 122001 (India)

First edition: October 2024

ISBN: 978-93-5954-874-6

Printed in India

CONTENTS

EVENTS

☑ **All Major Events**

AUGUST 2023

Parliament on 2 August cleared the Mines and Minerals (Development and Regulation) Amendment Bill 2023 to allow private companies to mine six of the twelve atomic minerals, including lithium.

Congress leader Rahul Gandhi's membership as MP was restored after the Supreme Court stayed his conviction in a defamation case.

The Lok Sabha cleared the Inter-Services Organisations (Command, Control & Discipline) Bill, 2023, empowering military commanders of tri-service organizations with full administrative and disciplinary powers.

Parliament on 7 August approved the Delhi Services Bill, which deals with transfers and postings of senior officers in the Delhi government. The Rajya Sabha passed the bill with a majority after a lengthy debate.

The Election Commission of Pakistan disqualified former Prime Minister Imran Khan from electoral politics for five years following his conviction in a graft case related to gifts retained from the Toshakhana.

The government moved three bills in the Lok Sabha to replace colonial-era codes, aiming to speed up trials, boost conviction rates, and provide relief to victims. These new codes introduce stricter punishment for crimes against women and children, seek to de-congest jails, define terrorism and mob lynching as new offenses, and hold cops accountable for arrests.

India beat Malaysia 4-3 to win their fourth Asian Championships Trophy in hockey.

The Supreme Court released a handbook to guide judges on gender-just language. According to the handbook, terms like 'spinster' will be replaced by 'unmarried woman', 'mistress' by 'woman with whom a man has had romantic or sexual relations outside of marriage', and 'prostitute' by 'sex worker'. 'Street sexual harassment' will replace 'eve teasing'.

A Russian robotic spacecraft headed to the southern region of the moon crashed into the lunar surface. This setback comes from a country that was the first to put a satellite, a man, and a woman in orbit during the Cold War.

On 23 August 2023, India became the first country to land in the southern polar region of the moon, with Chandrayaan-3 making a perfect touchdown.

PEOPLE METER

Former US President Donald Trump was indicted in connection with his efforts to overturn the 2020 national elections, following a federal investigation into his attempts to cling to power after losing the presidency.

Seventeen-year-old Aditi Swami became the youngest-ever world champion in archery, winning the individual women's compound event at the World Archery Championships in Berlin. She also won gold as a member of the women's compound team.

Antim Panghal made history by becoming the first Indian woman wrestler to win back-to-back junior world championship titles, securing a 4-0 victory in the 53 kg division.

Thai property mogul Srettha Thavisin was elected prime minister after a decisive win in a parliamentary election, set to take charge of a coalition government.

Olympic champion Neeraj Chopra became the first Indian to win a gold medal at the World Athletics Championships in Budapest, with his second attempt of 88.17 metres.

DEATHS

Veteran art director Nitin Desai, known for his work in Hindi and Marathi films, was found dead at fifty-seven years old. Desai, who had four National Awards, was best known for his work on *Lagaan* and *Devdas*.

Popular folk singer Gummadi Vittal Rao, also known as Gaddar, passed away at seventy-seven in Hyderabad.

Oscar-winning director William Friedkin, best known for *The French Connection* and *The Exorcist*, passed away at eighty-seven.

Bindeshwar Pathak, Sulabh International founder and crusader against manual scavenging, died at eighty.

Co-founder of Adobe Inc., John Warnock, passed away at eighty-two. He created the company with Charles Geschke in 1982 and served as CEO until 2000.

Actress Seema Deo, who acted in over eighty Hindi and Marathi films, passed away at eighty-one in Mumbai.

Lyricist Dev Kohli, associated with films like *Maine Pyar Kiya* and *Hum Aapke Hain Koun!*, passed away at eighty in Mumbai.

SEPTEMBER 2023

The government formed a six-member panel headed by former President Ram Nath Kovind to explore the feasibility of 'one nation-one election'.

The government granted deemed university status to the National Council of Educational Research and Training (NCERT). It will now be able to award its own graduate, postgraduate, and doctoral degrees.

Jet Airways founder Naresh Goyal was arrested by the Enforcement Directorate (ED) in connection with a ₹ 539 crore Canara Bank loan fraud case. The ED probe is based on a 3 May case filed by CBI on the complaint of Canara Bank.

Over 2,100 people were killed in Morocco's worst earthquake in more than six decades, which also damaged historic buildings in Marrakesh. Thousands of people were injured, most of them critically, in the 6.8 magnitude earthquake.

Former Andhra Pradesh Chief Minister and Telugu Desam President N. Chandrababu Naidu was arrested by the state CID in connection with a ₹ 371 crore scam in the AP Skill Development Corporation. The alleged scam occurred between 2014 and 2019 during Naidu's tenure as chief minister.

G20 भारत 2023 INDIA

India made history on September 9 by achieving consensus on over a hundred issues at the G20 meet, including the Russia-Ukraine war. G20 leaders adopted the New Delhi Leaders' Declaration after over 200 hours of intense negotiations. Prime Minister Narendra Modi's assertion that 'this is not the era of war', as echoed in the Bali Declaration, was also included.

India and Saudi Arabia on 11 September signed an MoU to work towards building an undersea interlink between their electricity grids, renewable power, and green hydrogen capacities.

Twenty-seven years after it was first introduced, the Narendra Modi government on 18 September cleared the women's quota bill. The bill proposed to reserve one-third of seats in Parliament and state legislatures across the country for women.

Canada accused India of playing a role in the murder of Khalistan Tiger Force chief Hardeep Singh Nijjar in the city of Surrey in June, deepening tensions between the two countries.

Statistics released by the US Census Board showed that legal and illegal immigrants together formed 13.9 per cent of the US population of about 33 crore in July 2022. This meant, one in every seven US residents was born outside the country.

PEOPLE METER

Actor-filmmaker R Madhavan was appointed the chairman of the Film and Television Institute of India (FTII) governing council on 1 September.

Tharman Shanmugaratnam, an Indian-origin Singapore-born economist, was elected Singapore President on 1 September.

With seventy-eight goals, Neymar became the top scorer for Brazil, surpassing the legendary three-time World Cup winner Pelé.

Tennis legend Novak Djokovic won a record twenty-fourth Grand Slam title by emerging victorious at the US Open.

Rupert Murdoch stepped down as chairman of the boards of Fox Corp and News Corp, ending a more than seven-decade career. His son, Lachlan Murdoch, will become sole chairman of News Corp and continue as executive chair and CEO of Fox.

Teenage sensation Coco Gauff won the US Open, which was also her first Grand Slam title. The nineteen-year-old American surged to her first major championship by coming back to defeat Aryna Sabalenka in the final.

DEATHS

Geneticist M.S. Swaminathan, who led India's push in the 1960s to become grain surplus and promoted the use of hybrid varieties and chemical fertilisers, passed away in Chennai on 28 September. He was ninety-eight.

Former international umpire Piloo Reporter passed away on 3 September in Thane, aged eighty-four.

Former Zimbabwe captain Heath Streak died on 3 September at the age of forty-nine.

Ian Wilmut, who played a critical part in the creation of Dolly the Cloned Sheep in 1996, passed away at the age of seventy-nine.

British-Irish actor Michael Gambon, best known for playing Professor Albus Dumbledore in the Harry Potter movie franchise, died aged eighty-two.

Egypt-born businessman Mohamed Al Fayed, whose son was killed in a car crash with Princess Diana, passed away at the age of ninety-four.

Actor David McCallum, who became a heartthrob in the hit series The Man From U.N.C.L.E. in the 1960s, passed away due to natural causes at ninety.

OCTOBER 2023

The World Health Organization recommended the use of a second malaria vaccine R21/Matrix-M for children.

The Pakistani government announced a major crackdown on illegal migrants, saying it will expel them. The move caused immediate alarm among foreigners, particularly 1.7 million Afghans who had taken refuge in the country without proper documents.

Israel on 7 October declared war with Hamas after Palestinian militants launched an early morning assault from the Gaza Strip on southern Israel. On the occasion of a major Jewish holiday, they invaded Israeli towns on bikes, trucks, paragliders, and boats, took dozens of civilians and soldiers hostage, and fired thousands of rockets toward cities as far away as Jerusalem. In retaliation, Israel launched airstrikes in Gaza. The war continued till the publishing of this book, reducing vast swathes of the Gaza Strip to rubble, claiming the lives of over 35,000 Palestinians and over 1,200 Israelis.

Undergraduate business education and computer application courses will be brought under the purview of the AICTE, reports in the media said.

Prime Minister Narendra Modi said India will officially bid to host the 2036 Olympics.

In a landmark decision, the Supreme Court rejected the plea to legalise same-sex marriages and extend the right of adoption to queer couples.

India's first semi-high-speed rail system was inaugurated by Narendra Modi, covering the distance from Sahibabad to Duhai Depot in the NCR. This section is part of the 82 km Delhi-Meerut corridor, set to be operational in 2025.

Cricket is making a comeback to the Olympics and is set to be included in the 2028 Los Angeles Games. Squash and baseball are among the other notable inclusions.

India's first all-women police station in Kerala's Kozhikode completed half a century on 25 October.

India became the only fourth Asian country after China, Japan, and South Korea to win over hundred medals in a single Asiad event. India achieved the feat for the first time, winning 107 medals—twenty-eight gold, thirty-eight silver, and forty-one bronze.

PEOPLE METER

Avinash Sable became the first Indian to win gold in men's steeplechase at the Asian Games in Hangzhou. The men's archery team won gold, while the women's team achieved the same feat.

At the Asian Games in Hangzhou, Satwiksairaj Rankireddy and Chirag Shetty won India's first-ever badminton gold.

Imprisoned Iranian activist Narges Mohammadi won the Nobel Peace Prize for her campaign for women's rights and democracy.

Conservative former businessman Christopher Luxon was elected the prime minister of New Zealand after a decisive victory in the country's polls.

Argentina football legend Lionel Messi won a record eighth Ballon d'Or for the best player in the world, pipping Norway's Erling Haaland.

DEATHS

Legendary Indian left-arm spinner Bishan Singh Bedi, who represented the country from 1966 to 1979, passed away aged seventy-seven.

Mohammad Amir Mohammad Khan, better known as the Raja of Mahmudabad, passed away aged eighty.

Former chief election commissioner M S Gill passed away in Delhi at the age of eighty-seven. The polls to the twelfth Lok Sabha in 1998 and the thirteenth Lok Sabha in 1999 were conducted during his tenure.

Actor Matthew Perry—star of the top-rated 1990s US television sitcom *Friends* as Chandler Bing—died at the age of fifty-four.

English soccer icon Bobby Charlton, who survived a plane crash and went on to become an integral part of the country's 1966 World Cup-winning team, passed away at eighty-six.

Nobel-winning poet Louise Glück, the first American-born poet to receive the honour in literature since T.S. Eliot in 1948, passed away in Cambridge aged eighty.

Burt Young, the Oscar-nominated actor best known for playing the role of Paulie in the iconic Rocky series, passed away aged eighty-three.

Richard Roundtree, considered the first Black action movie hero, who starred as private detective John Shaft in the 1971 film Shaft and its sequels in the early 1970s, passed away at eighty-one.

NOVEMBER 2023

The abbreviation of artificial intelligence (AI) was named the Collins Word of the Year for 2023. Lexicographers at Collins Dictionary said use of the term had 'accelerated' and had become the dominant conversation of 2023. Meanwhile, Merriam-Webster picked 'authentic' as its word of the year.

The BSE's market capitalisation went past the USD 4 trillion mark, or ₹ 333 lakh crore, scaling a new all-time high for the Indian market. With a US$ 4 trillion market cap, India became the fifth most-valued market in the world after the US, China, Japan, and Hong Kong. The Indian government decided to extend the free foodgrain scheme—the PM Garib Kalyan Ann Yojna (PMGKAY)—benefiting over 80 crore poor people, for five years.

The Union Government unveiled draft norms to help earn 'green credits' that can be generated via water harvesting and tree plantation in different states, and Union Territories.

The US approved the world's first vaccine for chikungunya: Ixchiq.

A portion of an under-construction tunnel of the Char Dham all-weather highway project collapsed between Silkayara and Polgaon villages in Uttarkashi, Uttarakhand. Forty-one people trapped for seventeen days were rescued by teams from the NDRF, SDRF, ITBP, and BRO. After multiple failed attempts to clear the debris, rat-hole miners manually dug through the rubble, successfully ending the marathon rescue mission.

The Indian team suffered a heartbreaking defeat in the cricket World Cup final, as they lost to Australia in Ahmedabad. The win gave Australia their sixth World Cup title.

Wealthy countries have decreased the amount of money they commit for helping developing countries cope with the effects of climate change, the United Nations said in a report.

Geert Wilders' Party for Freedom, a far-right outfit, became the single-largest party in the Netherlands House of Representatives, after winning 37 of the 150 seats. The performance of the party, which advocates banning the Quran, closing Islamic schools, and entirely halting the acceptance of asylum seekers, is a tectonic deviation from the country's traditionally liberal governments.

The Indian government decided to extend the free foodgrain scheme—the PM Garib Kalyan Ann Yojna (PMGKAY)—benefiting over 80 crore poor people, for five years.

PEOPLE METER

Courting India: England, Mughal India and the Origins of Empire, the debut novel of Indian-origin author Nandini Das won the eleventh British Academy Book Prize for Global Cultural Understanding.

Virat Kohli scored the forty-ninth one-day international (ODI) hundred on his 35th birthday to equal Sachin Tendulkar's world record of centuries in the format. Kohli achieved the feat against South Africa in the World Cup.

Sri Lanka senior player Angelo Mathews became the first international cricketer to be 'timed out' during the World Cup game against Bangladesh.

Javier Milei, a far-right libertarian was elected the Argentina president.

Irish writer Paul Lynch won the Booker Prize for his dystopian novel *Prophet Song* which tries to show the unrest in Western democracies and their indifference towards disasters.

Actor-comic Vir Das won the International Emmy Award in the best comedy category for his stand-up special *Vir Das: Landing.*

DEATHS

Prithvi Raj Singh Oberoi, the doyen of Indian hospitality and Chairman Emeritus of the Oberoi Group passed away on 14 November. He was ninety-four years old.

Former US Secretary of State Henry Kissinger, who played a pivotal role in US foreign policy during the Cold War, passed away at 100.

Dr Sengamedu Srinivasa Badrinath, an ophthalmologist who founded eyecare hospital Sankara Netralaya, died in Chennai. He was eighty-three.

Frank Borman, the commander of Apollo 8, whose crew became the first men to orbit the moon and capture the iconic 'Earthrise' image, passed away at ninety-five.

Former Reserve Bank of India Governor S Venkitaramanan, who served as finance secretary, died at ninety-two.

Charles Munger, who joined Warren Buffet as they transformed a textile company into renowned investment firm Berkshire Hathaway, passed away aged ninety-nine.

First woman Supreme Court judge and former Tamil Nadu governor Justice Fathima Beevi passed away in Kerala at ninety-six.

Dame Antonia Susan Duffy, who wrote under the pen name A.S. Byatt, passed away aged eighty-seven.

Renowned art historian and writer B. N. Goswamy passed away in Chandigarh at the age of ninety.

DECEMBER 2023

BJP defeated Congress in the assembly elections in Madhya Pradesh, Rajasthan, and Chhattisgarh, while Congress won in Telangana, dislodging two-term Chief Minister K Chandrasekhar Rao of BRS.

Penguins fall asleep thousands of times during each day, each just about a few seconds long, according to the report published in the journal *Science*.

'Rizz'—a colloquial term defined as 'style, charm or attractiveness'—was named as the word of the year for 2023 by Oxford University Press.

Bahujan Samaj Party (BSP) chief and former UP Chief Minister Mayawati designated her twenty-eight-year-old nephew Akash Anand as her political heir.

In a breach of security on 13 December, the twenty-second anniversary of the 2001 terror attack on Parliament, two men jumped down from the visitors' gallery of the Lok Sabha and opened coloured-smoke canisters. Four persons were held for their role in the incident.

The Lok Sabha on 20 December passed the Bharatiya Nyaya (Second) Sanhita, Bharatiya Nagarik Suraksha (Second) Sanhita, and Bharatiya Sakshya (Second) Bill, replacing the colonial-era Indian Penal Code, 1860; the Code of Criminal Procedure, 1898; and the Indian Evidence Act of 1872, respectively.

Eight Indian Navy veterans facing the death penalty in Qatar were reprieved after a higher court in that country commuted their sentences to an unspecified number of years in prison.

Barely a week after defeating England, the Indian women's team beat Australia for the first time. This was the eleventh Test match between the two sides, since the first in 1977. The Harmanpreet Kaur-led side achieved the feat in a Test at the Wankhede.

World population grew 75 million people in the last year and on New Year's Day, it will stand at more than 8 billion people, the US Census Bureau said. At the start of 2024, 4.3 births and two deaths are expected worldwide every second, according to the bureau.

PEOPLE METER

Bhajan Lal Sharma was made the chief minister of Rajasthan after BJP's win in the state, while Vishnu Deo Sai was named as the chief minister of Chhattisgarh.

Head of the Dawoodi Bohra community Dr Syedna Mufaddal Saifuddin received Pakistan's highest civilian honour, the 'Nishan-e-Pakistan'.

Abdel Fattah al-Sisi swept to a third six-year term as Egypt's President, winning 89.6 per cent of votes. However, Sisi did not face any serious challengers in the country's presidential elections.

The Lok Sabha expelled Trinamool Congress' Mahua Moitra after she was found guilty of 'unethical conduct' for accepting cash and gifts from businessman Darshan Hiranandani in lieu of asking questions in the House targeting his rival, the Adani Group.

Kolkata Knight Riders 'bought' Mitchell Starc for a record ₹ 24.75 crore in the Indian Premier League (IPL) auction, while Australia cricket captain Pat Cummins was 'sold' for ₹ 20.5 crore.

DEATHS

Shri Rashtriya Rajput Karni Sena president Sukhdev Singh Gogamedi, aged forty, was shot dead at his home in Jaipur.

Nayeem Sayyed, more popularly known as 'Junior Mehmood', who was a popular child actor and a dancing star in the 1960s and 1970s, passed away due to stomach cancer at sixty-seven.

Oscar-nominated actor Ryan O'Neal passed away at the age of eighty-two.

Andre Braugher, an Emmy Award-winning actor best known for playing stoic police officers on the television shows *Brooklyn Nine-Nine* and *Homicide: Life on the Street*, passed away. He was sixty-one.

Kuwait's ruling emir, Sheikh Nawaf Al Ahmad Al Sabah, passed away aged eighty-six.

South Korean actor Lee Sun-kyun who received global attention with his performance in the Oscar-winning film Parasite, was found dead in Seoul. He was forty-eight.

Tamil film star and DMDK chief Vijayakant passed away at the age of seventy-one.

JANUARY 2024

ISRO launched XPoSat (X-ray Polarimeter Satellite), the country's first satellite to research black holes and other celestial objects. With the launch, India became the second country in the world after the US to send a specialized astronomy observatory to study black holes and neutron stars in the galaxy.

The year 2023 was the second warmest ever recorded in India since 1901 when the recording of such data began. Extreme weather events claimed 2,376 lives, the Indian Meteorological Department (IMD) said.

The Indian cricket team became the first Asian side to win a Test match at Newlands, as the Rohit Sharma-led side beat South Africa in the shortest Test match in cricket history.

India placed a solar space observatory at a vantage point about 1.5 million km from earth to study the Sun. Equipped with a coronagraph, Aditya-L1 is designed and developed by the Indian Space Research Organisation (ISRO) and various other Indian Space Research Institutes to study the solar atmosphere.

Jharkhand Chief Minister Hemant Soren was arrested by the Enforcement Directorate (ED) in a corruption case.

Pench Tiger Reserve in Maharashtra earned the distinction of being named India's first 'International Dark Sky Park' by the International Dark-Sky Association (IDA), a global movement to promote astronomy.

The idol of Ram Lalla was consecrated in Ayodhya on 22 January, bringing to an end a saga that went on for centuries.

A diplomatic row erupted after Maldives ministers made sarcastic remarks on Prime Minister Narendra Modi over his visit to Lakshadweep, wherein he promoted the pristine islands and urged Indians to travel there. Three Maldives ministers were suspended and a huge number of Indians, including celebrities, cancelled their trips to the island nation.

Canada—one of the preferred destinations for Indian students and workers—decided to cap the number of student intake from around the world at 3.6 lakh for 2024 due to housing shortages and healthcare issues.

A new execution method was used for the first time in the US since the lethal injection was introduced in 1982. A man in Alabama was put to death using nitrogen gas. Kenneth Eugene Smith, fifty-eight, was sentenced to death for a murder for cash over thirty years ago.

PEOPLE METER

Lily Gladstone received the best actress award at the Golden Globe for her performance in the film *Killers of the Flower Moon*. She became the first indigenous person to achieve the feat.

Cillian Murphy was named the best actor for his role in the film *Oppenheimer* at the Golden Globes. The film, which was written, directed, and produced by Christopher Nolan, won five awards at the event.

Sheikh Hasina won the fourth straight term as Bangladesh's prime minister as her party Awami League won more than two-hundred of the three-hundred seats in the country's general elections.

Former Bhutanese Prime Minister Tshering Tobgay's party won the general elections in the country with almost a two-thirds majority.

Lai Ching-te, whom China had referred to as an 'instigator of war', was elected the president of Taiwan.

Socialist icon Karpoori Thakur was conferred the Bharat Ratna, the country's highest civilian honour. Thakur, as the chief minister of Bihar, was the first to implement an OBC quota with a sub-quota for Most Backward Classes (MBCs) in the north in 1978.

DEATHS

Brazilian soccer legend and former coach Mário Jorge Lobo Zagallo, a four-time World Cup champion as a player and coordinator of the national team, passed away at ninety-two.

Franz Beckenbauer, who lifted the World Cup for West Germany as a footballer in 1974 and coach in 1990, passed away aged seventy-eight.

Hindustani classical singer and music maestro Ustad Rashid Khan passed away in Kolkata on 9 January. He was fifty-five and was suffering from cancer.

Renowned classical singer and an icon of the Kirana gharana Dr Prabha Atre passed away in Pune. The Padma Vibhushan recipient was ninety-two years old.

Former world pole vault champion Shawn Barber of Canada passed away aged twenty-nine at his home in Texas.

Rana Talwar—the first Indian and Asian to helm a global bank—passed away at the age of seventy-six. He was the CEO of Standard Chartered Bank.

FEBRUARY 2024

Finance Minister Nirmala Sitharaman presented the interim Budget before the country's general elections in April-June.

The Lok Sabha passed 'The Public Examinations (Prevention of Unfair Means) Bill, 2024' which lays down strong punitive measures to curb paper leaks and other malpractices in competitive examinations.

The world experienced its warmest January on record, marking the first twelve-month period in which temperatures averaged more than 1.5 degrees above pre-industrial times.

Known for multiple flip-flops, Bihar Chief Minister Nitish Kumar decided to switch sides and return to the NDA fold, which is spearheaded by the BJP.

In a major diplomatic win for India, Qatar released former Indian Navy personnel who were sentenced to death, which was later commuted to imprisonment.

The Pakistan Muslim League-Nawaz (PML-N) and Pakistan People's Party entered into a coalition days after elections were held across Pakistan. Shahbaz Sharif became the prime minister.

The Supreme Court on 15 February struck down the electoral bond scheme introduced by the BJP government in 2018, calling it unconstitutional. The scheme allowed corporate contributions to political parties anonymously.

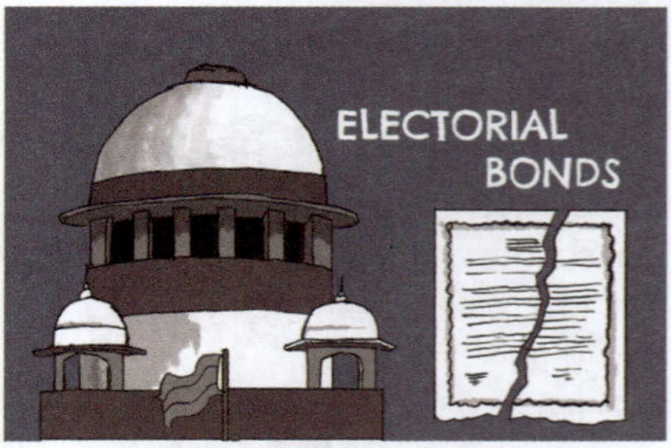

Greece became the first Orthodox Christian country to legalise same-sex marriage and give equal parental rights to same-sex couples.

NASA's commercial partner, Intuitive Machines (IM), made history by becoming the first private firm to land on the moon, marking the first American lunar soft landing in fifty-two years.

A record twenty-three candidates scored 100 percentile (NTA score 100) in the first session of Paper 1 of JEE-Main for admission to BE and BTech courses. Telangana accounted for the highest number of toppers with seven.

Hungary's Parliament voted to approve Sweden as a new member of Nato. Sweden Prime Minister Ulf Kristersson said the country is leaving 200 years of neutrality and military non-alignment behind to join Nato and defend itself amid the prolonged Russian aggression in Ukraine.

PEOPLE METER

BJP patriarch Lal Krishna Advani was conferred the Bharat Ratna, India's highest civilian honour. This was seen as a recognition of the contributions of the veteran BJP leader, who played a crucial role in turning the party into a major political force.

Former Prime Minister Chaudhary Charan Singh was awarded the Bharat Ratna posthumously.

Jasprit Bumrah became the first Indian pacer to top the ICC's Test rankings.

Senior spinner Ravichandran Ashwin became only the second Indian bowler to take 500 Test wickets. He also became the first Indian all-rounder, and the only third overall, to take 500 Test wickets and score 3,000 runs for his side.

Renowned scholar and writer Jagadguru Rambhadracharya and veteran poet-lyricist Sampooran Singh Kalra 'Gulzar' were named the recipients of the 58th Jnanpith Award for 2023.

DEATHS

Alexei Navalny, Russian President Vladimir Putin's fiercest critic, died in a prison in the country. He was forty-seven.

Actress Kavitha Choudhary, known for playing an IPS officer in the serial *Udaan*, passed away after suffering a heart attack. She was sixty-seven.

Former Netherlands Prime Minister Dries van Agt died by euthanasia along with his wife. Both were ninety-three.

Arguably one of the most popular radio announcers in India's history, Ameen Sayani, who achieved immense fame across the nation for his programme Binaca Geetmala, passed away at ninety-one.

Eminent jurist and senior Supreme Court advocate Fali Nariman—a recipient of the Padma Bhushan and the Padma Vibhushan—passed away aged ninety-five.

Popular ghazal singer Pankaj Udhas, who lent his voice to songs of many films, passed away at the age of seventy-two. Some of his iconic songs included 'Chitthi Aai Hai', 'Chandi Jaisa Rang Hai Tera', and 'Na Kajre Ki Dhar', among many more.

Suhani Bhatnagar, who played the role of young Babita Phogat in Aamir Khan-starrer *Dangal*, passed away at nineteen. Suhani was suffering from dermatomyositis.

Renowned Jain seer Acharya Vidyasagar Maharaj attained samadhi through the practice of 'Sallekhna', a voluntary fast unto death for spiritual purification.

Iconic chef Imtiaz Qureshi, credited with reviving the old Lucknowi tradition of dum pukht style cooking, passed away at ninety-three.

MARCH 2024

A ship attacked by Yemen's Houthi rebels sank in the Red Sea, becoming the first vessel to be fully destroyed as part of their 'campaign' against Israel's war in Gaza.

China announced a 7.2 per cent increase in its defence budget for the next fiscal. The country's defence budget is the second highest in the world after the US at 1.6 trillion yuan ($222 billion).

Sweden formally joined NATO on 7 March to become its thirty-second member.

President Joe Biden and former President Donald Trump secured delegates to clinch the nominations for the Democrats and the Republicans, respectively, for the US presidential elections. This will be the first time in sixty-eight years the polls in the US will see a rematch.

The State Bank of India, following the Supreme Court's orders, published the details of the electoral bonds. The BJP was the highest recipient of the donations, followed by the Trinamul Congress, and the Congress. Future Gaming was the biggest donor, with ₹ 1,365 crore.

India beat England in the fifth Test to win the series 4-1 and remain unbeaten at home for a record-extending seventeen consecutive series.

Royal Challengers Bangalore (RCB) women's team won the Women's Premier League by defeating Delhi Capitals in the final.

Finland remained the world's happiest country for a seventh straight year, the UN-sponsored World Happiness Report said. Nordic countries kept their places among the ten most cheerful, with Denmark, Iceland, and Sweden following Finland. India ranked at 126.

The 2023 World Air Quality report by Swiss tech company IQAir ranked India's air quality as the third worst in the world after Bangladesh and Pakistan. The report ranked Delhi as the worst capital and Bihar's Begusarai as the most polluted city globally.

PEOPLE METER

Vladimir Putin won his fifth term as the Russian president and is set to surpass Joseph Stalin's tenure at the helm and become the longest-serving Russian president in 200 years.

Delhi Chief Minister Arvind Kejriwal was arrested by the Enforcement Directorate in the Delhi liquor scam case. Kejriwal became the first sitting chief minister to be arrested.

Tarun Kumar Vashisth, forty-two, became the first visually impaired person to earn a PhD at IIM Ahmedabad.

Writer Amitav Ghosh received the Erasmus Prize 2024 for his writings on climate change. Erasmus Prize, launched in 1958 and awarded annually to a person or institution for contributions to humanities, social sciences, or arts in Europe and beyond, consists of a cash prize of 150,000 euros.

Former IAS officers Gyanesh Kumar and Sukhbir Singh Sandhu were appointed as election commissioners, barely a month before the Lok Sabha elections.

DEATHS

Japanese manga comic creator Akira Toriyama, best known for his *Dragon Ball* series that inspired widely popular films, video games, and TV shows, passed away. He was sixty-eight.

Daniel Kahneman, who pioneered a psychologically-based branch of the field that led to a Nobel in economic science in 2002, passed away at ninety.

Louis Gosset Jr, who won an Oscar as the best supporting actor for An Officer and a Gentleman, died aged eighty-seven. Gossett was the first Black performer to win an Oscar in the category.

Eric Carmen, the iconic lead singer of the Raspberries, who gave voice to multiple hits such as 'All By Myself' and 'Hungry Eyes', passed away. He was seventy-four.

Former chairman of the Pakistan Cricket Board, Shaharyar Khan, passed away at the age of eighty-nine.

Ramakrishna Math and Mission president Swami Smarananananda ji Maharaj died at a Kolkata hospital. He was ninety-four.

Eminent mathematician of Indian origin, Dr. T. N. Subramaniam, passed away in Michigan at the age of seventy-six.

APRIL 2024

India ranked first among countries with the highest percentage of dope offenders in 2022, the World Anti-Doping Agency (WADA) said.

The Supreme Court granted bail to Aam Admi Party MP Sanjay Singh after the Enforcement Directorate did not oppose the leader's petition. Singh had been in jail for six months in connection with an alleged scam relating to changes in excise policy.

The ruling BJP released its Lok Sabha election manifesto, promising to turn India into a developed country by 2047, but avoided offering freebies.

Israel dismissed two officers for killing seven aid workers in Gaza in an air raid after mistaking them as Hamas gunmen.

The Supreme Court disapproved its April 2019 order imposing a blanket restriction on overhead power transmission lines in 90,000 sq km. The previous verdict had crippled solar energy generating units in prime harvesting areas in Rajasthan and Gujarat and threatened to derail India's target of increasing renewable energy capacity to 450 GW by 2030.

For the first time in its 128-year history, forty-eight Olympic gold medal winners at the Athletics events in Paris will receive $50,000 each. The announcement was made by World Athletics President Sebastian Coe.

Iran launched a large aerial attack on Israel on 14 April, firing at least 300 drones and missiles. It was the first direct attack from Iranian territory after decades of shadow warfare between the two countries.

Vast swathes of Dubai went under water as the city received an unprecedented amount of rainfall (255 mm) in a single day on 17 April. While some said the deluge was triggered by cloud seeding, scientists blamed climate change.

The US blocked the UN Security Council from moving forward on a Palestinian bid to be recognized as a full member state at the UN.

The seven-phase Lok Sabha elections across India began on 19 April.

The Supreme Court ruled against the return to the ballot system of voting and said the distrust in EVMs was blind.

PEOPLE METER

Novak Djokovic, thirty-six, surpassed Roger Federer as the oldest man to become the number one in ATP Tour's rankings.

Mohamed Muizzu's pro-China People's National Congress (PNC) won the Maldives election with a heavy majority, winning over sixty seats in the ninety-three-member Parliament.

India's men's recurve team of Dhiraj Bommadevara, Tarundeep Rai, and Pravin Jadhav defeated Olympic champions to win the gold medal in the archery World Cup after fourteen years.

Seventeen-year-old Gukesh Dommaraju became the youngest chess player to win the Candidates tournament. Gukesh, who broke a forty-year-old record held by Garry Kasparov, will now get a chance to challenge China's world champion Ding Liren later in the year.

Naima Khatoon became the first woman to be appointed as the Vice-Chancellor of Aligarh Muslim University (AMU) in its 123-year history.

DEATHS

Senior commander in the Quds Force General Mohamad Reza Zahedi, sixty-five, who oversaw Iran's covert military operations in Syria and Lebanon, was killed in Israeli airstrikes on the Iranian consulate in Damascus.

Michael Dewayne, forty-one, who was convicted of shooting and killing two people, including an Indian, in Oklahoma in 2002, was executed in the US.

Nobel Laureate British physicist Peter Higgs, who shed light on 'Dark Matter' and proposed the existence of 'God Particle' passed away. He was ninety-four.

OJ Simpson, former football star and actor, who was acquitted of killing his former wife and her friend in a sensational trial in 1995 in Los Angeles, passed away due to prostate cancer. He was seventy-six.

Italian fashion designer Roberto Cavalli, popular as the 'king of leopard print', died at the age of eighty-three.

The oldest living conjoined twins, Lori and George Schappell, passed away aged sixty-two. The twins had distinct brains but were joined at the skull.

MAY 2024

In a sudden escalation in the tariff war between the US and China, President Joe Biden sharply hiked tariffs on Chinese electric vehicles (EVs), cells and chips, etc.

The national capital recorded its highest-ever temperature of 49.9°C on 28 May, nine notches above normal. A day later, a maximum temperature of 52.9°C at Mungeshpur in Delhi sent shockwaves across the country.

As Israel's offensive in Gaza entered the seventh month, the US, for the first time, acknowledged that civilians have died by bombs it supplied.

The Supreme Court on 10 May granted a twenty-one-day bail to Delhi Chief Minister Arvind Kejriwal, who had been lodged in Tihar Jail since 1 April on charges of corruption and money laundering in the Delhi government's excise policy for 2021-22. The bail allowed Kejriwal to campaign for the ongoing Lok Sabha elections.

The United Nations General Assembly on 10 May overwhelmingly adopted a resolution declaring that Palestinians qualify for full-member status at the United Nations. The resolution was approved by a vote of 143 to 9, with twenty-five nations abstaining. India voted in favour of the resolution, while the US voted against it.

Richard 'Rick' Slayman—the first recipient of a genetically modified pig kidney transplant—died nearly two months after he underwent the procedure.

Former US President Donald Trump was found guilty of falsifying documents to cover up a sex scandal that could have derailed his presidential campaign in 2016. With this, Trump became the first former US president to be convicted of a crime.

The Reserve Bank of India moved about 100 tonnes of gold from the UK to its vaults in India. This was the first time since 1991 that such a large amount of gold had been brought to India.

At 250,000, Indians made up the highest number of people to immigrate to Britain in 2023, followed by Nigerians, Chinese, and Pakistanis.

Prajwal Revanna, JDS MP and grandson of former Prime Minister HD Deve Gowda, was arrested in Bengaluru on his return from Germany in connection with sexually assaulting three women.

PEOPLE METER

Filmmaker Payal Kapadia scripted history as her film *All We Imagine as Light* won the Grand Prix award at the 2024 Cannes.

Vladimir Putin started his fifth term as the Russian president for the next six years. The US and its allies boycotted the event.

Slovakia PM Robert Fico was shot multiple times at a political event, leaving him very seriously injured. Seventy-one-year-old Juraj C. was arrested for the crime. After battling life-threatening injuries, Fico made his first public appearance more than a month later.

Andhra-born Gopi Thotakura became the first Indian citizen to enter space as a tourist. He was part of the crew for Blue Origin's NS-25 mission.

Kairos, a novel written by Jenny Erpenbeck about a love affair in the final years of East Germany, won the International Booker Prize.

Melinda Gates resigned as the co-chair of the Bill and Melinda Gates Foundation to focus on the groups working on women and family issues.

DEATHS

Iranian President Ebrahim Raisi was killed in a helicopter crash, along with foreign minister Hossein Amirabdollahian on 19 May. The incident took place when they were returning from a visit to the border with Azerbaijan in Iran's northwest. Raisi, sixty-three, had met with Azerbaijan's President Ilham Aliyev earlier in the day.

British actor Bernard Hill, best known for his supporting roles in *Titanic* and *The Lord of the Rings* trilogy, died at the age of seventy-nine.

Renowned mathematician and one of the most successful Wall Street investors ever, James 'Jim' Simmons, passed away at eighty-six.

Roger Corman, the Oscar-winning 'King of the Bs' who helped turn out low-budget classics such as Little Shop of Horrors and Attack of the Crab Monsters, passed away at ninety-eight.

Former Bihar Deputy Chief Minister and senior BJP leader Sushil Kumar Modi passed away after a battle with cancer. He was seventy-two.

Nobel-winning Canadian writer Alice Munro, a globally acclaimed master of the short story, died at ninety-two.

Paul Auster, a novelist, screenwriter, and filmmaker who rose to fame in the 1980s and became one of the signature New York writers of his generation, passed away. He was seventy-seven.

JUNE 2024

The seven-phase 2024 Lok Sabha elections ended on 1 June with lower turnouts as compared with 2019.

On 4 June, Narendra Modi became only the second person to remain prime minister for three straight terms after Jawaharlal Nehru as the BJP-led NDA crossed the majority mark of 272 in the Lok Sabha elections. The National Democratic Alliance (NDA) won 291 seats, while the opposition, led by the Congress, won 234.

Sensex surged a record 2,507 points on June 3, registering its biggest gain in a day, a day after exit polls forecast a third term for BJP-led NDA with brute majority. Sensex would go on to tumble a day later as the actual results were different from what was predicted.

Om Birla was elected the Speaker of the 18th Lok Sabha.

The BJP won the assembly elections in Odisha and Arunachal Pradesh that were held alongside the LS polls. The BJP's victory in Odisha brought to an end the twenty-four-year regime of popular Chief Minister Naveen Patnaik.

The Supreme Court on 11 June said the sanctity of NEET-UG 2024 exam was compromised. The top court sought explanation from National Testing Agency (NTA) on reported irregularities in conducting the test, including allegations of a paper leak.

President Emmanuel Macron dissolved the French Parliament and called for snap elections after his party was heavily defeated by the far right in European Parliament elections.

The government replaced National Testing Agency (NTA) Director General Subodh Singh amid a controversy over alleged irregularities in competitive exams NEET and NET.

Twenty-three people were killed in Kenya after police fired at rioters who were protesting the government's decision to raise taxes. A part of the country's Parliament building was set on fire.

India won the T20 cricket World Cup in a nail-biting thriller by defeating South Africa by just 7 runs in the final, to end a global trophy drought that lasted eleven years (2013 Champions Trophy). India last won a World Cup in 2011 (50 overs), while brought home the inaugural T20 WC title in the inaugural edition in 2007. Jasprit Bumrah was declared the player of the tournament for his phenomenal performance with the ball, while Virat Kohli was adjudged the player of the match in the final. Three of India's biggest players—Rohit Sharma, Virat Kohli, and Ravindra Jadeja—announced their retirements after winning the trophy.

PEOPLE METER

Claudia Sheinbaum, a climate scientist and former mayor of Mexico City, became the first woman to be elected president of her country. Sheinbaum, sixty-one, won, in what the Mexico authorities said saw the highest number of voters turning up to cast their franchise in the country's history.

Puja Tomar, twenty-eight, became the first Indian MMA fighter to win at UFC.

Women's world no. 1 tennis player Iga Swiatek defeated Italian Jasmine Paolini to win the French Open. This was Swiatek's fourth title.

All India Football Federation sacked senior men's team head coach Igor Stimac after India failed to go past the second round of the FIFA World Cup qualifiers.

Eighteen-year-old Divya Deshmukh defeated Bulgaria's Beloslava Keasteva to win the title at the World Junior Girls' Chess Championship.

After two aborted bids, two NASA scientists, including Sunita Williams, lift off for ISS in Starliner spacecraft built by Boeing.

DEATHS

Cherukuri Ramoji Rao, who dominated the Telugu media and film industry for half a century, and founded his Ramoji Film City, passed away at eighty-seven.

Malawi's Vice-President Saulos Klaus Chilima, fifty-one, was killed in a plane crash. Nine others in the aircraft were also killed.

French film actress Anouk Aimee, best known for Claude Lelouch's 1966 romance A Man and a Woman, passed away. She was ninety-two.

Former India fast bowler David Johnson passed away after falling from the fourth floor of his Bengaluru apartment. He was fifty-two.

Legendary actor Donald Sutherland, was a part of many memorable performances in films, including The Dirty Dozen, Klute, The Eagle Has Landed, and The Hunger Games passed away at the age of eighty-eight.

JULY 2024

The ancient practice of yoga was included in future Asian Games According to media reports, yoga is set to be included as a demonstration sport at the 2026 Asian Games to be held in Nagoya, Japan, and is likely to become a competitive sport with medal rounds at Doha in 2030.

French elections threw up an unprecedented situation with no party in clear majority in the 577-member House. The results to the country's elections gave a broad leftist coalition to the National Assembly, the more important of the two houses of Parliament.

Nepal saw a change in regime with former Prime Minister K P Sharma Oli returning to power after incumbent PM Pushpa Kamal Dahal 'Prachanda' failed to win a trust vote in Parliament.

Spain beat England 2-1 in football to become champions of Europe. This was the fourth Curo for the country. In Miami, world champions Argentina, led by legendary Lionel Messi, retained the Copa America by defeating Colombia 1-0.

Over 105 people were killed, and many more injured in violent clashes in Bangladesh against job quotas. A nationwide curfew was imposed as protests spread throughout the day.

Labour leader Sir Keir Starmer became the new prime minister of Britain after his party won more than 400 of the 650 seats in the general election. The victory brought the Labour Party back to office after fourteen years in opposition.

Republican presidential candidate Donald Trump picked Senator JD Vance as the party's vice-presidential candidate for the upcoming US presidential polls. Vance is the husband of Usha Chilukuri Vance, a person of Indian origin, whose parents moved to the US in the 1980s.

Former US President Donald Trump survived an assassination attempt as a bullet fired at him during a rally missed him by centimetres, cutting through his ears. The assailant was shot dead, and another person were killed in the incident.

Over 120 people were killed in a stampede at a satsang conducted by a local godman 'Bhole Baba' at Hathras in Uttar Pradesh.

The world witnessed an unprecedented IT outage on 19 July, affecting almost every business—from airlines to healthcare, financial markets and government agencies running Microsoft computers. The chaos was triggered after CrowdStrike, a cloud-based cybersecurity platform whose software is used by scores of industries around the world, released a flawed update of its Falcon Sensor software.

PEOPLE METER

Hemant Soren returned as the Jharkhand Chief Minister after he was released on bail in the alleged money laundering case which saw him go to jail.

Rahul Dravid officially retired as the coach of the Indian cricket team following India's T20 Worlde Cup win. Former cricketer Gautam Gambhir, who played a crucial part in India's T20 World Cup win in 2007 and in the 50 Over WC three years later, was appointed the coach.

Legendary England cricketer James Anderson retired from Test cricket after taking 704 wickets—the highest by a fast bowler. He is the third highest wicket taker in Tests after Muthiah Muralitharan and Shane Warne.

With his 9th win at Silverstone, Lewis Hamilton broke Legendary Michael Schumacher's record for most wins in a single track in F1 history.

Barbora Krejcikova won her second women's singles Grand Slam title at the Wimbledon, defeating Jasmine Paolini. Carlos Alcaraz defeated Novak Djokovic to lift the men's singles title.

DEATHS

Pal Enger, a Norwegian soccer player-turned celebrity art thief who pulled off the 1994 heist of Edvard Munch's famed 'The Scream' painting from the National Gallery in Oslo, passed away. He was fifty-seven.

Pro-Khalistan terrorist Gajinder Singh, wanted in India since he hijacked Delhi-Srinagar Indian Airlines flight IC 423 in 1981, died at seventy-three in Lahore.

Movie star Shelley Duvall, known for her parts in films of Robert Altman and who co-starred in Stanley Kubrick's *The Shining*, died at seventy-five.

Former Indian cricketer and coach Anshuman Gaekwad passed away after losing a long battle with cancer. He was seventy-one.

AWARDS

☑ INTERNATIONAL AND NATIONAL AWARDS

The Padma Awards 2024

The 'Padmas'—Padma Vibhushan, Padma Bhushan and Padma Shri—are India's highest civilian awards, awarded for exceptional and distinguished service in all fields and disciplines. This year 132 awards were given.

Padma Vibhushan

- Vyjayantimala Bali - **Art**
- Konidela Chiranjeevi - **Art**
- M Venkaiah Naidu - **Public Affairs**
- Bindeshwar Pathak (Posthumous) - **Social Work**
- Padma Subrahmanyam - **Art**

Padma Subrahmanyam

Padma Bhushan

- M Fathima Beevi (Public Affairs)
- Hormusji N Cama (Literature & Education - Journalism)
- Mithun Chakraborty (Art)
- Sitaram Jindal (Trade & Industry)
- Young Liu (Trade & Industry)
- Ashwin Balachand Mehta (Medicine)
- Satyabrata Mookherjee (Public Affairs)
- Ram Naik (Public Affairs)
- Tejas Madhusudan Patel (Medicine)
- Olanchery Rajagopal (Public Affairs)
- Dattatray Ambadas Mayaloo alias Rajdutt (Art)
- Togdan Rinpoche (Others - Spiritualism)
- Pyarelal Sharma (Art)
- Chandreshwar Prasad Thakur (Medicine)
- Usha Uthup (Art)
- Vijaykanth (Art)
- Kundan Vyas (Literature & Education - Journalism)

PADMA SHRI

110 people were awarded Padma Shri this year. Notable awardees include India's first female elephant trainer and caretaker, Parbati Baruah, an international mallakhamb coach, Uday Vishwanath Deshpande, as well as a bamboo craftsman of the Lepcha tribe, Jordan Lepcha.

Parbati Baruah

NOBEL PRIZE 2023

Nobel Prize for Economics: U.S. economist Claudia Goldin won this year's Nobel Prize for Economics for research on the historical and contemporary role of women in the labour market, revealing major sources impacting the current gender gap.

Claudia Goldin

Nobel Prize for Peace: Imprisoned Iranian human rights advocate Narges Mohammadi won the 2023 Nobel Peace Prize for fighting against the oppression of women in Iran and promoting freedom for all.

Nobel Prize for Literature: Norwegian author Jon Fosse won the 2023 Nobel Prize in Literature for his 'innovative plays and prose' and diverse body of work that give voice to the unspeakable.

Nobel Prize in Chemistry: Scientists Moungi G. Bawendi, Louis E. Brus, and Aleksey Yekimov won the 2023 Nobel Prize in Chemistry for the discovery and development of quantum dots, the smallest components of nanotechnology.

Nobel Prize in Physics: Scientists Pierre Agostini, Ferenc Krausz, and Anne L'Huillier won the 2023 Nobel Prize in Physics for experiments to study electron dynamics in matter.

Nobel Prize in Physiology or Medicine: Katalin Karikó and Drew Weissman won the 2023 Nobel Prize in Physiology or Medicine for their research that enabled the development of effective mRNA vaccines against COVID-19 at an unprecedented rate.

PRADHAN MANTRI RASHTRIYA BAL PURASKAR 2024

The award is bestowed for different categories which include innovation, scholastic, social service, art and culture, science and technology, sports and bravery. The award was presented in January 2024 to nineteen recipients:

Art & Culture: Anushka Pathak (Uttar Pradesh), Arijeet Banerjee (West Bengal), Armaan Ubhrani (Chattisgarh), Hetvi Kantibhai Khimsuriya (Gujarat), Ishfaq Hamid (Jammu & Kashmir), Md Hussain (Bihar), Pendyala Laxmi Priya (Telangana)

Innovation: Suhani Chauhan (Delhi)

Social Service: Avnish Tiwari (Madhya Pradesh), Garima (Haryana), Jyotsna Aktar (Tripura), Saiyam Mazumder (Assam)

Sports: Aaditya Yadav (Uttar Pradesh), Charvi A (Karnataka), Jesicca Neyi Saring (Arunachal Pradesh), Linthoi Chanambam (Manipur), R Surya Prasad (Andhra Pradesh)

Bravery: Aaditya Vijay Bramhane (Maharashtra)

Science & Technology: Aryan Singh (Rajasthan)

THE LAUREUS WORLD SPORTS AWARDS 2024

Laureus World Sportsman of the Year:
Novak Djokovic (Serbia)

Laureus World Sportswoman of the Year:
Aitana Bonmatí (Spain)

Laureus World Team of the Year:
Spain Women's Football Team

Laureus World Breakthrough of the Year:
Jude Bellingham (UK)

Laureus World Comeback of the Year:
Simone Biles (USA)

Simone Biles

Laureus World Action Sportsperson of the Year:
Arisa Trew (Australia)

Laureus World Sportsperson of the Year With a Disability: Diede De Groot (The Netherlands)

IMPORTANT AWARDEES:

Roger Federer holds the record for winning the most awards. The Swiss tennis player has won six awards, five for Sportsman of the Year and one for Comeback of the Year.

Serena Williams holds the record for winning the most award by a female.

Lionel Messi – who led Argentina to the World Cup in 2022 – became the first athlete to win the Laureus World Sportsman of the Year and also pick up the Laureus World Team of the Year Award in the same year i.e, 2023.

The Oscars 2024

Emma Stone

Best Actor: Cillian Murphy, *Oppenheimer*
Best Actress: Emma Stone, *Poor Things*
Best Picture: *Oppenheimer*
Best Animated Feature: *The Boy and the Heron*
Best Supporting Actor: Robert Downey Jr., *Oppenheimer*
Best Supporting Actress:
Da'vine Joy Randolph, *The Holdovers*
Best Documentary Feature: *20 Days in Mariupol*
Best International Film: *The Zone of Interest* (UK)
Best Documentary Short Film: *The Last Repair Shop*
Best Animated Short: *War Is Over!*
Best Adapted Screenplay: *American Fiction*
Best Sound: *The Zone of Interest*
Best Original Song: 'What Was I Made For?' from *Barbie*
Best Editing: Jennifer Lame, *Oppenheimer*
Best Director: Christopher Nolan, *Oppenheimer*

The Grammy Awards 2024

Billie Eilish

Album of the year: *Midnights* (Taylor Swift)
Best new artist: Victoria Monét
Record of the year: *Flowers* (Miley Cyrus)
Song of the year: 'What Was I Made For?' (Billie Eilish)
Best pop solo performance: 'Flowers' (Miley Cyrus)
Best dance/electronic album: *Actual Life 3 (January 1 - September 9 2022)* by Fred Again..
Best pop duo/group performance: 'Ghost In The Machine' (SZA and Phoebe Bridgers)
Best country album: *Bell Bottom Country* (Lainey Wilson)
Best R&B song: 'Snooze' (SZA)
Best pop vocal album: *Midnights* (Taylor Swift)
Best R&B performance: 'ICU' (Coco Jones)
Best R&B album: *JAGUAR II* (Victoria Monét)
Best rap song: *'SCIENTISTS & ENGINEERS' (Killer Mike, André 3000, Future and Eryn Allen Kane)*

Taylor Swift

THE GOLDEN GLOBES 2024

Best Motion Picture Drama: *Oppenheimer*

Best Motion Picture Musical or Comedy: *Poor Things*

Best Motion Picture Non-English Language: *Anatomy of a Fall*

Best Motion Picture Animated: *The Boy and the Heron*

Best Director Motion Picture: Christopher Nolan, *Oppenheimer*

Christopher Nolan

Best Performance by an Actor in a Motion Picture Drama: Cillian Murphy, *Oppenheimer*

Best Performance by an Actress in a Motion Picture Drama: Lily Gladstone, *Killers of the Flower Moon*

Best Performance by an Actor in a Motion Picture Musical or Comedy: Paul Giamatti, *The Holdovers*

Best Performance by an Actress in a Motion Picture Musical or Comedy: Emma Stone, *Poor Things*

Robert Downey Jr.

Best Performance by an Actor in a Supporting Role in any Motion Picture: Robert Downey Jr., *Oppenheimer*

Best Performance by an Actress in a Supporting Role in any Motion Picture: Da'Vine Joy Randolph, *The Holdovers*

Best Original Score Motion Picture: Ludwig Göransson, *Oppenheimer*

Best Original Song Motion Picture: 'What Was I Made For?' by Billie Eilish, Finneas O'Connell from *Barbie*

Best Television Series Drama: *Succession*

Best Performance by an Actress in a Supporting Role in a Series, Limited Series or Motion Picture Made for Television: Ali Wong, *Beef*

Crunchyroll Anime Awards 2024

Anime of the Year: *JUJUTSU KAISEN* Season 2

Best Continuing Anime Series: *One Piece*

Best Comedy Anime: *SPY x FAMILY* Season 1 Cour 2

Best Fantasy Anime: *Demon Slayer: Kimetsu no Yaiba Swordsmith Village Arc*

Best Slice of Life Anime: *BOCCHI THE ROCK!*

Best Anime Film: *Suzume*

Best Anime Song: 'Idol' by YOASOBI from *OSHI NO KO*

Pulitzer Prize 2024

Joseph Pulitzer was one of the most influential journalists of the late nineteenth and early twentieth centuries in America. The Pulitzer Prizes for journalism, books, music and letters were instituted at Columbia University, as per his will, in 1917.

Journalism: *ProPublica* (Public Service) for reporting on billionaires seeking support of the US Supreme Court through gifts.

The New York Times (Investigative Reporting) for reporting on migrant child labour across the US.

Reuters (Breaking News Photography) for photos from the initial attacks of Hammas and retailation from Israel.

Fiction: *Night Watch* by Jayne Anne Phillips (Knopf)

Drama: *Primary Trust* by Eboni Booth, a play about an emotionally damaged man who finds a new job, new friends and a new sense of worth.

History: Freedom's No *Right to an Honest Living: The Struggles of Boston's Black Workers in the Civil War Era* by Jacqueline Jones (Basic Books)

Eboni Booth

INTERNATIONAL BOOKER PRIZE 2024

International Booker Prize was awarded to the English translation of the novel, *Kairos*, written by German author, Jenny Erpenbeck, and translated into English by Michael Hofmann.

This book, set in 1980s East Berlin, depicts a destructive love affair between a young woman and an older man, reflecting East Germany's shattered idealism and eventual dissolution. It raises complex questions about love, loyalty, freedom, and power. The £50,000 prize was equally shared between Erpenbeck and Hofmann.

INDIA

- ☑ States and Union Territories
- ☑ Important Office holders
- ☑ Organisations and Commissions
- ☑ Indian Politics
- ☑ Overview of the Economy
- ☑ Landmark Judgements
- ☑ Indian History Timeline

Andhra Pradesh

- *Capital*: Amaravati
- *Date of formation*: 1 November 1956
- *Governor*: Biswabhusan Harichandan
- *Chief minister*: Y S Jagan Mohan Reddy
- *Tourist attractions*: R K Beach, Borra Caves, Tirumala Venkateswara Temple, Thotlakonda, Horsley Hills, Kolleru Lake, Kanakadurga Temple, Dolphin House
- *Festivals*: Shivaratri, Pongal, Vinayaka Chaturthi, Jan-Makara Sankranti, Ugadi
- *Major dance and music forms*: Kuchipudi, Bhamakalpam, Dappu
- *Arts and crafts*: Kalamkari cotton, ikat handlooms, banjara embroidery
- *Size*: 1,62,968 sq km
- *Population*: 5,31,56,000
- *Rivers*: Godavari, Krishna, Tungabhadra, Palar, Pennar
- *Forests and wildlife sanctuaries*: Rajiv Gandhi NP, Papikonda NP, Pulicat Lake and WS
- *State animal*: Blackbuck
- *State bird*: Rose-ringed parakeet
- *State flower*: Jasmine
- *State tree*: Neem
- *Major crops*: Jowar, rice, bajra

Interesting Trivia

- Sea turtles have made a nesting ground in Andhra Pradesh's east coast.
- Cured and dried goatskin is coloured with vegetable dyes to make *Tholu Bommalatta* or leather puppets.

Arunachal Pradesh

- *Capital*: Itanagar
- *Date of formation*: 20 February 1987
- *Governor*: Brig (Dr) B D Mishra (Rtd)
- *Chief minister*: Pema Khandu
- *Tourist attractions*: Tawang Gompa, Dirang, Bomdila
- *Festivals*: Losar, Si-Donyi, Reh, Mopin and Solung
- *Major dance and music forms*: Lion dance, Peacock dance, Ponung, Roppi, Wancho dance
- *Arts and crafts*: Khamptis are especially good wood carvers; women in Arunachal are expert weavers
- *Languages*: Monpa, Miki, Aka, Sherdukpen, Apatani, Adi, Hill Miri
- *Size*: 83,743 sq km
- *Population*: 15,62,000
- *Rivers*: Brahmaputra, Siang, Lohit, Kameng, Tirap, Dibang, Subansiri, Drangme Chhu, Papumpare
- *Forests and wildlife sanctuaries*: Namdapha Tiger Reserve, Mouling NP
- *State animal*: Mithun
- *State bird*: Great Indian hornbill
- *State flower*: Lady's Slipper
- *State tree*: Hollong
- *Major crop*: Rice, maize, millet

Interesting Trivia

- Considered to be a unit of wealth, the mithun roams free till it is sacrificed on special occassions and eaten.
- Arunachal Pradesh has the lowest population density in India.

KARNATAKA

- *Capital*: Bengaluru
- *Date of formation*: 1 November 1956
- *Governor*: Thaawar Chand Gehlot
- *Chief minister*: Siddaramaiah
- *Tourist attractions*: Mysore City Palace, Chamundi Hills, Stone Chariot in Hampi
- *Festivals*: Ugadi, Ganesh Chaturthi, Kar Hunnive, Hampi Utsav
- *Major dance and music forms*: Carnatic music, Yakshagana
- *Arts and crafts*: Bidri, wood chiselling, Ganjifa (specialized card game)
- *Languages*: Kannada, Kodava, Tulu
- *Size*: 1,91,791 sq km
- *Population*: 6,83,62,000
- *Rivers*: Krishna, Tungabhadra, Kaveri, Kabini
- *Forests and wildlife sanctuaries*: Bandipur NP, Rajiv Gandhi (Nagarhole) NP, Bannerghatta NP
- *State animal*: Elephant
- *State bird*: Indian roller
- *State flower*: Lotus
- *State tree*: Sandalwood
- *Major crops*: Rice, jowar, coffee

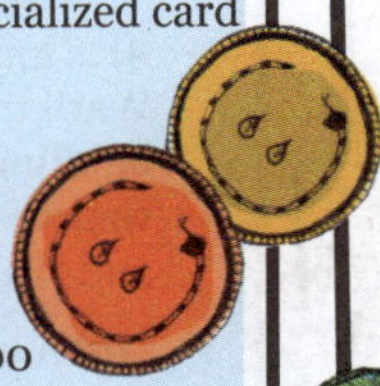

Interesting Trivia

- Karunadu is another name for Karnataka.
- The Gol Gumbaz of Bijapur, the central dome of Muhammad Adil Shah's tomb, is the second largest in the world.

KERALA

- *Capital*: Thiruvananthapuram
- *Date of formation*: 1 November 1956
- *Governor*: Arif Mohammed Khan
- *Chief minister*: Pinarayi Vijayan
- *Tourist attractions*: Kovalam, Wayanad, Kannur
- *Festivals*: Snake boat races, Chinakathoor, Onam
- *Major dance and music forms*: Mohiniattam, Kathakali
- *Arts and crafts*: Kalamezhuthu paintings; murals in temples using 'pure' colours such as white, red, black, green; bell metal idols, lamps, etc.
- *Language*: Malayalam
- *Size*: 38,863 sq km
- *Population*: 3,60,03,000
- *Rivers*: Periyar, Bharathappuzha
- *Forests and wildlife sanctuaries*: Periyar NP, Wayanad WS, Silent Valley NP
- *State animal*: Elephant
- *State bird*: Great Indian hornbill
- *State flower*: Golden shower tree
- *State tree*: Coconut
- *Major crops*: Coconut, rubber, tea, coffee

Interesting Trivia

- Edakkal caves in Ambukutty Mala have rock carvings believed to have been made during the Neolithic Age.
- Kalaripayattu, an ancient martial arts discipline, is derived from 'kalari' or battlefield and 'payattu' or practice.

Madhya Pradesh

- *Capital*: Bhopal
- *Date of formation*: 1 November 1956
- *Governor*: Mangubhai Chhaganbhai Patel
- *Chief minister*: Mohan Yadav
- *Tourist attractions*: Sanchi Stupa, Gwalior Fort, Orchha Fort, Khajuraho, Ujjain
- *Festivals*: Gana-Gour, Ganga Dashami, Hareli
- *Major dance and music forms*: Karma dance, Muria dance, Relo songs
- *Arts and crafts*: Wall paintings by the Chiteras, Chippa community's hand-block printing, Battubai dolls
- *Language*: Hindi
- *Size*: 3,08,252 sq km
- *Population*: 8,82,12,000
- *Rivers*: Narmada, Tapti, Betwa, Son, Chambal
- *Forests and wildlife sanctuaries*: Bandhavgarh NP, Kanha NP, Pench NP, Kheoni WS
- *State animal*: Barasingha
- *State bird*: Indian paradise flycatcher
- *State flower*: Madonna Lily
- *State tree*: Banyan
- *Major crops*: Rice, wheat, soybean, mustard

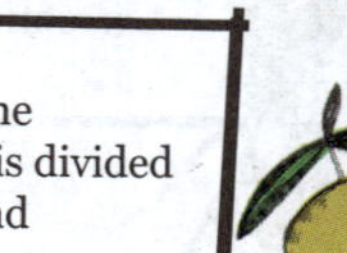

Interesting Trivia

- Bhawani Mandi station on the Mumbai–Delhi railway line is divided between Madhya Pradesh and Rajasthan.
- Pench, Kanha and Bandhavgarh are all tiger reserves.

Maharashtra

- *Capital*: Mumbai
- *Date of formation*: 1 May 1960
- *Governor*: Ramesh Bais
- *Chief minister*: Eknath Shinde
- *Tourist attractions*: Gateway of India, Murud-Janjira Fort, Elephanta Caves, Ajanta and Ellora Caves
- *Festivals*: Makar Sankranti, Ganesh Chaturthi
- *Major dance and music forms*: Vasudev dance, Lavni dance, Dhangari Gaja
- *Arts and crafts*: People of the Warli tribe create ritualistic paintings on cowdung-plastered walls; Paithani saris; Mashroo and Himroo fabrics
- *Language*: Marathi
- *Size*: 3,07,713 sq km
- *Population*: 12,79,28,000
- *Rivers*: Godavari, Painganga, Krishna, Tapti, Pravara, Mula
- *Forests and wildlife sanctuaries*: Pench NP, Tadoba NP, Nagzira WS, Nawegoan NP, Chandoli NP, Gugamal NP
- *State animal*: Giant squirrel
- *State bird*: Yellow-footed green pigeon
- *State flower*: Jarul
- *State tree*: Mango
- *Major crops*: Paddy, wh[illegible] sugarcane, cotton

Interesting Trivia

- There are seven caves in Gharapuri with rock carvings made in 6th and 7th centuries AD.
- Kolis were among the first inhabitants of the archipelago that has now become Mumbai.

MANIPUR

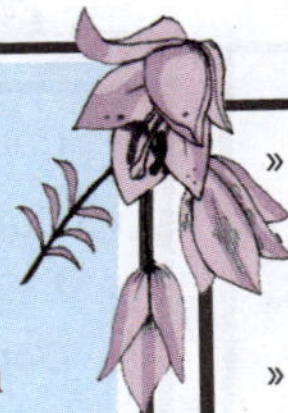

- *Capital*: Imphal
- *Date of formation*: 21 January 1972
- *Governor*: Anusuiya Uikey
- *Chief minister*: Nongthombam Biren Singh
- *Tourist attractions*: Loktak Lake, Sendra Island
- *Festivals*: Heikru-Hidongba boat races, Baruni
- *Major dance and music forms*: Ras Lila, Lai Haraoba Ishei music, Nongdai Jagoi
- *Arts and crafts*: Bamboo baskets, fishing baskets, umbrellas, musical instruments, Kauna mats, etc.

- *Languages*: Manipuri, Thado, Tankhul
- *Size*: 22,327 sq km
- *Population*: 32,67,000
- *Rivers*: Manipur, Barak
- *Forests and wildlife sanctuaries*: Keibul Lamjao NP, Khonghampat Orchidarium
- *State animal*: Sangai
- *State bird*: Mrs Hume's pheasant
- *State flower*: Siroi Lily
- *State tree*: Uningthou
- *Major crops*: Paddy, wheat, maize, pulses

Interesting Trivia

- The pung is the Manipuri version of the mridanga, an ancient drum, and is played during the Ras Lila.
- Imphal's Ima Keithal is an all-women's market.

MEGHALAYA

- *Capital*: Shillong
- *Date of formation*: 21 January 1972
- *Governor*: Phagu Chauhan
- *Chief minister*: Conrad K Sangma
- *Tourist attractions*: Nohkalikai Waterfalls, Living Root Bridges, Tura, Butterfly Museum, Capt. Williamson Sangma State Museum
- *Festivals*: Wangala, Behdeinkhlam
- *Major dance and music forms*: Shad Suk Mynsiem, Shad Nongkrem and Doregata dances
- *Arts and crafts*: Eri silk is used to make colourful wraps and shawls; woven baskets known as khok, cone-shaped bamboo rain shields known as knup are also popular

- *Languages*: Khasi, Garo, Jaintia, Bengali, Assamese, English
- *Size*: 22,720 sq km
- *Population*: 33,94,000
- *Rivers*: Simsang, Someswari, Jinjiram, Kalu, Myntdu, Didram
- *Forests and wildlife sanctuaries*: Nokrek Ridge NP, Balpakram NP, Nongkhyllem WS, Siju Bird Sanctuary
- *State animal*: Clouded leopard
- *State bird*: Hill myna
- *State flower*: Lady's slipper orchid
- *State tree*: Gamhar
- *Major crops*: Potato, cotton, pineapple, orange

Interesting Trivia

- Nartiang contains a collection of megaliths and monoliths.
- Wangala, or the dance of hundred hrums, is used by the Garos to celebrate a good harvest in November.

MIZORAM

» *Capital*: Aizawl
» *Date of formation*: 20 February 1987
» *Governor*: Dr Hari Babu Kambhampati
» *Chief minister*: PU Lalduhoma
» *Tourist attractions*: Phawngpui Hills, Sibuta Lung, Philpui Grave, Palak Lake

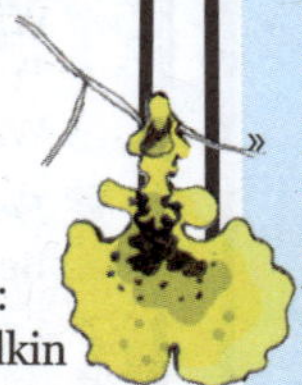

» *Festivals*: Chapchar Kut, Mim Kut, Pawl Kut
» *Major dance and music forms*: Khal Lam, Chai, Chhilam, Sawlkin
» *Arts and crafts*: Puan (traditional dress), cane and bamboo baskets, pipes, toys
» *Languages*: Mara, Mizo, Bengali, English
» *Size*: 21,081 sq km

» *Population*: 12,55,000
» *Rivers*: Tlwang, Tlau, Chhimtuipui, Tuichang, Tuirial
» *Forests and wildlife sanctuaries*: Lengteng WS, Murlen NP, Phawngpui NP, Thorangtlang WS
» *State animal*: Serow

» *State bird*: Mrs Hume's pheasant
» *State flower*:Red vanda
» *State tree*: Iron wood
» *Major crops*: Paddy, maize, sugarcane, oil palm

NAGALAND

» *Capital*: Kohima
» *Date of formation*: 1 December 1963
» *Governor*: La. Ganesan Iyer
» *Chief minister*: Neiphiu Rio
» *Tourist attractions*: Kohima War Cemetery, Bara Basti, State Museum
» *Festivals*: Moatsu Mong, Sekrenyi, Hornbill
» *Major dance and music forms*: Zeliang, Hereileu song

» *Arts and crafts*: Naga baskets, cup violin made using bamboo and gourd, bamboo trumpet
» *Languages*: Ao, Sema, Konyak, Angami, Chakhesang, Chang, Khiamniungan, Kuki
» *Size*: 16,579 sq km
» *Population*: 22,64,000
» *Rivers*: Milak, Barak, Dhansiri, Doyang, Dikhu, Zungki, Tizu
» *Forests and wildlife sanctuaries*: Intanki NP
» *State animal*: Mithun
» *State bird*: Blyth's tragopan
» *State flower*: Rhododendron
» *State tree*: Alder
» *Major crops*: Rice, maize, millet, sugarcane

Interesting Trivia

- Cheraw is a popular form of dancing that uses bamboos.
- Pukzing cave, near Aizawl, stands at 25m. Legends say that Mualzavata, a very strong man, carved it out with a hair pin.

Interesting Trivia

- Nagaland is home to around 360 orchid species.
- Sekrenyi, the Angami festival, is celebrated over a period of ten days.

ODISHA

- *Capital*: Bhubaneswar
- *Date of formation*: 1 April 1936
- *Governor*: Raghubar Das
- *Chief minister*: Mohan Charan Majhi
- *Tourist attractions*: Sun Temple, Jagannath Temple, Taptapani
- *Festivals*: Rath Yatra, Dol Jatra, Patua Jatra, Chandak Puja
- *Major dance and music forms*: Odissi, Chitrapada, Dhruvapada, Panchal music
- *Arts and crafts*: Pattachitras, palm-leaf ganjifa cards, intricate combs made using bamboo, lac and fabric, Sambalpuri double ikat
- *Language*: Oriya
- *Size*: 1,55,707 sq km
- *Population*: 4,67,36,000
- *Rivers*: Mahanadi, Baitarni, Brahmani, Tel, Sabari
- *Forests and wildlife sanctuaries*: Chilka Lake Sanctuary, Simlipal NP, Bhitarkanika NP
- *State animal*: Sambar
- *State bird*: Indian roller
- *State flower*: Ashoka
- *State tree*: Peepal Tree
- *Major crops*: Paddy, mustard, ragi, maize

Interesting Trivia

- The thirty-three sandstone caves on the Udaygiri and Khandagiri hills near Bhubaneshwar were probably carved during King Kharavela's reign.
- Odisha has sixty-two tribes including the Santhals, Suras, Juangs, Gonds, Bondas, etc.

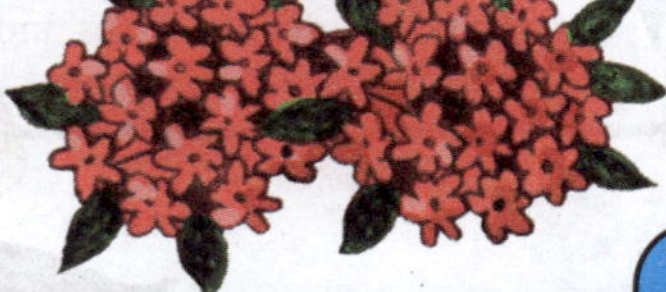

PUNJAB

- *Capital*: Chandigarh
- *Date of formation*: 1 November 1966
- *Governor*: Shri Banwarilal Purohit
- *Chief minister*: Bhagwant Mann
- *Tourist attractions:* Golden Temple, Jallianwalla Bagh, Anandpur Sahib Fort, Rajmahal
- *Festivals*: Lohri, Baisakhi, Gurpurab
- *Major dance and music forms*: Bhangra, Giddha
- *Arts and crafts*: Phulkari or flower embroidery, wood inlay of Hoshiarpur on black shisham wood.
- *Language*: Punjabi
- *Size*: 50,362 sq km
- *Population*: 3,10,41,000
- *Rivers:* Beas, Sutlej, Ravi
- *Forests and wildlife sanctuaries:* Bir Moti Bagh WS, Bir Bhunerhari WS, Bir Dosanjh WS
- *State animal:* Blackbuck
- *State bird*: Northern goshawk
- *State flower*: Gladiolus
- *State tree:* Shisham
- *Major crops*: Wheat, gram, barley, oil seeds

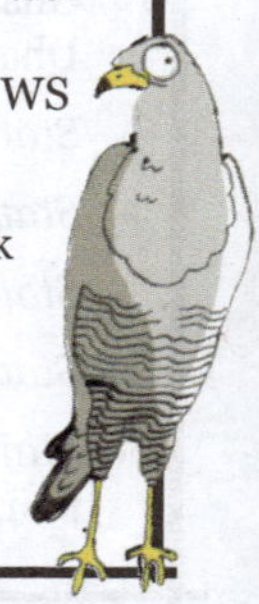

Interesting Trivia

- Sikhism, a dominant religion in Punjab, was founded by Guru Nanak. The word 'Sikh' translates to 'learner'.
- Punjab, one of India's most fertile states, is also called the 'Granary of India'.

RAJASTHAN

- *Capital*: Jaipur
- *Date of formation*: 30 March 1949
- *Governor*: Kalraj Mishra
- *Chief minister*: Bhajan Lal Sharma
- *Tourist attractions*: Mount Abu, City Palace Jaipur, Hawa Mahal, Jaisalmer Fort, Birla Temple, Pushkar
- *Festivals*: Teej, Gangaur, Bikaner Camel Festival, Marwar Festival
- *Major dance and music forms*: Ghoomar and Kalbeliya dances, Panihari songs, Bhopa-Bhopi songs
- *Arts and crafts*: Rajasthani miniature paintings such as Mewar, Marwar, Jaipur, etc., Pichwai paintings, hand-block printing
- *Languages*: Rajasthani, Hindi
- *Size*: 3,42,239 sq km
- *Population*: 8,24,06,000
- *Rivers*: Luni, Banas, Kali Sindh, Chambal
- *Forests and wildlife sanctuaries*: Sariska Tiger Reserve, Keoladeo Ghana NP, Ranthambore NP, Dhawa Doli WS
- *State animal*: Camel, Chinkara
- *State bird*: Great Indian bustard
- *State flower*: Rohida
- *State tree*: Khejri
- *Major crops*: Jowar, pulses, maize, gram

Interesting Trivia

- Jaipur has an Elephant Festival which includes a tug-of-war between humans and elephants.
- Rats are revered and fed in the Karni Mata temple in Bikaner.

SIKKIM

- *Capital*: Gangtok
- *Date of formation*: 16 May 1975
- *Governor*: Lakshman Acharya
- *Chief minister*: Prem Singh Tamang (a.k.a. P S Golay)
- *Tourist attractions*: Tsuklakhang Palace, Dubdi Gompa, Gurudongmar Lake, Deorali, Orchid Sanctuary, Tathagata Tsal
- *Festivals*: Pang Lhabsol, Losoong
- *Major dance and music forms*: Enchey Chaam mask dance, Kali Topi
- *Arts and crafts*: Thangkas or religious scroll paintings, Choktse tables, hand-knotted carpets
- *Languages*: Lepcha, Bhutia, Limbu, Nepali, Hindi
- *Size*: 7,096 sq km
- *Population*: 6,99,000
- *Rivers*: Teesta, Rangeet
- *Forests and wildlife sanctuaries*: Khanchendzonga NP, Fambong Lho WS
- *State animal*: Red panda
- *State bird*: Blood pheasant
- *State tree*: Rhododendron
- *State flower*: Noble Orchid
- *Major crops*: Maize, paddy, wheat, barley

Interesting Trivia

- The red panda, which is highly endangered, is found in Sikkim.
- Sikkim is home to around 200 monasteries or gompas. The red-robed lamas chant to drums, horns and trumpets in these monasteries.

Tamil Nadu

- *Capital*: Chennai
- *Date of formation*: 1 November 1956
- *Governor*: R N Ravi
- *Chief minister*: M K Stalin
- *Tourist attractions*: Marina Beach, Mahabalipuram Beach, Ooty
- *Festivals*: Pongal, Vaikasi Visakam, Avani Moola
- *Major dance and music forms*: Bharatnatyam, Parai Attam, Naiyandi Melam
- *Arts and crafts*: Tanjore style of painting, Kanchipuram silk, Puthululi (embroidered shawls)
- *Language*: Tamil
- *Size*: 1,30,058 sq km
- *Population*: 7,72,22,000
- *Rivers*: Kaveri, Palar, Periyar, Bhavani
- *Forests and wildlife sanctuaries*: Mudumalai NP, Mukurthi NP, Indira Gandhi (Annamalai) NP, Kalakad WS
- *State animal*: Nilgiri tahr
- *State bird*: Emerald dove
- *State flower*: Glory lily or Kandhal
- *State tree*: Palmyra palm
- *Major crops*: Paddy, millets, pulses, tea

Interesting Trivia

- Mamallapuram, a group of rock-cut monuments and temples in Mahabalipuram, were carved between 7th and 8th centuries AD.
- The Pandyas built the Meenakshi temple in Madurai.

Telangana

- *Capital*: Hyderabad
- *Date of formation*: 2 June 2014
- *Governor*: C.P Radhakrishnan
- *Chief minister*: Revanth Reddy
- *Tourist attractions*: Charminar, Golconda Fort, Qutb Shahi Tombs, Chowmahalla Palace, Falaknuma Palace, Bhongir Fort
- *Festivals*: Bathukamma, Ramzan, Vinayaka Chavithi
- *Major dance and music forms*: Kuchipudi, Bhamakalpam, Dappu
- *Arts and crafts*: Kalamkari cotton; the nakashis of Cheriyal village paint vibrantly coloured scrolls.
- *Languages*: Telugu, Urdu, English
- *Size*: 1,12,077 km
- *Population*: 3,83,63,000
- *Rivers*: Godavari, Krishna, Musi, Tungabhadra, Bhima, Manjira, Pranhitha, Wardha
- *Forests and wildlife sanctuaries*: Kawal WS, Manjira WS, Nagarjunasagar-Srisailam Tiger Reserve
- *State animal*: *Spotted Deer*
- *State bird*: Indian roller
- *State flower*: Tangedu
- *State tree*: Jammi Chettu
- *Major crops*: Groundnut, rice, maize, pulses

Interesting Trivia

- Patronage by Qutb Shahi and Asafjahi rulers led to the growth of mushairas, ghazals and qawali in Hyderabad.

TRIPURA

- *Capital*: Agartala
- *Date of formation*:
- 21 January 1972
- *Governor*: Indrasena Reddy Nallu
- *Chief minister*: Manik Saha
- *Tourist attractions*: Ujjayanta Palace, Chaturdas Devata Temple, Neer Mahal, Jampui Hills
- *Festivals*: Kharchi Puja, Ker Puja, Garia Puja, Pous-Sankranti Mela
- *Major dance and music forms*: Bizu dance, Garia dance, Sumui music
- *Arts and crafts*: Bamboo mats, clothes with snakeskin designs known as Ponmongvom, garments called the Risa and the Rignai
- *Languages*: Kokborok, Bengali, English
- *Size*: 10,491 sq km
- *Population*: 42,03,000
- *River*: Gumti, Longai, Manu
- *Forests and wildlife sanctuaries*: Sipahijala WS, Trishna WS, Rowa WS, Rajbari NP
- *State animal*: Phayre's langur
- *State bird*: Green imperial pigeon
- *State flower*: Nageswar
- *State tree*: Agarwood
- *Major crops*: Paddy, wheat, pineapple, orange, maize

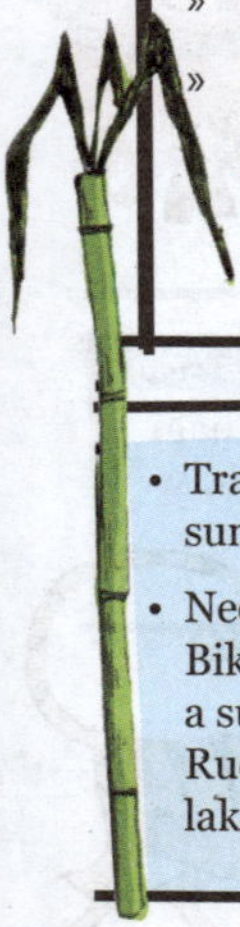

Interesting Trivia

- Traditional instruments include the sumui, sarinda and chongpreng.
- Neermahal, built by Maharaja Bir Bikram Kishore Manikya Bahadur as a summer resort, is located in Lake Rudrasagar. It is the only palace in a lake in eastern India.

UTTAR PRADESH

- *Capital*: Lucknow
- *Date of formation*: 24 January 1950
- *Governor*: Anandiben Patel
- *Chief minister*: Yogi Adityanath
- *Tourist attractions*: Taj Mahal, Sangam, Varanasi
- *Festivals*: Karva Chauth, Annakoot, Sheetala Ashtami, Eid
- *Major dance and music forms*: Kathak, Lucknow and Benares Gharanas of music
- *Arts and crafts*: Chikankari or shadow-work embroidery, Baranasi brocades, Sanjhi (the art of paper-cutting)
- *Languages*: Hindi, Urdu
- *Size*: 2,40,928 sq km
- *Population*: 23,94,72,000
- *Rivers*: Ganga, Yamuna, Gomti, Ghaghra, Ramganga, Betwa
- *Forests and wildlife sanctuaries*: Dudhwa NP, Ranipur WS
- *State animal*: Swamp deer
- *State bird*: Sarus crane
- *State flower*: Palash
- *State tree*: Ashoka
- *Major crops*: Wheat, rice, potato, sugarcane

Interesting Trivia

- The ancient Dhamek Stupa in Sarnath is the spot where Buddha gave his first sermon.
- The Taj Mahal took about twenty-two years to build.

Uttarakhand

- *Capital*: Dehradun
- *Date of formation*: 9 November 2000
- *Governor*: Gurmit Singh
- *Chief minister*: Pushkar Singh Dhami
- *Tourist attractions*: Rishikesh, Nainital, Almora, Mussoorie, Nanda Devi
- *Festivals*: Bagwal Mela, Nanda Devi Mela, Purnagiri Mela
- *Major dance and music forms*: Bhotia dance, Barada Nati dance, Chancheri dance
- *Arts and crafts*: Kholi woodcarving, Aipan (rangoli)
- *Languages*: Hindi, Garhwali, Kumaoni
- *Size*: 53,483 sq km
- *Population*: 1,18,24,000
- *Rivers*: Ganga, Yamuna, Ramganga, Kali
- *Forests and wildlife sanctuaries*: Nanda Devi NP, Rajaji NP, Corbett NP
- *State animal*: White-bellied musk deer
- *State bird*: Monal
- *State flower*: Brahma kamal
- *State tree*: Burans
- *Major crops*: Rice, wheat, soyabean, pulses, oilseed

Interesting Trivia

- Kedarnath temple is situated at a height of 3,584m above sea level.
- Rock-paintings dating back to the Mesolithic period have been found here.

West Bengal

- *Capital*: Kolkata
- *Date of formation*: 26 January 1950
- *Governor*: CV Ananda Bose
- *Chief minister*: Mamata Banerjee
- *Tourist attractions*: Victoria Memorial, Vidyasagar Setu, Shantiniketan, Darjeeling
- *Festivals*: Durga Puja, Rabindra Jayanti
- *Major dance and music forms*: Gaudiya Nritya, Baul, Rabindrasangeet
- *Arts and crafts*: Terracotta Bankura horses, Kalighat style of painting, hand-woven Baluchari silk textiles
- *Languages*: Bengali, Hindi
- *Size*: 88,752 sq km
- *Population*: 9,98,43,000
- *Rivers*: Hooghly, Teesta, Torsa, Subarnarekha, Damodar
- *Forests and wildlife sanctuaries*: Sunderbans NP, Jaldapara NP
- *State animal*: Fishing cat
- *State bird*: White-breasted kingfisher
- *State flower*: Shiuli
- *State tree*: Devil tree or Chatim
- *Major crops*: Rice, potato, jute, tea

Interesting Trivia

- Bengali literature developed early thanks to the cultural awakening brought about by the Brahmo Samaj.
- Rabindranath Tagore, the first Asian to win the Nobel Prize for Literature, was from Bengal.

ANDAMAN AND NICOBAR ISLANDS

- *Capital*: Port Blair
- *Date of formation*: 1 November 1956
- *Lieutenant Governor*: Admiral Devendra Kumar Joshi
- *Tourist attractions*: Cellular Jail, Ross Island, Havelock Island, Samudrika Museum
- *Festivals*: Island Tourism Festival, Janamashtami
- *Languages*: Hindi, Nicobarese, Bengali, Tamil, Malayalam, Telugu
- *Size*: 8,249 sq km
- *Population*: 4,05,000
- *Rivers*: Kalpong, Galathea, Dagmar
- *State animal*: Dugong (Sea Cow)
- *State bird*: Andaman wood pigeon
- *State flower*: Andaman pyinma
- *State tree*: Andaman Padauk
- *Major crops*: Paddy, coconut, nuts, banana, mango

Interesting Trivia

- It is located in the Bay of Bengal.
- It is composed of 572 islands.

CHANDIGARH

- *Capital*: Chandigarh
- *Date of formation*: 1 November 1966
- *Administrator*: Banwarilal Purohit
- *Tourist attractions*: Rock Garden, Sukhna Lake, Open-hand monument in Capitol Complex, Rose Garden
- *Festivals*: Festival of Gardens, Mango Festival, Teej
- *Languages*: Hindi, Punjabi, English
- *Size*: 114 sq km
- *Population*: 12,50,000
- *State animal*: Indian grey mongoose
- *State bird*: Indian grey hornbill
- *State tree*: Mango
- *State flower*: Dhak
- *Major crops*: Wheat, maize, paddy

Interesting Trivia

- Chandigarh derives its name from the goddess Chandi.
- Swiss-born architect Le Corbusier (Charles-Edouard Jeanneret) planned the city.

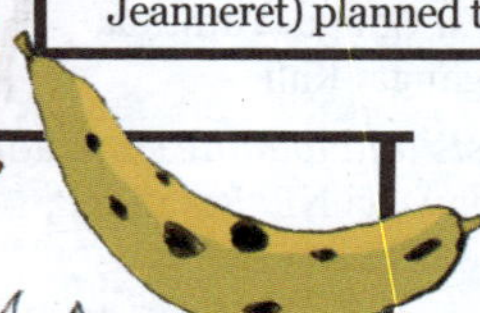

DELHI

- *Capital*: New Delhi
- *Date of formation*: 1 November 1956
- *Lieutenant Governor*: Vinai Kumar Saxena
- *Chief minister*: Arvind Kejriwal
- *Tourist attractions*: Qutub Minar, Humayun's Tomb, Jantar Mantar, Red Fort, India Gate
- *Festivals*: Diwali, Holi, Eid
- *Languages*: Hindi, English, Urdu, Punjabi
- *Size*: 1,484 sq km
- *Population*: 2,19,82,000
- *River*: Yamuna
- *State animal*: Nilgai
- *State bird*: House sparrow
- *State flower*: Alfalfa
- *State tree:* Gulmohar
- *Major crops*: Rice, millet, mustard

Interesting Trivia

- The National Capital Region or NCR is believed to be one of the world's biggest urban clusters.
- It is believed that Delhi was destroyed and rebuilt many times.

Daman and Diu, and Dadra and Nagar Haveli

- *Capital*: Daman
- *Date of formation*: 26 January 2020
- *Administrator*: Praful Patel
- *Tourist attractions*: Somnath Mahadev Temple, Devka Beach, Diu Fort, Pani Kotha, Nagoa Beach, Tadkeshwar Temple, Van Vihar Tourist Complex, Silvassa Vasona Lion Safari, Dudhani Lake
- *Festivals*: Gangaji Fair, Holi, Diwali, Garba Festival, Folk Dance Festival, Barash (Diwali), Ivaso, Bhawada
- *Languages*: Gujarati, Hindi, Marathi, Konkani
- *Size*: 603 sq km
- *Population*: 6,50,880
- *Rivers*: Damanganga, Kolak, Kalai, Silvassa, Khanvel
- *Major crops*: Paddy, ragi, millet, pulses, jowar, groundnut, pulses

Interesting Trivia

- Daman is believed to have belonged to the Mauryan Empire.
- The ancient river Damanganga is possibly the source of the name of the region of Daman.

Interesting Trivia

- The Koknas are known for their body and forehead tattoos.
- The ghangal, a musical instrument that is part of Warli religious rituals, is made from bamboo, a gourd and iron strings.

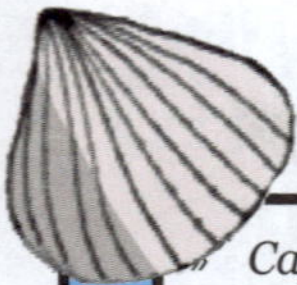

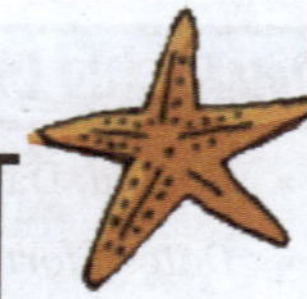

LAKSHADWEEP

- *Capital*: Kavaratti
- *Date of formation*: 1 November 1956
- *Administrator*: Praful Patel
- *Tourist attractions*: Kavaratti Kadamat, Kalpeni, Minicoy Lighthouse, Bangaram islands
- *Festivals*: Muharram, Eid
- *Languages*: Malayalam, Mahl, Hindi, Tamil
- *Size*: 32 sq km
- *Population*: 69,000
- *State animal*: Butterfly fish
- *State bird*: Sooty tern
- *State tree*: Breadfruit
- *Major crop*: Coconut

Interesting Trivia

- Lakshadweep has been ruled by Kerala dynasties such as the Kulashekharas and the Kolathiris.
- Mahi or Mahl (a dialect of Dhiveli—the national language of Maldives) is only spoken on the island of Minicoy.

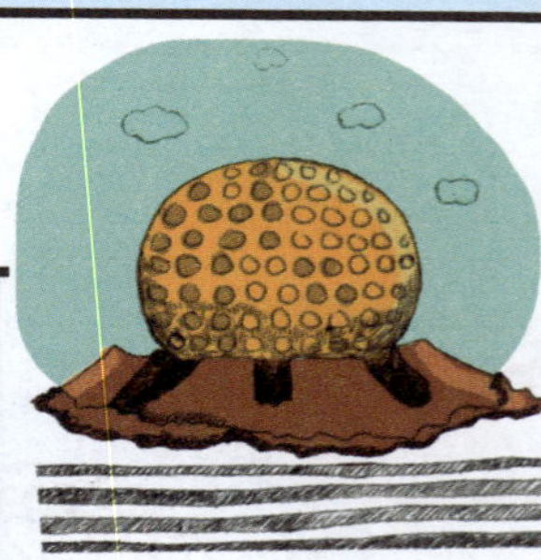

PUDUCHERRY

- *Capital*: Puducherry
- *Date of formation*: 7 January 1963
- *Lieutenant Governor*: C.P Radhakrishnan
- *Chief minister*: N Rangaswamy
- *Tourist attractions*: Serenity Beach, Paradiso Beach, Karaikal Beach, Place du Gouvernement, Aurobindo Ashram
- *Festivals*: Fire-Walk festival, Sedal, Mascarade festival
- *Languages*: Tamil, Telugu, Malayalam, English and French
- *Size*: 479 sq km
- *Population*: 17,04,000
- *Rivers*: Gingee, Guduvaiyar, Malattar, Pambaiyar, Pennaiyar
- *State animal*: Indian Palm Squirrel
- *State bird*: Asian koel
- *State tree*: Bael
- *State flower*: Cannonball
- *Major crops*: Paddy, pulses, coconut, areca nut, spices

Interesting Trivia

- Mahe is also known as Mayyazhi or the 'sea's eyebrow'.
- The ancient town of Arikamedu traded terracotta objects, beads, precious stones and spices with the Romans in exchange for wine, cups and other ceramic items

Jammu and Kashmir

- *Capital*: Srinagar (summer), Jammu (winter)
- *Date of Formation*: 31 October 2019
- *Lieutenant Governor*: Manoj Sinha
- *Tourist attractions*: Dal Lake, Shalimar Bagh, Pahalgam, Gulmarg, Vaishno Devi
- *Festivals*: Makar Sankranti, Eid, Shab-e-Miraj
- *Languages*: Urdu, Hindi, Punjabi, Kashmiri, Dogri, Gojri
- *Population:* 1,37,58,000
- *Rivers*: Chenab, Jhelum, Tawi, Ravi
- *State animal*: Hangul
- *State bird*: Kalij pheasant
- *State flower*: Rhododendron
- *State tree*: Chinar
- *Major crops*: Rice, maize, barley, wheat

Interesting Trivia

- The erstwhile state of Jammu and Kashmir has been divided into two union territories: Jammu & Kashmir and Ladakh.
- While Jammu and Kashmir will have a legislature, Ladakh will not.

Ladakh

- *Capital*: Leh, Kargil
- *Date of Formation*: 31 October 2019
- *Lieutenant Governor*: B.D. Mishra
- *Tourist attractions*: Lamayuru, Pangong Lake, Nubra, Zanskar, Drass, Suru Valley
- *Festivals*: Hemis, Saka Dawa, Losar, Ladakh
- *Languages*: Bhoti, Ladakhi, Tibetan, Urdu, Balti, Purig, Hindi
- *Population:* 3,03,000
- *Rivers*: Zanskar, Indus, Shyok, Nubra, Suru
- *State animal*: Snow Leopard
- *State bird*: Black-necked crane
- *Major crops*: Wheat, barley

Interesting Trivia

- The Indian Astronomical Observatory at Hanle is the second-highest optical telescope in the world. It is set up at a height 4,500m.
- The rare two-humped camel or Bactrian camel are found only in Ladakh in India.

Presidents (past and present)

Dr Rajendra Prasad: 1950–1962
Dr Sarvepalli Radhakrishnan: 1962–1967
Dr Zakir Hussain: 1967–1969
Varahagiri Venkata Giri: May–July 1969 (Acting)
Justice Mohammad Hidayatullah: July–Aug 1969 (Acting)
Varahagiri Venkata Giri: 1969–1974
Fakhruddin Ali Ahmed: 1974–1977
B D Jatti: Feb–July 1977 (Acting)
Neelam Sanjiva Reddy: 1977–1982
Giani Zail Singh: 1982–1987
R Venkataraman: 1987–1992
Dr Shankar Dayal Sharma: 1992–1997
K R Narayanan: 1997–2002
Dr A P J Abdul Kalam: 2002–2007
Pratibha Patil: 2007–2012
Pranab Mukherjee: 2012–2017
Ram Nath Kovind: 2017–2022
Droupadi Murmu: 2022—present

Gyani Zail Singh
Zakir Hussain

Prime Ministers (past and present)

Jawaharlal Nehru: 1947–1964
Gulzari Lal Nanda: May–June 1964 (Acting)
Lal Bahadur Shastri: 1964–1966
Gulzari Lal Nanda: 11–24 Jan 1966 (Acting)
Indira Gandhi: 1966–1977
Morarji Desai: 1977–1979
Charan Singh: 1979–1980
Indira Gandhi: 1980–1984
Rajiv Gandhi: 1984–1989
Vishwanath Pratap Singh: 1989–1990
Chandrasekhar: 1990–1991
P V Narasimha Rao: 1991–1996
Atal Bihari Vajpayee: May–June 1996
H D Deve Gowda: June 1996–April 1997
Inder Kumar Gujral: April 1997–March 1998
Atal Bihari Vajpayee: 1998–2004
Dr Manmohan Singh: 2004–2014
Narendra Modi: May 2014–present

Rajiv Gandhi
Atal Bihari Vajpayee

Important Indian Office Holders

Chief Justice: Dhananjaya Yeshwant Chandrachud
Chief of Defence Staff: General Anil Chauhan
Chief of the Army Staff: General Manoj Pande
Chief of the Naval Staff: Admiral Dinesh K Tripathi
Chief of the Air Staff: Air Chief Marshal Vivek Ram Chaudhari
Attorney General: R. Venkataramani
Chief Election Commissioner: Rajiv Kumar
Comptroller and Auditor-General: Girish Chandra Murmu
Foreign Secretary: Vinay Mohan Kwatra
Speaker of the Lok Sabha: Om Birla
RBI Governor: Shaktikanta Das
Finance Secretary: T V Somanathan
R&AW Chief: Ravi Sinha
NCC Director General: Lt. Gen. Gurbirpal Singh

Shaktikanta Das

Important Industrialists

Mukesh D Ambani *(Reliance Industries Limited)*
Dilip Shanghvi *(Sun Pharmaceuticals)*
Azim H Premji *(Wipro Limited)*
Lakshmi N Mittal *(Arcelor Mittal)*
Srichand P Hinduja *(Hinduja Group)*
Shiv Nadar *(HCL Technologies)*
Adi B Godrej *(Godrej Group)*
Kumar Mangalam Birla *(Aditya Birla Group)*
Sunil Mittal *(Bharti Enterprises)*
Cyrus Poonawalla *(Poonawalla Group)*
Anil D Ambani *(Reliance ADA Group)*
Rahul Bajaj *(Bajaj Group)*
Nandan Nilekani *(Infosys Technologies)*
Gautam Adani (*Adani Enterprises Limited*)
Natarajan Chandrasekaran *(Tata Group)*

Shiv Nadar

Gautam Adani

Important Organisations

- Anthropological Survey of India
- Archaeological Survey of India
- Department of Public Enterprises
- Central Board of Film Certification
- Comptroller and Auditor-General
- Council of Scientific and Industrial Research
- Defence Research and Development Organisation
- Dental Council of India
- Film and Television Institute of India
- Forest Survey of India
- Geological Survey of India
- Indian Council of Agricultural Research
- Indian Council for Cultural Relations
- Indian Council of Historical Research
- Indian Council of Medical Research
- Indian Council of Philosophical Research
- Indian Council of Social Science Research
- Indian Farmers Fertilizers Cooperative Ltd.
- Indian Institute of Advanced Study
- Indian Institute of Forest Management
- Indian Institute of Mass Communication
- Indian Space Research Organisation
- Indira Gandhi National Centre for the Arts
- Indira Gandhi National Open University
- Industrial Development Bank of India
- Industrial Investment Bank of India
- National Archives of India
- National Bank for Agriculture and
- Rural Development
- National Book Trust
- National Council of Educational Research and Training
- National Development Council
- National Film Festival
- National Informatics Centre
- National Sample Survey Organisation
- National School of Drama
- Press Council of India
- Press Information Bureau
- Reserve Bank of India
- Zoological Survey of India

Important Commissions

- Atomic Energy Commission
- Commission for Agricultural Costs and Prices
- Census Commission
- National Forest Commission
- Central Information Commission
- Central Water Commission
- Earth Commission
- Election Commission
- Finance Commission
- Indo-Bangladesh Joint Rivers Commission
- Khadi and Village Industries Commission
- Law Commission
- Mandal Commission
- National Commission on Farmers
- National Commission to Review the Working of the Constitution
- National Knowledge Commission
- National Statistical Commission
- NITI Aayog
- Staff Selection Commission
- Union Public Service Commission
- University Grants Commission
- Venkataswami Commission
- National Commission for Protection of Child Rights
- Digital Communications Commission

NEW PARLIAMENT BUILDING

Prime Minister Narendra Modi inaugurated the new Parliament building, also known as Sansad Bhavan, in New Delhi on 28 May 2023, as part of the Central Vista Redevelopment Project. The new Parliament house, a triangular-shaped building, is a modernized version of the old structure, with state-of-the-art facilities and security details. It houses the Lok Sabha (lower house of Parliament) and the Rajya Sabha (upper house of Parliament), along with various offices for members of Parliament and staff. The new Parliament building is adjacent to the old Parliament house, flanked by the India Gate and the National War Memorial.

G20 SUMMIT: SEPTEMBER 2023

India was the proud host of the 18th G20 Summit, a grouping of the world's top twenty leading countries, in September 2023 held at the Bharat Mandapam in New Delhi. With the theme of 'One Earth, One Family, One Future', G20 nations unanimously adopted the 'New Delhi Leaders Declaration'. Some of the key outcomes of the historic summit were:

- The African Union joined the grouping as a permanent member
- Countries launched a new body called the 'Global Biofuel Alliance' to push the green energy initiatives
- India-Middle East-Europe Economic Corridor: India, Saudi Arabia, the UAE, Jordan, Israel, and the EU resolved to build a rail and shipping corridor to link our country with the Middle East and Europe to boost trade

After the formal conclusion of India's G20 Presidency, Prime Minister Narendra Modi formally handed over the baton to the president of Brazil.

PARLIAMENT SECURITY BREACH AND THE SUSPENSION OF OPPOSITION MPS

A security breach occurred in the Lok Sabha (the lower house of Parliament) on 13 December 2023, when two individuals, Manoranjan D and Sagar Sharma, made their way inside via the public gallery. One trespasser leaped over the tables occupied by the Members of Parliament and let off a yellow-coloured smoke canister while the other yelled slogans. The Parliament proceedings were immediately adjourned due to the confusion and panic that ensued. There were about 100 leaders present during the breach, including Congress MP Rahul Gandhi and Defence Minister Rajnath Singh. Several MPs protested, following which 146 members of the opposition were suspended.

WOMEN'S RESERVATION BILL

The Women's Reservation Bill, or the Constitution (One Hundred and Sixth Amendment) Act, 2023, is a massive milestone in India's journey towards gender equality in governance and politics as it reserves for women one-third of the seats in Rajya Sabha (upper house) and Lok Sabha (lower house) of Parliament, and also all state legislative assemblies. The legislation aims to augment the representation and participation of women in decision-making processes at the highest levels of governance. The Lok Sabha passed the bill with 454 votes in favour of it on 20 September 2023, while the Rajya Sabha unanimously passed the bill with 214 votes in favour the very next day. Subsequently, President Droupadi Murmu signed the bill into law a week later on 28 September. It must be noted here that the reservation will be in effect for fifteen years from the date of enactment.

ASSEMBLY ELECTIONS

2023 saw a plethora of state elections, a litmus test of sorts for several national and regional parties in the run up to the 2024 general elections. While the Bharatiya Janata Party (BJP) and the Congress were straight contenders in some states, the others saw regional powerhouses battle it out in close contests.

In Chhattisgarh, the BJP defied predictions to win a majority, making Vishnu Deo Sai the fourth chief minister, while Congress won only 35 seats. The Zoram People's Movement won a majority in Mizoram, reducing Congress to one seat. In Madhya Pradesh, the BJP won 163 seats, appointing Mohan Yadav as chief minister, while Congress secured 66. Rajasthan saw a BJP landslide with 115 seats, with Bhajan Lal Sharma becoming chief minister, as Congress managed 70 seats. In Telangana, Congress triumphed, with Revanth Reddy becoming chief minister, while K Chandrasekhar Rao faced a complete defeat. The National Democratic Alliance won 164 seats in Andhra Pradesh, with N Chandrababu Naidu as chief minister, as the YSR Congress Party won 11. In Odisha, the BJP won 78 seats, ending the Biju Janata Dal's 24-year rule, and Mohan Charan Majhi became the fifteenth chief minister.

SUPREME COURT UPHOLDS ABROGATION OF ARTICLE 370

The Supreme Court of India, on 11 December 2023, unanimously upheld the abrogation of Article 370, which stripped the special status of Jammu and Kashmir in 2019. This move by the BJP-led central government paved the way for the reorganization of the state of J&K into two Union Territories—Jammu & Kashmir, and Ladakh. While delivering its verdict, the apex court, led by Chief Justice of India DY Chandrachud, validated the Narendra Modi government's decision and said that Article 370 was 'deemed a temporary provision' when India attained Independence.

RAM MANDIR INAUGURATION

Prime Minister Narendra Modi inaugurated the long-awaited Ram Mandir in Ayodhya, the abode of Lord Ram, on 22 January 2024. The consecration ceremony, attended by several religious leaders, was telecast live for everyone to witness the unveiling of the idol of Lord Ram. The very next day, over 3,00,000 devotees flocked to the temple for a 'darshan' of the 'murti'. Managed by the Shri Ram Janmabhoomi Teerth Kshetra Trust, the temple soon became a place of pilgrimage for crores of Hindus.

LOK SABHA ELECTIONS

The largest electoral exercise in the world's biggest democracy began on 19 April and concluded on 1 June. Stakes were high as both the ruling dispensation and the opposition alliance (the INDIA bloc) fought tooth and nail to woo voters. To make it a historic moment, over 968 million people in India cast their ballot this year, the highest ever, as more than 70 per cent of India's population voted. The number of first-time voters were the most this year, so was the participation of women. Prime Minister Narendra Modi returned to power for a third consecutive term after his BJP-led NDA government won 293 seats out of the total 543 in the Lok Sabha. The Congress-led INDIA (Indian National Developmental Inclusive Alliance) bloc continues to be in the opposition.

UTTARAKHAND ASSEMBLY PASSES UNIFORM CIVIL CODE

The Himalayan state became the first in the country to enact the uniform legal framework that aims to apply a common set of laws for every citizen. With the Uniform Civil Code of Uttarakhand Act, 2024, the state brought about common laws for several matters such as marriage, divorce, adoption, inheritance, etc., regardless of the religion, gender, caste, or sex of its citizens. President Droupadi Murmu gave her written assent, following which the law was enacted on 7 February 2024. The law also strictly bans child marriages and prohibits polygamy.

DELHI EXCISE POLICY CASE: KEJRIWAL, SISODIA, KAVITHA CONTINUE TO BE IMPRISONED

Delhi Chief Minister Arvind Kejriwal, Deputy Chief Minister Manish Sisodia, and Bharat Rashtra Samithi leader K Kavitha, continue to be in prison in connection with the alleged Delhi liquor excise policy scam case. The three politicians, along with several businessmen and middlemen, are facing probe by the Central Bureau of Investigation and the Enforcement Directorate, both levelling charges on Kejriwal as the kingpin of the alleged scam that they estimate goes into crores of rupees as kickbacks. Kejriwal, however, was granted a brief bail during the later stages of the parliamentary elections. But his campaigning did not bear fruit as his Aam Aadmi Party failed to win even a single seat in the Delhi Lok Sabha constituencies.

NEET CONTROVERSY

Several inconsistencies during the National Eligibility cum Entrance Test (Undergraduate) raised suspicions of a possible leak in the largest medical entrance exam in India. The National Testing Agency (NTA), which conducts the examination, initially denied the claims but social media posts went viral claiming that NEET-UG questions were leaked. The matter put the newly-formed NDA government in a major soup, forcing Union education minister Dharmendra Pradhan to admit in the Parliament that there were discrepancies in the conduct of the exam. Federal probe agencies began investigations and arrested many suspects from Bihar and the matter is now in the Supreme Court.

NEW CRIMINAL LAWS

India introduced three new criminal laws to replace the British-era justice system in the country. Here's a brief look at what these entail:

Bharatiya Nyaya Sanhita: This replaced the 163-year-old Indian Penal Code. This includes several everyday criminal provisions, such as for trial and judgement on absconding people, mandatory summary trial for petty cases, examination of the accused via video conferencing, e-FIR, videography made mandatory for crime scenes, forensic examination for grave offences, recording the statement of rape victims by female police personnel, a minimum of twenty years imprisonment for raping a minor girl below twelve years of age, etc.

Bharatiya Nagarik Suraksha Sanhita: This replaced the 126-year-old Code of Criminal Procedure. It enlists provisions on arrest, trial, and procedural matters.

Bharatiya Sakshya Adhiniyam: This replaced the 151-year-old Indian Evidence Act, which will now dictate guidelines on evidence in legal proceedings.

By **MURUKESH KRISHNAN**

GAMING, ONLINE BETTING GET DEARER

The Goods and Services Tax (GST) Council decided to impose a uniform 28 per cent tax on online money gaming, casinos, and horse racing. The tax will be applicable on the face value of the chips purchased in casinos, on the full value of horse racing bets, and on the full value of bets placed in online gaming. The 28 per cent rate came into effect on 1 October 2023.

TELECOM TALKS

I) PARLIAMENT PASSES TELECOMMUNICATIONS BILL

The Rajya Sabha on 21 December 2023 passed the Telecommunications Bill 2023, aiming to reform the country's century-old telecom law. The bill sought to make the telecom sector investor-friendly, prioritize user protection, and extend powers to the government to intercept communications. The bill superseded the archaic regulatory framework for the telecommunication sector, based on the Indian Telegraph Act, 1885, the Wireless Telegraphy Act, 1933, and the Telegraph Wires (Unlawful Possession) Act, 1950. The bill excluded broadcasting and over-the-top services, such as WhatsApp and Telegram.

II) THE 'DAMP' SPECTRUM AUCTION

The latest round of spectrum auction to sell airwaves, held in the last week of June 2024, ended in two days with mobile companies purchasing spectrum worth ₹ 11,341 crore. The amount was lower than estimates of the government, which offered 10GHz of spectrum worth ₹ 96,238 crore at the base price. In this round of auctions, Bharti Airtel bought nearly 60 per cent of the spectrum, followed by Vodafone and Jio.

III) JIO ON THE TOP

India's leading telecom operator Reliance Jio surpassed China Mobile to become the world's largest consumer of data traffic. Jio also has the world's second-largest 5G subscriber base with 108 million users.

LIC: INDIA'S MOST-VALUED PSU

Life Insurance Corporation of India (LIC) surpassed India's largest bank, the State Bank of India (SBI) in market cap to become the country's most-valued public sector unit (PSU) stock. LIC's market value crossed ₹ 5.75 lakh crore in January 2024, while the SBI's was around ₹ 5.65 lakh crore.

LIC
भारतीय जीवन बीमा निगम
LIFE INSURANCE CORPORATION OF INDIA

MARKET MATTERS

I) THE BIG JP MORGAN EM BOND INDEX ENTRY

On 28 June 2024, Indian Government Bonds joined the JP Morgan Emerging Market

(EM) Bond Index. The announcement for the big inclusion was made in September 2023. This is expected to lead to inflows of several billion dollars in the ongoing 2024-25 fiscal year itself.

II) D-STREET IS 5TH BIGGEST MARKET

India consolidated its position as the fifth biggest equity market in the world, just after Hong Kong, as the country's global market capitalisation (m-cap) hit a record 3.8 per cent in December 2023. India added over $900 billion in m-cap in 2023, equivalent to the entire market cap of countries such as Brazil, Sweden, and the Netherlands. The US is the biggest contributor to the world's market cap with a share of 45.6 per cent, followed by China (8.6 per cent), Japan (5.6 per cent), and Hong Kong (4.3 per cent). A record fifty-eight companies raising ₹ 53,016 crore from the market via initial public offerings (IPO) added $50 billion to the m-cap. Market cap is the total value of a company's stock that can be arrived at by multiplying the stock price with the number of shares.

III) BSE, NSE DIAL T+0

India's stock exchanges – the BSE and the NSE – on 28 March launched the same-day transaction settlement, or T+0, with twenty-five stocks. In doing this, India joined a handful of countries, such as Russia and South Korea, to follow the superfast, same-day trade settlement system.

TATA'S TRYST WITH IPHONE

The Tata Group's manufacturing wing—Tata Electronics Pvt Ltd—acquired Wistron's operations in India for $125 million (₹ 1,000 crore), making it the first Indian company to manufacture Apple iPhones. The buy was significant, as it is likely to spur the next cycle of investment in the Indian electronics manufacturing ecosystem.

6. THE BIG MEDIA MERGER

Reliance Industries and Walt Disney on 28 February signed an agreement to merge their media operations in India in an $8.5-billion deal. The pact created a behemoth having 120 TV channels and two digital OTT platforms. Reliance Foundation Chairperson Nita Ambani will lead the board of the merged company.

SCALING NEW PEAKS

I) NO STOPPING SENSEX, M-CAP

The thirty-share BSE benchmark climbed 391.26 points, or 0.49 per cent, to settle at a new closing peak of 80,351.64 on 9 July. The m-cap of BSE-listed firms also hit a fresh lifetime high of ₹ 451.27 lakh crore on the same day. Both Sensex and m-cap have been on an upward swing for the past several months. The BSE Sensex breached the 75,000-level during the Lok Sabha polls, before crossing the 78,000-mark on 25 June and 79,000 on 27 June.

II) THE AVIATION HIGH

After seeing consecutive years of slump following the outbreak of COVID-19, domestic and international air traffic in India crossed the pre-pandemic peak of 2018-19 in 2023-24. The international air traffic in India stood at 69.7 crore passengers in 2023-24 as against 69.5 million in 2018-19. Meanwhile, the domestic air traffic was at 153.4 million passengers in 2023-24, higher than 137.6 million in 2018-19.

III) FOREX RESERVES JUMP

India's forex reserves increased US$ 4.3 billion to a new all-time high of US$ 655.8 billion in June. A strong forex reserves position is good for an economy as it helps it prepare for internal and external shocks.

IV) GST COLLECTIONS

Gross Goods and Services Tax (GST) collections hit a record high of ₹ 2.10 lakh crore in April 2024, 12.4 per cent higher than a year earlier.

LOAN NORMS GET STRINGENT

The Reserve Bank of India asked lenders to increase the risk weights on consumer credit exposure of commercial banks by 25 per cent to 125 per cent. Risk weights mean the amount of capital that banks need to keep aside to cover credit risk from a particular loan segment. This hike includes personal loans, while housing loans, education loans, vehicle loans and loans secured by gold and gold jewellery were kept out of the directive. The higher the risk weight, the more capital a bank needs to set aside for the loans.

By THIRUMOY BANERJEE

CONSTITUTIONAL ISSUES

The reservation for Other Backward Classes has included sub-classification in various states. However, the reservations for Scheduled Castes and Scheduled Tribes have not had any such sub-classification after the Supreme Court had previously held that sub-classification in SC and ST is not permissible. This year, a seven-judge bench of the Supreme Court in 'State of Punjab vs. Davinder Singh' overruled the previous decision and held that sub classification is indeed permissible.

When a company is dissolved, the assets are to be divided among the various persons who have valid claims against the company. Of these, the claims of the government and the employees take priority. Section 327(7) of the Companies Act makes this priority subject to the provisions of the insolvency and bankruptcy code which limits the priority for employee dues to a period of two years. Workmen's Union challenged this in 'Moserbaer Karamchari Union vs. Union of India'. The Supreme Court upheld validity of Section 327(7) of the Companies Act, 2013.

When granting bail to persons accused of serious offences, the courts look to balance the right of the accused person to liberty with the need for securing their presence before the court for the trial. In 'Frank Vitus vs. NCB', the trial court granted bail to a Nigerian national, with the condition that he provide his live location pin to the Narcotics Control Bureau. The Supreme Court held that such a bail condition requiring constant tracking of live location is not permissible as it infringes upon the accused person's right to privacy.

The Right to Property was a fundamental right under the constitution. Then by amendments in the 1970s its status as a fundamental right was taken away and it remained as a Constitutional Right. The Supreme Court in 'Kolkata Municipal Corporation vs. Bimal Kumar Shah' identified seven sub rights of the constitutional right to property, which the state should protect during land acquisition. Acquisition should be for a public purpose. The person whose land is acquired should have notice, be heard, be given a reasoned decision, get fair compensation, and an expeditious process which concludes properly by the state taking possession of the property.

Since 2017, a new mode of political finance was seen in India. This was a system of anonymized money bonds by which any person could donate any amount of money to any registered political party without being traced. The Supreme Court in 'Association for Democratic Reforms vs. Union of India' set aside the Electoral Bond Scheme. The court also directed the disclosure of details of all persons who had purchased electoral bonds since 2019.

Article 370 of the constitution which conferred a special status on Jammu and Kashmir was abrogated in 2019. The constitutionality of the abrogation was challenged before the Supreme Court. A five-judge bench of the court in 'In Re: Abrogation of Article 370 of the Constitution' held that the abrogation was valid noting that Article 370 was intended as a transitory measure.

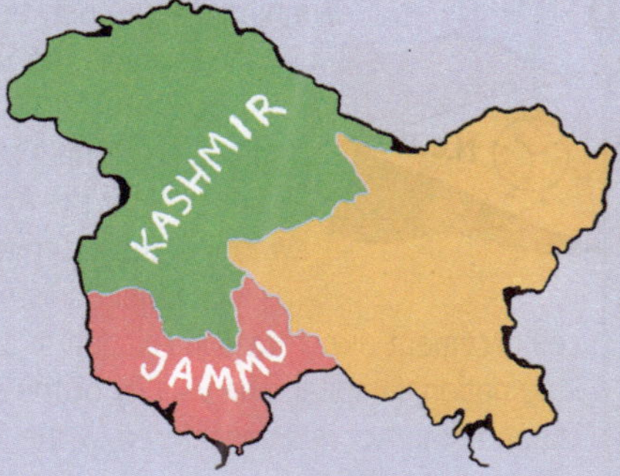

INTERNATIONAL COURT OF JUSTICE

The war between Israel and Hamas has been widely acknowledged as humanitarian disaster. In 'South Africa vs. Israel' the International Court of Justice passed a provisional ruling directing the prevention of genocide in Palestine, providing humanitarian assistance, and directing Israel to stop acts which would destroy evidence.

POLITICS

The foundations of one of the oldest and largest constitutional democracies in the world was shaken when a group of rioters in Washington D.C., USA, overwhelmed the capitol in January 2021 in a bid to undo the results of the presidential elections that took place the previous November. A grand jury had indicted the former president Donald Trump on four counts of conduct that led to the January uprising. In 'Trump vs. United States' the former president and current presidential contender was held to have immunity from prosecution for his acts as president by the Supreme Court of the United States of America.

Rahul Gandhi, one of the leaders of the largest opposition party was convicted by a court for defamation. As a result, he was disqualified from being a member of parliament. The first appellate court, and the High Court had declined to stay the conviction. The Supreme Court in 'Rahul Gandhi vs. Purnesh Ishwarbhai Modi' noted the adverse impact of the disqualification of the MP on the constituents and stayed the conviction enabling Rahul Gandhi to discharge his duty as an MP once again.

The mayoral elections of Chandigarh Municipal Corporation ran into troubled waters with allegations that they had been rigged. The footage of the election officer deliberately marking some ballots became available which added to the doubts of those claiming foul play. The Supreme Court in 'Kuldeep Kumar vs. State (UT of Chandigarh)' set aside the tainted election.

The Nationalist Congress Party has successfully contested several elections using the clock as its symbol. After a recent split in the party, there has been a

running dispute between the two factions as to who gets to use the symbol. The Supreme Court in 'Sharad Pawar vs. Ajit Anantrao Pawar' directed the Election Commission to reserve a symbol, i.e., a man blowing a trumpet, for the Sharad Pawar faction and for the Ajit Pawar faction to declare that the clock symbol is subject to the dispute in the court.

The Chief Minister of Delhi was arrested by the enforcement directorate in relation to an alleged scam in the liquor policy of the national capital. The validity of the arrest under the Prevention of Money Laundering Act was considered by the Supreme Court in 'Arvind Kejriwal vs. Directorate of Enforcement'. The court held that when examining the validity of an arrest, the court could look into the reasons which necessitated the arrest and whether arrest was the proportionate response. Considering these factors, the court released Mr Kejriwal on interim bail.

CORPORATE AND COMMERCIAL

The Insolvency and Bankruptcy Code has been implemented in stages. The insolvency process for corporates was implemented at the very outset and the validity of that part of the code had been upheld by the Supreme Court. However, when it comes to individuals, the validity of insolvency process against personal guarantors was considered by the Supreme Court separately and upheld in 'Dilip B. Jiwrajka vs. Union of India'.

Arbitration is seen as an alternate to the mainstream dispute resolution process of the courts. One of the stated advantages of this process is the finality of the awards of the arbitral tribunal, as no appeal is permissible against such awards. The award can only be set aside on very narrow grounds. The Supreme Court in 'DMRC vs. Delhi Airport Metro Express Pvt. Ltd.' in a curative petition, i.e., the sixth round of adjudication, set aside the award of the arbitral tribunal. This judgment has raised fresh questions about the finality of arbitral awards.

Arbitration is a process of adjudication which can be imposed upon a party only if the party agrees to have the dispute resolved by arbitration. This means that only the signatories to an arbitration agreement can be involved in an arbitration. But what about connected parties, such as sister companies of signatory? A five-judge bench of the Supreme Court in 'Cox and Kings vs. SAP India', noting that major businesses operate as conglomerates or Groups of Companies, held that parties who are connected to the signatory entities to an arbitration could also be involved in the arbitration depending on the facts of the case.

An arbitration agreement is an expression of the will of the parties to resolve their disputes by arbitration. Once the agreement is signed, all disputes between the parties on the issue, including the validity of the arbitration itself, have to be resolved by arbitration. Previously the Supreme Court had held that if the arbitration agreement is unstamped it would not be valid till the requisite stamp duty was paid. Then in December 2023, a seven-judge bench of the Supreme Court held that arbitration agreements were not invalid merely because they are unstamped and that lack of stamping an agreement is a curable defect.

CRIMINAL LAW AND BAIL

A case of rape and murder during the Gujarat riots of 2002 was noted by the entire nation for its brutality. The trial took place in Mumbai and several persons were convicted. In 2022, the Gujarat government granted remission and early release to the convicts. The Supreme Court in 'Bilkis Yakub Rasool vs. Union of India' held that the order of the Government of Gujrat to release the convicts was invalid.

ENVIRONMENT AND FORESTS

Large development projects have to obtain environmental clearance from the government. In some cases, the projects had been given environmental clearance retrospectively, i.e., after the project had been implemented. The Supreme Court had previously held that such ex-post facto clearance is not permissible. Thereafter in 'Vanashakti vs. Union of India', the Supreme Court clarified that this direction would not come in the way of modification of environmental clearance already given.

The National Green Tribunal is the regulatory and adjudicatory body for environmental issues. It often passes orders of far reaching consequences. The Supreme Court in 'Veena Gupta vs. Central Pollution Control Board' advised the National Green Tribunal against passing orders without hearing the parties.

STRANGE BUT TRUE PILS

- In October 2023, a petitioner before the Supreme Court attempted to challenge the oath taken by the Bombay High Court. The court promptly dismissed the PIL as a frivolous attempt to get publicity for the petitioners and imposed costs of Rs. 5 lakhs.
- A petitioner before the Delhi High Court sought that reference to 'Central Government' in all laws be replaced by 'Union Government'. The High Court dismissed the PIL.
- Being an election year, there were several PILs related to the polls. Once such petition sought that the Supreme Court bar candidates with similar names not be permitted to contest from the same constituency. The claim of the petitioner that it would lead to confusion was denied by the court.
- The Supreme Court in 2023 had dismissed a PIL that claimed that there is a danger to the Hindu religion. In 2024, the petitioner again approached the court seeking that the previous order be recalled and was once again dismissed by the court.
- Mr Raj Kumar, petitioner in a PIL before the Supreme Court said that Charles Darwin and Albert Einstein were wrong in their conclusions. The Supreme Court promptly dismissed the PIL.

By **VIKRAM HEGDE**

INDIAN HISTORY TIMELINE

3000 BC
The Indus Valley Civilization is established.

543 BC
Bimbisara, later a follower of Gautama Budhha, conquers and becomes the king of Magadha (modern Bihar).

400 – 200 BC
Mahabharata, the great Sanskrit epic, composed.

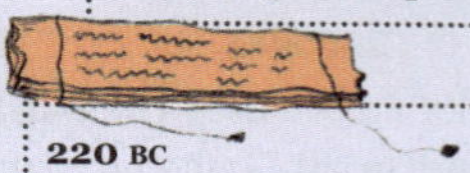

220 BC
Mauryan dynasty expands to almost all of India.

800 – 300 BC
The Upanishads, cornerstone philosophical texts of Hinduism, composed around this time.

265 BC
After the bloodbath at the battle of Kalinga, Emperor Ashoka embraces Buddhism.

1500 BC
The Aryans arrive from Europe and a unique Indo-Aryan culture develops.

273 BC
Ashoka is the new Mauryan Emperor.

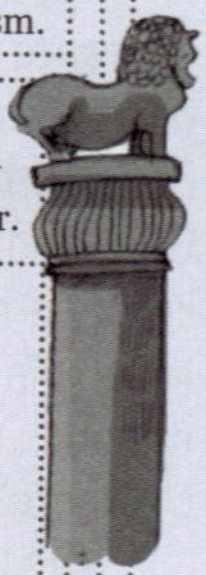

2000 BC
The Indus Valley Civilization begins to decline.

1200 BC
Indo-Aryans start using iron tools. This is dubbed the Iron Age.

500 BC
Prince Mahavira establishes Jainism in northern India.

000 BC — 1500 BC — 500 BC — 0 BC

1500 BC
One of the oldest books in Sanskrit or any Indo-Eurpoean language, the Rig Veda, is composed.

326 BC
Alexander the Great of Macedonia wins the famous battle against Porus, a ruler in Eastern Punjab.

73 BC
Sunga dynasty declines.

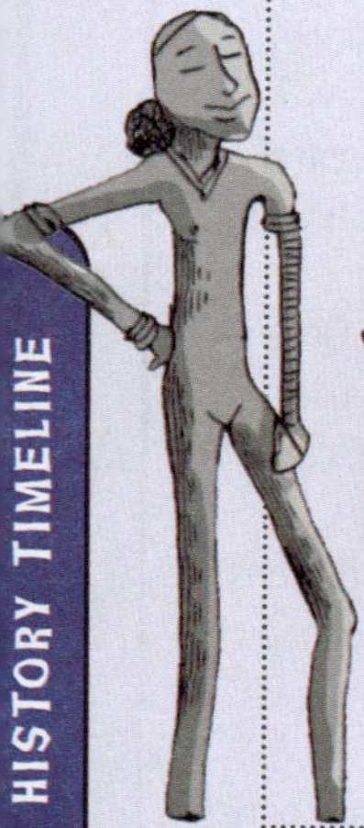

527 BC
Prince Siddhartha Gautama establishes Buddhism and is known as the Buddha.

322 BC
Mauryan Empire founded by Chandragupta Maurya.

185 BC
Mauryan dynasty collapses; Sunga dynasty established.

304 BC
Ramayana, the famous Sanskrit epic, is composed.

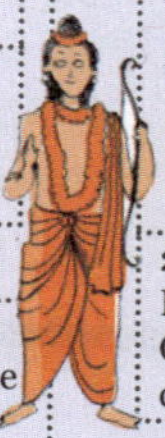

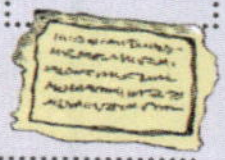

2500 BC
Cities of Harappa and Mohenjo-Daro in the Indus Valley start flourishing.

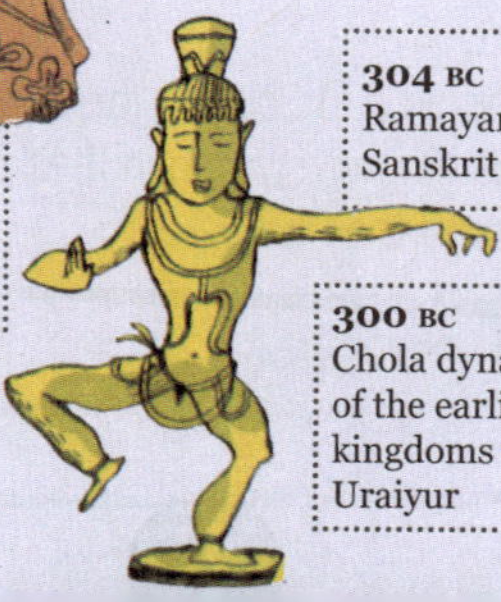

300 BC
Chola dynasty establishes one of the earliest South Indian kingdoms with its capital at Uraiyur

200 BC
Bhagavad Gita is composed.

50 AD
First Buddha stupa constructed at Sanchi.

300 AD
Pallava dynasty established in Kanchi.

350 AD
Sangam compiled in Tamil in the kingdom of Madurai, and the Puranas composed.

390 AD
Chandra Gupta II extends Gupta kingdom to Gujarat.

402 AD
Chinese scholar Fa-Hsien reaches India.

427 AD
Monastic university of Nalanda is built.

499 AD
Aryabhatta writes the *Aryabhatiya*, a compendium of mathematics and astronomy.

500 AD
Beginning of Bhakti cult in Tamil Nadu.

543 AD
Chalukyan kingdom established in central India with Badami as the capital.

550 AD
Downfall of Gupta Empire due to continuous barbaric invasions.

600 AD
Pallavan dynasty governs southern India from Kanchi.

606 AD
Harshavardhana, a Buddhist king, unites the kingdoms of Thanesar and Kanauj.

655 AD
Pallavas of Kanchipuram are defeated by the Chalukyas.

753 AD
Rashtrakutas overthrow the Chalukyas.

788 AD
Birth of Shankaracharya.

850 AD
Cholas get back their independence from the Pallavas.

888 AD
Cholas put an end to the Pallava dynasty.

985 AD
Rajaraja Chola extends the Chola Empire to all of South India. He would go on to construct the temple of Thanjavur.

1001 AD
Mahmud of Ghazni raids northern India.

1010 AD
Chola king Rajaraja builds the Brihadeshvara Temple in Thanjavur.

0 AD — 500 AD — 750 AD — 1000 AD

Not to scale.

1017 AD
Al-Biruni, Persian mathematician, travels to India.

1100 AD
Chandelas, Cholas, Kadambas and Rashtrakutas reign in different parts of India.

1190 AD
Chalukya Empire is split among Hoysalas, Yadavas and Kakatiyas.

1192 AD
Mohammad of Ghori captures Delhi and establishes a Muslim Sultanate at Delhi.

1206 AD
Qutub-ud-din Aibak becomes the first Sultan of Delhi.

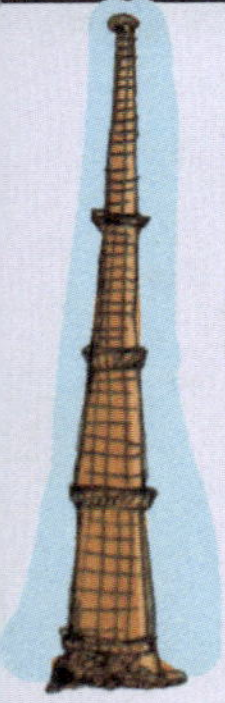

1279 AD
Chola dynasty comes to an end.

1290 AD
Establishment of the Khilji Sultanate at Delhi.

1292 AD
Marco Polo comes to India.

1325 AD
Turks invade and Muhammad bin Tughlaq becomes Sultan of Delhi.

1336–1565 AD
Vijayanagar Empire is established.

1347 AD
Bahmani kingdom established in the Deccan.

1371 AD
Vijayanagar kingdom takes over the Muslim Sultanate of Madura in Tamil Nadu.

1490 AD
Guru Nanak Dev Ji establishes Sikhism.

1526 AD
Babur, an Afghan ruler, establishes the Mughal dynasty in India.

1530 AD
Babur dies and his son Humayun is the next Mughal emperor.

1540 AD
Humayun loses the empire to Afghan leader Sher Shah and goes into exile.

1555 AD
Humayun fights Sher Shah and regains India.

1556 AD
Humayun dies and his son Akbar becomes one of the greatest rulers of India.

1010 AD — 1250 AD — 1450 AD — 1600 AD

1605 AD
Jahangir succeeds his father Akbar.

1611 AD
East India Company is established in India by the British.

1628 AD
Shah Jahan succeeds Jahangir.

1707 AD
Aurangzeb dies, Mughal Empire destabilized, Bahadur Shah I comes to the throne.

1757 AD
British defeat Siraj-ud-daulah at the Battle of Plassey in Bengal.

1793 AD
Permanent Settlement of Bengal—reorganisation of the tax laws by the British.

1799 AD
British defeat Tipu Sultan.

1818 AD
End of the Maratha Empire—British control extends over most of India.

1829 AD
Prohibition of Sati by law.

1848 AD
Lord Dalhousie becomes the Governor-General of India.

1851-1853 AD
Railway, postal services and telegraph line introduced in India.

1650 AD — 1700 AD — 1800 AD — 1899 AD

1618–1656 AD
Shah Jahan builds Taj Mahal, Jama Masjid and Red Fort.

1658 AD
Shah Jahan's son Aurangzeb seizes power.

1674 AD
Shivaji's coronation takes place and Maratha Empire established.

1761 AD
Marathas rule over most of northern India.

1769 AD
A famine kills ten million people in Bengal and the East India Company is ineffectual.

1773 AD
Warren Hastings, Governor of Bengal, establishes a monopoly on the sale of opium.

1831 AD
Administration of Mysore is taken over by East India Company.

1857 AD
First War of Indian Independence also known as Revolt of 1857 or Sepoy Mutiny.

1877 AD
Queen of England is proclaimed the Empress of India.

1885 AD
Formation of the Indian National Congress.

1899 AD
Lord Curzon becomes Governor-General and Viceroy of India.

1919 AD
The Jallianwalla Bagh massacre takes place due to protests against the Rowlatt Act.
1920 AD
Non-cooperation Movement formally launched.
SIMON GO BACK
1928 AD
Lala Lajpat Rai killed by the British during a peaceful protest.
1912 AD
The Imperial capital shifts from Calcutta to Delhi.
1928 AD
Simon Commission comes to India and is boycotted by all parties.
1930 AD
Salt Satyagraha is launched as an agitation against salt tax.
1900 AD
1920 AD
1935 AD
1906 AD
Muslim League is formed.
1930–31 AD
First Round Table Conference in London to discuss constitutional reforms for India.
1931 AD
Second Round Table Conference takes place and Irwin–Gandhi Pact is signed.
1905 AD
The Partition of Bengal takes place.
1934 AD
Civil Disobedience Movement is called off.

1942 AD
Quit India Movement is launched.

1942 AD
Indian National Army is formed with Netaji Subhash Chandra Bose spearheading the movement.

1942 AD
Cripps Mission deputed by British Parliament to contain political crisis in India.

1947 AD
Partition of India and Independence from British rule.

1951 AD
First General Elections and Jawaharlal Nehru of the Congress Party elected prime minister.

1965 AD
Second war with Pakistan over Kashmir.

1966 AD
Indira Gandhi, Nehru's daughter, elected prime minister.

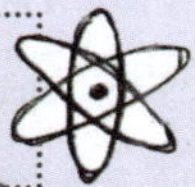

1971 AD
Third war with Pakistan over creation of Bangladesh.

1971 AD
Soviet Union and India sign twenty-year treaty of friendship.

1974 AD
India's first underground nuclear test is carried out.

1940 AD — 1960 AD — 1975 AD

1947 – 48 AD
Widespread communal riots during and after the Partition into two nations: India and Pakistan.

1948 AD
First war over Kashmir with Pakistan.

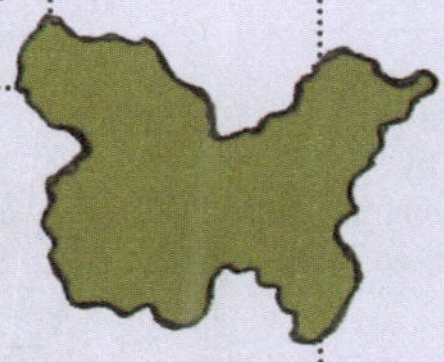

1948 AD
Mahatma Gandhi assassinated by Nathuram Godse.

1962 AD
The main pretext for the India–China War is a disputed Himalayan border.

1964 AD
Lal Bahadur Shastri becomes prime minister after Nehru's death.

1975 AD
Indira Gandhi declares Emergency—considered the darkest hour of Indian democracy.

1977 AD
Indira Gandhi loses the General Elections.

1980 AD
Indira Gandhi returns to power.

1987 AD
India sends troops for peacekeeping operations in Sri Lanka's civil conflict with the LTTE.

1989 AD
Congress defeated in General Elections. V P Singh is prime minister.

1991 AD
Rajiv Gandhi assassinated by suicide bomber.

1991 AD
Economic reform begun by Prime Minister P V Narasimha Rao and Finance Minister Manmohan Singh.

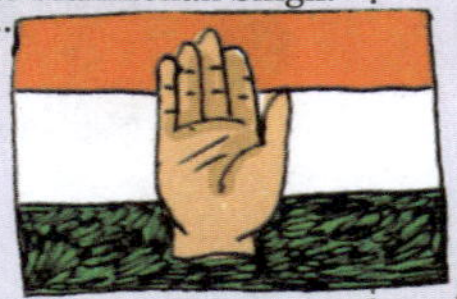

1992 AD
Hindu extremists demolish Babri mosque in Ayodhya, triggering widespread Hindu–Muslim violence.

1998 AD
India conducts five nuclear tests, closely followed by Pakistan.

1980 AD — 1990 AD — 1998 AD

1984 AD
Gas leak at Union Carbide pesticides plant in Bhopal. Thousands are killed.

UNION CARBIDE

1984 AD
Indira Gandhi assassinated by bodyguards, sparking off anti-Sikh riots in Delhi.

1984 AD
Troops storm Golden Temple in Amritsar, the hide-out of Sikh militants demanding self-rule.

1983 AD
India wins the cricket Prudential World Cup under the captaincy of Kapil Dev.

1996 AD
Congress suffers worst ever electoral defeat as the BJP emerges as single largest party.

2001 AD
Massive earthquakes hit Gujarat, leaving at least 30,000 dead.

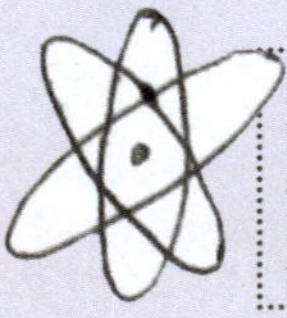

2006 AD
US president George W Bush signs agreement with Indian PM for sharing nuclear technology with India.

2007 AD
Pratibha Patil becomes India's first woman president.

2001 AD
US lifts sanctions imposed on India and Pakistan after they staged nuclear tests in 1998.

2008 AD
Terrorists of Pakistani origin execute large-scale attack on various busy spots in Mumbai.

2010 AD
The largest ever multi-sport event to be staged in India, the 2010 Commonwealth Games, are held in New Delhi from 3–14 October.

2000 AD
The billionth Indian citizen is born.

2002 AD
Retired scientist and architect of India's nuclear programme, A P J Abdul Kalam is elected president of India.

2003 AD
India and Pakistan agree to resume air links, banned for years.

2011 AD
India wins the Cricket World Cup again after twenty-eight years, beating Sri Lanka by six wickets. The last World Cup victory came in 1983.

1999 AD
Cyclone devastates Odisha, leaving at least 10,000 dead.

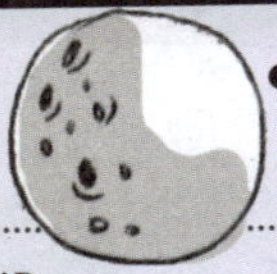

2009 AD
India's lunar mission, *Chandrayaan-I,* discovers traces of water on the moon. This is India's greatest space discovery so far, opening the possibility of setting up future lunar colonies.

2009 AD
The world's cheapest car, Nano, manufactured in India, hits the roads.

1999 AD
War with Pakistan-backed forces in the Kargil region of India-held Kashmir.

1999 AD
Prime Minister Vajpayee takes the bus to Pakistan to sign bilateral Lahore peace declaration.

2004 AD
Whole islands and tribes in the Andaman and Nicobar Islands disappear due to tsunami.

2005 AD
At least 1,000 people are killed in floods and mudslides in Maharashtra.

2004 AD
A huge earthquake in Indonesia triggers a tsunami. India's southern coast severely affected.

2004 AD
Manmohan Singh becomes prime minister.

2013 AD
The 163-year-old telegram service breathed its last, marking the end of an era.

2014
India's low-cost Mars Mission, *Mangalyaan*, successfully entered the Mars orbit on its maiden attempt.

2012 AD
Former finance minister Pranab Mukherjee becomes new president of India.

2017 AD
Ram Nath Kovind becomes the 14th president of India.

2016 AD
The government announced a 'Demonitisation Drive' to eradicate black money, corruption and fake currency from the country.

2019 AD
The state of Jammu and Kashmir is divided into two union territories: Jammu & Kashmir and Ladakh.

2020 AD
Covid-19 pandemic hits India with the first case emerging in Kerala on January 30.

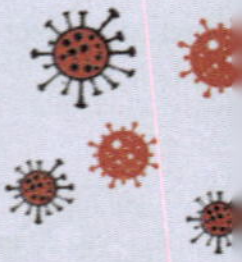

2023 AD
Chandrayaan-3 makes history with soft landing on the Moon's south pole on August 23rd 2023.

2012 AD — 2015 AD — 2023 AD

2011–2012 AD
Widespread corruption in government exposed in 2G scam and Coalgate.

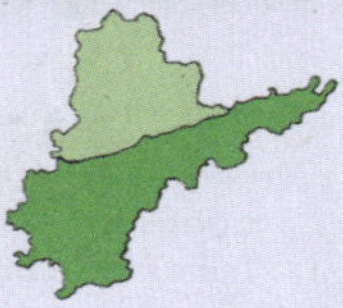

2014 AD
The 29th Indian state—Telangana—came into being, with the division of Andhra Pradesh.

2013 AD
India's cricketing god, Sachin Tendulkar, announced retirement from all forms of cricket.

2017 AD
GST, a universal taxation system for the country, was rolled out on 1 July 2017.

2016 AD
Mother Teresa canonized at a ceremony at the Vatican by Pope Francis. She will now be called Saint Teresa.

2015 AD
The people's president, A P J Abdul Kalam, also called the Missile Man of India, died on 27 July.

2024 AD
Arvind Kejriwal becomes the first sitting Chief Minister of India to be placed under arrest. He was arrested by the ED in the Delhi liquor policy case.

2021 AD
Covid-19 vaccine rollout begins on 16 January with Covishield and Covaxin.

2021 AD
Indian hockey team bags an Olympic medal in Tokyo breaking a 41-year jinx.

WORLD

- ☑ Countries of the World
- ☑ International Organizations
- ☑ Important Office Holders
- ☑ World Round-up
- ☑ World History Timeline

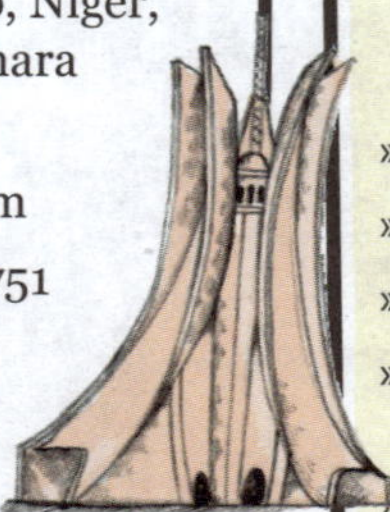

ALGERIA

- *Location*: Northern Africa
- *Neighbours*: Libya, Mali, Mauritania, Morocco, Niger, Tunisia, Western Sahara
- *Capital*: Algiers
- *Area*: 23,81,741 sq km
- *Population*: 46,278,751
- *Languages*: Arabic, French, Berber
- *Dominant religion*: Islam
- *Time zone*: +1
- *Currency*: Algerian Dinar
- *Current head of state*: Abdelmadjid Tebboune
- *Current head of government*: Nadir Larbaoui
- *Type of government*: Presidential Republic
- *Literacy rate*: 79.61%
- *GDP*: US$ 266.78 billion
- *HDI ranking*: 93

ANGOLA

- *Location*: Southern Africa
- *Neighbours*: DR of the Congo, Republic of the Congo, Namibia, Zambia
- *Capital*: Luanda
- *Area*: 12,46,700 sq km
- *Population*: 37,804,634
- *Languages*: Portuguese, Umbundu, Kimbundu
- *Dominant religions*: Christianity, indigenous beliefs
- *Time zone*: +1
- *Currency*: Angolan Kwanza
- *Current head of state and government*: João Lourenço
- *Type of government*: Presidential Republic
- *Literacy rate*: 71.1%
- *GDP*: US$ 92.12 billion
- *HDI ranking*: 150

BENIN

- *Location*: Western Africa
- *Neighbours*: Burkina Faso, Niger, Nigeria, Togo
- *Capital*: Porto-Novo (constitutional capital); Cotonou (seat of government)
- *Area*: 1,14,763 sq km
- *Population*: 14,080,072
- *Languages*: French, Fon, Yoruba
- *Dominant religions*: Christianity, Islam, Vodoun
- *Time zone*: +1
- *Currency*: West African CFA Franc
- *Current head of state and government*: Patrice Talon
- *Type of government*: Presidential Republic
- *Literacy rate*: 38.45%
- *GDP*: US$ 21.37 billion
- *HDI ranking*: 173

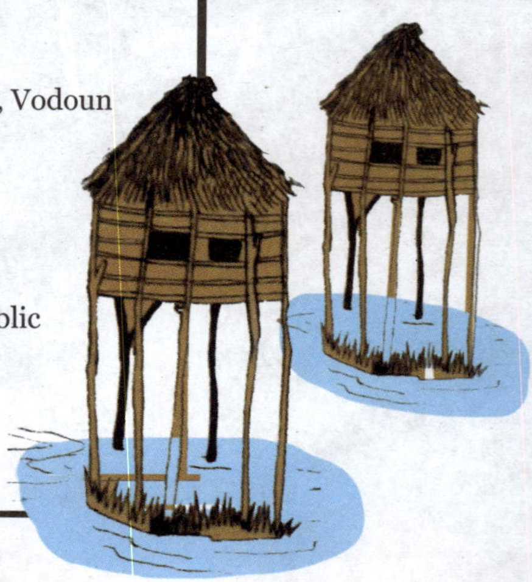

BOTSWANA

- *Location*: Southern Africa
- *Neighbours*: Namibia, South Africa, Zambia, Zimbabwe
- *Capital*: Gaborone
- *Area*: 5,81,730 sq km
- *Population*: 2,719,694
- *Languages*: English, Setswana, Sekalanga
- *Dominant religion*: Christianity
- *Time zone*: +2
- *Currency*: Botswana Pula
- *Current head of state and government*: Mokgweetsi Eric Masisi
- *Type of government*: Parliamentary Republic
- *Literacy rate*: 88.2%
- *GDP*: US$ 21.42 billion
- *HDI ranking*: 114

BURUNDI

- *Location*: Central Africa
- *Neighbours*: Rwanda, Tanzania, DR of Congo
- *Capital*: Gitega (political capital), Bujumbura (commercial capital)
- *Area*: 27,834 sq km
- *Population*: 13,591,657
- *Languages*: Kirundi, French, English
- *Dominant religion*: Christianity
- *Time zone*: +2
- *Currency*: Burundian Franc
- *Current head of state and government*: Evariste Ndayishimiye
- *Type of government*: Presidential Republic
- *Literacy rate*: 85.5%
- *GDP*: US$ 3.08 billion
- *HDI ranking*: 187

BURKINA FASO

- *Location*: Western Africa
- *Neighbours*: Benin, Cote d'Ivoire, Ghana, Mali, Niger, Togo
- *Capital*: Ouagadougou
- *Area*: 2,74,200 sq km
- *Population*: 23,840,247
- *Languages*: French, Moore
- *Dominant religions*: Islam, Catholicism, Animism
- *Time zone*: GMT
- *Currency*: West African CFA Franc
- *Current head of state*: Ibrahim Traoré
- *Current head of government*: Joachim Kyélem de Tambèla
- *Type of government*: Presidential Republic
- *Literacy rate*: 37.7%
- *GDP*: US$ 21.9 billion
- *HDI ranking*: 185

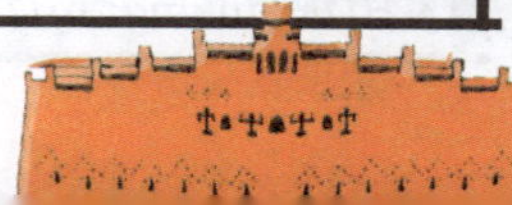

CAMEROON

- *Location*: Central Africa
- *Neighbours*: Central African Republic, Chad, Republic of the Congo, Equatorial Guinea, Gabon, Nigeria
- *Capital*: Yaoundé
- *Area*: 475,440 sq km
- *Population*: 29,394,433
- *Languages*: French, English, African languages
- *Dominant religions*: Indigenous beliefs, Christianity, Islam
- *Time zone*: +1
- *Currency*: Central African CFA Franc
- *Current head of state*: Paul Biya
- *Current head of government*: Joseph Dion Ngute
- *Type of government*: Presidential Republic
- *Literacy rate*: 74.99%
- *GDP*: US$ 53.21 billion
- *HDI ranking*: 151

CENTRAL AFRICAN REPUBLIC

- *Location*: Central Africa
- *Neighbours*: Cameroon, Chad, DR of the Congo, Republic of the Congo, South Sudan, Sudan
- *Capital*: Bangui
- *Area*: 6,22,984 sq km
- *Population*: 5,915,627
- *Languages*: French, Sangho
- *Dominant religions*: Indigenous beliefs, Christianity, Islam
- *Time zone*: +1
- *Currency*: Central African CFA Franc
- *Current head of state*: Faustin Archange Touadéra
- *Current head of government*: Félix Moloua
- *Type of government*: Presidential Republic
- *Literacy rate*: 36.75%
- *GDP*: US$ 2.81 billion
- *HDI ranking*: 191

CABO VERDE

- *Location*: Western Africa
- *Capital*: Praia
- *Area*: 4,033 sq km
- *Population*: 604,461
- *Languages*: Portuguese, Crioulo
- *Dominant religion*: Roman Catholicism
- *Time zone*: -1
- *Currency*: Cape Verdean Escudo
- *Current head of state*: José Maria Pereira Neves
- *Current head of government*: José Ulisses de Pina Correia e Silva
- *Type of government*: Parliamentary Republic
- *Literacy rate*: 90.78%
- *GDP*: US$ 2.72 billion
- *HDI ranking*: 131

CHAD

- *Location*: Central Africa
- *Capital*: N'Djamena
- *Neighbours*: Cameroon, Central African Republic, Libya, Niger, Nigeria, Sudan
- *Area*: 12,84,000 sq km
- *Population*: 18,847,148
- *Languages*: Arabic, French
- *Dominant religions*: Islam, Christianity
- *Time zone*: +1
- *Currency*: Central African CFA Franc
- *Current head of state and government*: Mahamat Idriss Déby Itno
- *Type of government*: Presidential Republic
- *Literacy rate*: 40.2%
- *GDP*: US$ 18.7 billion
- *HDI ranking*: 189

COMOROS

- *Location*: Southern Africa
- *Capital*: Moroni
- *Area*: 2,235 sq km
- *Population*: 867,605
- *Languages*: Arabic, French, Shikomoro
- *Dominant religion*: Islam
- *Time zone*: +3
- *Currency*: Comorian Franc
- *Current head of state and government*: Azali Assoumani
- *Type of government*: Federal Presidential Republic
- *Literacy rate*: 61.99%
- *GDP*: US$ 1.42 billion
- *HDI ranking*: 152

REPUBLIC OF THE CONGO

- *Location*: Central Africa
- *Neighbours*: Angola, Cameroon, Central African Republic, DR of the Congo, Gabon
- *Capital*: Brazzaville
- *Area*: 3,42,000 sq km
- *Population*: 6,244,547
- *Languages*: French
- *Dominant religion*: Christianity
- *Time zone*: +1
- *Currency*: Central African CFA Franc
- *Current head of state*: Denis Sassou Nguesso
- *Current head of government*: Anatole Collinet Makosso
- *Type of government*: Presidential Republic
- *Literacy rate*: 79.31%
- *GDP*: US$ 15.5 billion
- *HDI ranking*: 149

DEMOCRATIC REPUBLIC OF THE CONGO

- *Location*: Central Africa
- *Neighbours*: Angola, Burundi, Central African Republic, Republic of the Congo, Rwanda, South Sudan, Tanzania, Uganda, Zambia
- *Capital*: Kinshasa
- *Area*: 23,45,410 sq km
- *Population*: 105,625,114
- *Languages*: French, Lingala
- *Dominant religion*: Christianity
- *Time zone*: +1, +2
- *Currency*: Congolese Franc
- *Current head of state*: Félix Tshisekedi
- *Current head of government*: Sama Lukonde Kyenge
- *Type of government*: Semi-Presidential Republic
- *Literacy rate*:77.22%
- *GDP*: US$ 73.76 billion
- *HDI ranking*: 180

EGYPT

- *Location*: Northern Africa
- *Neighbours*: Gaza Strip, Israel, Libya, Sudan
- *Capital*: Cairo
- *Area*: 10,01,450 sq km
- *Population*: 114,484,252
- *Languages*: Arabic, English
- *Dominant religion*: Islam
- *Time zone*: +2
- *Currency*: Egyptian Pound
- *Current head of state*: Abdel Fattah Saeed Hussein Khalil Al-Sisi
- *Current head of government*: Mostafa Madbouly
- *Type of government*: Semi-Presidential Republic
- *Literacy rate*: 75.8%
- *GDP*: US$ 347.59 billion
- *HDI ranking*: 105

DJIBOUTI

- *Location*: Eastern Africa
- *Neighbours*: Eritrea, Somalia, Ethiopia
- *Capital*: Djibouti
- *Area*: 23,200 sq km
- *Population*: 1,152,329
- *Languages*: French, Arabic
- *Dominant religion*: Islam
- *Time zone*: +3
- *Currency*: Djiboutian Franc
- *Current head of state*: Ismaïl Omar Guelleh
- *Current head of government*: Abdoulkader Kamil Mohamed
- *Type of government*: Semi-Presidential Republic
- *Literacy rate*: 67.9%
- *GDP*: US$ 4.36 billion
- *HDI ranking*: 171

EQUATORIAL GUINEA

- *Location*: Central Africa
- *Neighbours*: Cameroon, Gabon
- *Capital*: Malabo
- *Area*: 28,051 sq km
- *Population*: 1,754,993
- *Languages*: Spanish, French
- *Dominant religion*: Roman Catholicism
- *Time zone*: +1
- *Currency*: Central African CFA Franc
- *Current head of state*: Teodoro Obiang Nguema Mbasogo
- *Current head of government*: Manuela Roka Botey
- *Type of government*: Presidential Republic
- *Literacy rate*: 95.2%
- *GDP*: US$ 10.71 billion
- *HDI ranking*: 133

ERITREA

- *Location*: Eastern Africa
- *Neighbours*: Djibouti, Ethiopia, Sudan
- *Capital*: Asmara
- *Area*: 1,17,600 sq km
- *Population*: 3,817,651
- *Language*: Arabic, Tigrinya, English
- *Dominant religion*: Islam
- *Time zone*: +3
- *Currency*: Eritrean Nakfa
- *Current head of state and government*: Isaias Afwerki
- *Type of government*: Presidential Republic
- *Literacy rate*: 77%
- *GDP*: US$ 2.7 billion
- *HDI ranking*: 175

ESWATINI

- *Location*: Southern Africa
- *Neighbours*: Mozambique, South Africa
- *Capital*: Mbabane (administrative capital); Lobamba (royal and legislative capital)
- *Area*: 17,364 sq km
- *Population*: 1,222,075
- *Languages*: English, SiSwati
- *Dominant religion*: Christianity
- *Time zone*: +2
- *Currency*: Swazi Lilangeni
- *Current head of state*: King Msawti III
- *Current head of government*: Russell Mmemo Dlamini
- *Type of government*: Absolute Monarchy
- *Literacy rate*: 87.4%
- *GDP*: US$ 5.09 billion
- *HDI ranking*: 142

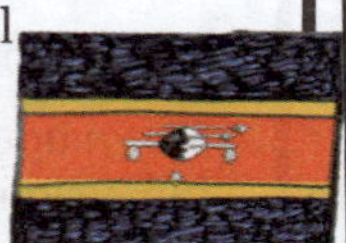

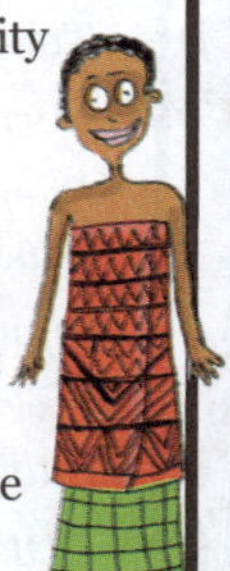

ETHIOPIA

- *Location*: Eastern Africa
- *Neighbours*: Djibouti, Eritrea, Kenya, Somalia, South Sudan, Sudan
- *Capital*: Addis Ababa
- *Area*: 1,104,300 sq km
- *Population*: 129,719,719
- *Languages*: Oromo, Amharic, Somali, Tigrigna, Afar, English
- *Dominant religion*: Christianity
- *Time zone*: +3
- *Currency*: Ethiopian Birr
- *Current head of state*: Sahle-Work Zewde
- *Current head of government*: Abiy Ahmed
- *Type of government*: Federal Parliamentary Republic
- *Literacy rate*: 49.03%
- *GDP*: US$ 205.13 billion
- *HDI ranking*: 176

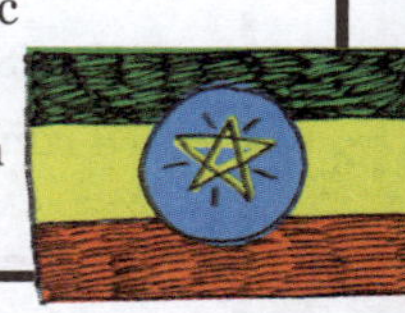

GABON

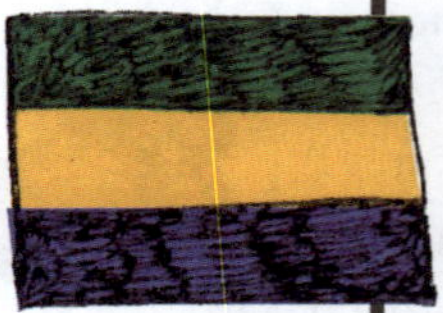

- *Location*: Central Africa
- *Neighbours*: Cameroon, Republic of the Congo, Equatorial Guinea
- *Capital*: Libreville
- *Area*: 2,67,667 sq km
- *Population*: 2,484,557
- *Languages*: French, Fang
- *Dominant religions*: Christianity, Islam
- *Time zone*: +1
- *Currency*: Central African CFA Franc
- *Current head of state*: Brice Clotaire Oligui Nguema
- *Current head of government*: Raymond Ndong Sima
- *Type of government*: Presidential Republic
- *Literacy rate*: 83.2%
- *GDP*: US$ 21.01 billion
- *HDI ranking*: 123

GHANA

- *Location*: Western Africa
- *Neighbours*: Cote d'Ivoire, Burkina Faso, Togo
- *Capital*: Accra
- *Area*: 2,38,533 sq km
- *Population*: 34,777,522
- *Languages*: Asante, Ewe, Fante
- *Dominant religion*: Christianity
- *Time zone*: GMT
- *Currency*: Ghanaian Cedi
- *Current head of state and government*: Nana Addo Dankwa Akufo-Addo
- *Type of government*: Presidential Republic
- *Literacy rate*: 76.58%
- *GDP*: US$ 75.24 billion
- *HDI ranking*: 145

THE GAMBIA

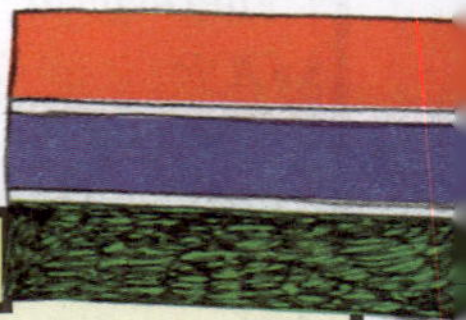

- *Location*: Western Africa
- Neighbour: Senegal
- *Capital*: Banjul
- *Area*: 11,300 sq km
- *Population*: 2,841,803
- *Languages*: English, indigenous languages
- *Dominant religion*: Islam
- *Time zone*: GMT
- *Currency*: Gambian Dalasi
- *Current head of state and government*: Adama Barrow
- *Type of government*: Presidential Republic
- *Literacy rate*: 58.06%
- *GDP*: US$ 2.69 billion
- *HDI ranking*: 174

GUINEA

- *Location*: Western Africa
- *Neighbours*: Cote d'Ivoire, Guinea-Bissau, Liberia, Mali, Senegal, Sierra Leone
- *Capital*: Conakry
- *Area*: 245,857 sq km
- *Population*: 14,528,770
- *Language*: French
- *Dominant religion*: Islam
- *Time zone*: GMT
- *Currency*: Guinean Franc
- *Current head of state*: Mamady Doumbouya
- *Current head of government*: Mamadou Oury Bah
- *Type of government*: Presidential Republic
- *Literacy rate*: 30.4%
- *GDP*: US$ 25.45 billion
- *HDI ranking*: 181

GUINEA-BISSAU

- *Location*: Western Africa
- *Neighbours*: Guinea, Senegal
- *Capital*: Bissau
- *Area*: 36,125 sq km
- *Population*: 2,194,023
- *Languages*: Portuguese, Criuolo
- *Dominant religions*: Islam, Christianity
- *Time zone*: GMT
- *Currency*: West African CFA Franc
- *Current head of state*: Umaro Sissoco Embaló
- *Current head of government*: Rui Duarte De Barros
- *Type of government*: Semi-Presidential Republic
- *Literacy rate*: 59.7%
- *GDP*: US$ 2.15 billion
- *HDI ranking*: 179

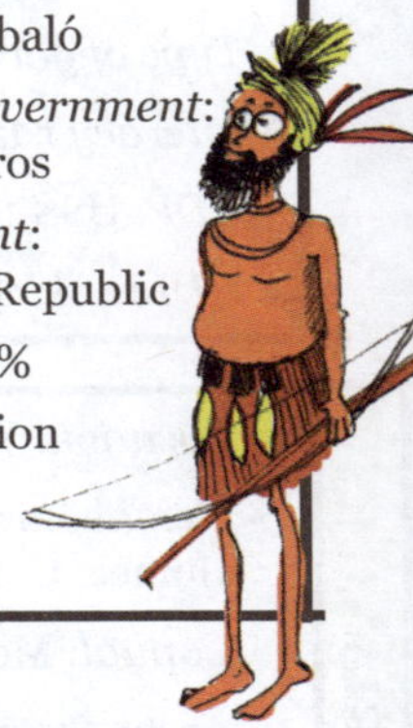

CÔTE D'IVOIRE

- *Location*: Western Africa
- *Neighbours*: Burkina Faso, Ghana, Guinea, Liberia, Mali
- *Capital*: Yamoussoukro (legislative capital), Abidjan (administrative capital)
- *Area*: 3,22,463 sq km
- *Population*: 29,981,758
- *Languages*: French, Dioula
- *Dominant religions*: Islam, Christianity, indigenous beliefs
- *Time zone*: GMT
- *Currency*: West African CFA Franc
- *Current head of state*: Alassane Dramane Ouattara
- *Current head of government*: Robert Beujre Mambe
- *Type of government*: Presidential Republic
- *Literacy rate*: 43.2%
- *GDP*: US$ 86.91 billion
- *HDI ranking*: 166

KENYA

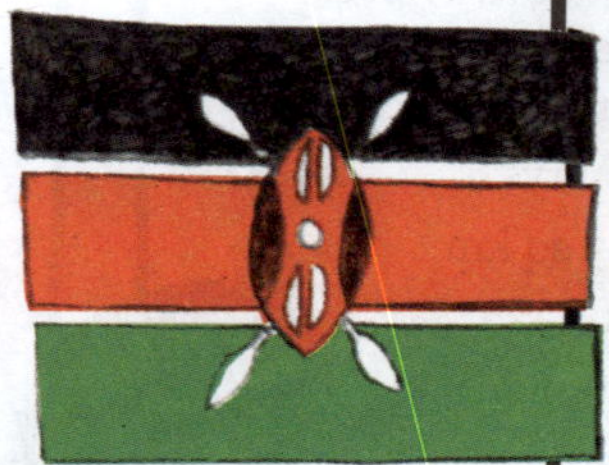

- *Location*: Eastern Africa
- *Neighbours*: South Sudan, Uganda, Ethiopia, Somalia, Tanzania
- *Capital*: Nairobi
- *Area*: 5,80,367 sq km
- *Population*: 56,203,030
- *Languages*: English, Kiswahili
- *Dominant religion*: Christianity
- *Time zone*: +3
- *Currency*: Kenyan Shilling
- *Current head of state and government*: William Ruto
- *Type of government*: Presidential Republic
- *Literacy rate*: 78.02%
- *GDP*: US$ 104 billion
- *HDI ranking*: 146

LIBERIA

- *Location*: Western Africa
- *Neighbours*: Sierra Leone, Guinea, Cote d'Ivoire
- *Capital*: Monrovia
- *Area*: 1,11,369 sq km
- *Population*: 5,536,949
- *Languages*: English, ethnic languages
- *Dominant religions*: Christianity, Islam, indigenous beliefs
- *Time zone*: GMT
- *Currency*: Liberian Dollar
- *Current head of state and government*: Joseph Boakai
- *Type of government*: Presidential Constitutional Republic
- *Literacy rate*: 47.6%
- *GDP*: US$ 4.75 billion
- *HDI ranking*: 177

LESOTHO

- *Location*: Southern Africa
- *Neighbours*: South Africa
- *Capital*: Maseru
- *Area*: 30,355 sq km
- *Population*: 2,356,083
- *Languages*: Sesotho, English
- *Dominant religion*: Christianity
- *Time zone*: +2
- *Currency*: Lesotho Loti
- *Current head of state*: King Letsie III
- *Current head of government*: Ntsokoane Samuel Matekane
- *Type of government*: Parliamentary Constitutional Monarchy
- *Literacy rate*: 79.3%
- *GDP*: US$ 2.4 billion
- *HDI ranking*: 168

LIBYA

- *Location*: Northern Africa
- *Neighbours*: Algeria, Chad, Egypt, Niger, Sudan, Tunisia
- *Capital*: Tripoli
- *Area*: 17,59,540 sq km
- *Population*: 7,361,263
- *Languages*: Arabic, Italian, English
- *Dominant religion*: Islam
- *Time zone*: +2
- *Currency*: Libyan Dinar
- *Current head of state*: Mohamed al-Menfi
- *Current head of government:* Abdul Hamid Dbeibeh
- *Type of government*: In transition
- *Literacy rate*: 91.3%
- *GDP*: US$ 48.22 billion
- *HDI ranking*: 92

MADAGASCAR

- *Location*: Southern Africa
- *Capital*: Antananarivo
- *Area*: 5,87,041 sq km
- *Population*: 31,056,610
- *Languages*: Malagasy, English, French
- *Dominant religions*: Indigenous faiths, Christianity
- *Time zone*: +3
- *Currency*: Malagasy Ariary
- *Current head of state*: Andry Rajoelina
- *Current head of government*: Christian Ntsay
- *Type of government*: Semi-Presidential Republic
- *Literacy rate*: 64.6%
- *GDP*: US$ 16.47 billion
- *HDI ranking*: 177

MALAWI

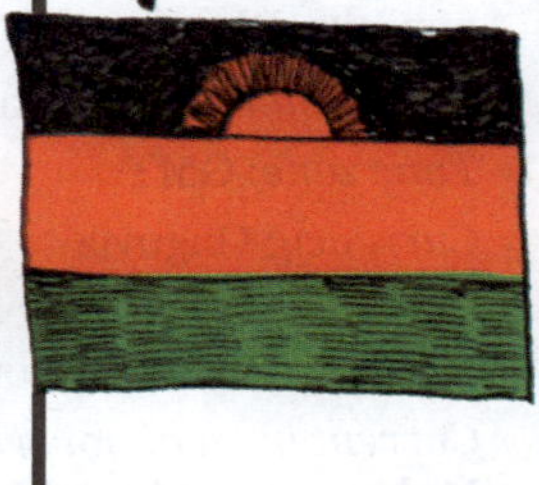

- *Location*: Southern Africa
- *Neighbours*: Mozambique, Tanzania, Zambia
- *Capital*: Lilongwe
- *Area*: 1,18,484 sq km
- *Population*: 21,475,962
- *Languages*: English, Chichewa
- *Dominant religion*: Christianity
- *Time zone*: +2
- *Currency*: Malawian Kwacha
- *Current head of state and government*: Lazarus McCarthy Chakwera
- *Type of government*: Presidential Republic
- *Literacy rate*: 65.9%
- *GDP*: US$ 11.24 billion
- *HDI ranking*: 172

MALI

- *Location*: Western Africa
- *Neighbours*: Algeria, Burkina Faso, Guinea, Cote d'Ivoire, Mauritania, Niger, Senegal
- *Capital*: Bamako
- *Area*: 12,40,192 sq km
- *Population*: 24,015,789
- *Languages*: Bambara, French
- *Dominant religion*: Islam
- *Time zone*: GMT
- *Currency*: West African CFA Franc
- *Current head of state*: Assimi Goita
- *Current head of government:* Choguel Kokalla Maïga
- *Type of government*: Semi-Presidential Republic
- *Literacy rate*: 33.07%
- *GDP*: US$ 21.66 billion
- *HDI ranking*: 188

MAURITANIA

- *Location*: Western Africa
- *Neighbours*: Algeria, Mali, Senegal, Western Sahara
- *Capital*: Nouakchott
- *Area*: 10,30,700 sq km
- *Population*: 4,993,922
- *Languages*: Arabic, Pulaar, Soninke, Wolof
- *Dominant religion*: Islam
- *Time zone*: GMT
- *Currency*: Ouguyia
- *Current head of state*: Mohamed Ould Ghazouani
- *Current head of government*: Mohamed Ould Bilal
- *Type of government*: Presidential Republic
- *Literacy rate*: 52.1%
- *GDP*: US$ 10.63 billion
- *HDI ranking*: 164

MAURITIUS

- *Location*: Southern Africa
- *Capital*: Port Louis
- *Area*: 2,040 sq km
- *Population*: 1,301,978
- *Languages*: Creole, French, Bhojpuri, English
- *Dominant religions*: Hinduism, Christianity
- *Time zone*: +4
- *Currency*: Mauritian Rupee
- *Current head of state*: Prithvirajsing Roopun
- *Current head of government*: Pravind Kumar Jugnauth
- *Type of government*: Parliamentary Republic
- *Literacy rate*: 90.6%
- *GDP*: US$ 16.36 billion
- *HDI ranking*: 72

MOROCCO

- *Location*: Northern Africa
- *Neighbours*: Algeria, Spain, Western Sahara
- *Capital*: Rabat
- *Area*: 4,46,550 sq km
- *Population*: 38,211,459
- *Language*: Arabic, Tamazight
- *Dominant religion*: Islam
- *Time zone*: +1
- *Currency*: Moroccan Dirham
- *Current head of state*: King Mohammed VI
- *Current head of government*: Aziz Akhannouch
- *Type of government*: Parliamentary Constitutional Monarchy
- *Literacy rate*: 71.7%
- *GDP*: US$ 152.38 billion
- *HDI ranking*: 120

MOZAMBIQUE

- *Location*: Southeastern Africa
- *Neighbours*: Zimbabwe, South Africa Malawi, Eswatini, Tanzania, Zambia
- *Capital*: Maputo
- *Area*: 7,99,380 sq km
- *Population*: 34,858,402
- *Languages*: Portuguese, Emakhuwa, Tsonga
- *Dominant religions*: Christianity, Islam
- *Time zone*: +2
- *Currency*: Mozambican Metical
- *Current head of state and government*: Filipe Jacinto Nyusi
- *Type of government*: Presidential Republic
- *Literacy rate*: 58.84%
- *GDP*: US$ 22.98 billion
- *HDI ranking*: 183

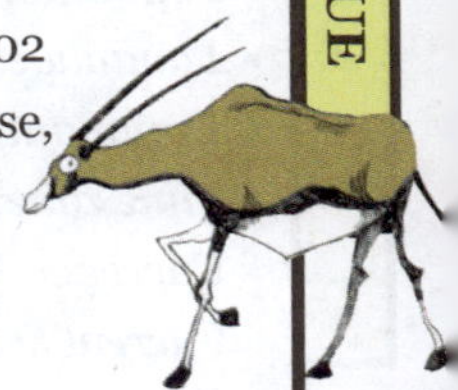

NAMIBIA

- *Location*: Southern Africa
- *Neighbours*: Angola, Botswana, South Africa, Zambia
- *Capital*: Windhoek
- *Area*: 8,24,292 sq km
- *Population*: 2,645,805
- *Languages*: English, Oshiwambo languages
- *Dominant religion*: Christianity
- *Time zone*: +2
- *Currency*: Namibian Dollar
- *Current head of state and government*: Nangolo Mbumba
- *Type of government*: Presidential Republic
- *Literacy rate*: 90.8%
- *GDP*: US$ 12.77 billion
- *HDI ranking*: 142

NIGER

- *Location*: Western Africa
- *Neighbours*: Algeria, Benin, Burkina Faso, Chad, Libya, Mali, Nigeria
- *Capital*: Niamey
- *Area*: 12,67,000 sq km
- *Population*: 28,238,972
- *Languages*: French, Hausa, Djerma
- *Dominant religion*: Islam
- *Time zone*: +1
- *Currency*: West African CFA Franc
- *Current head of state*: Abdourahame Tiani
- *Current head of government*: Ali Mahaman Lamine Zeine
- *Type of government*: Semi-Presidential Republic
- *Literacy rate*: 59.5%
- *GDP*: US$ 18.82 billion
- *HDI ranking*: 189

NIGERIA

- *Location*: Western Africa
- *Neighbours*: Benin, Cameroon, Chad, Niger
- *Capital*: Abuja
- *Area*: 9,23,768 sq km
- *Population*: 229,152,217
- *Languages*: English, Hausa
- *Dominant religions*: Islam, Christianity
- *Time zone*: +1
- *Currency*: Nigerian Naira
- *Current head of state and government*: Bola Ahmed Adekunle Tinubu
- *Type of government*: Federal Presidential Republic
- *Literacy rate*: 62%
- *GDP*: US$ 252.74 billion
- *HDI ranking*: 161

RWANDA

- *Location*: Central Africa
- *Neighbours*: Burundi, DR of the Congo, Tanzania, Uganda
- *Capital*: Kigali
- *Area*: 26,338 sq km
- *Population*: 14,414,910
- *Languages*: Kinyarwanda, French, English, Swahili
- *Dominant religion*: Christianity
- *Time zone*: +2
- *Currency*: Rwandan Franc
- *Current head of state*: Paul Kagame
- *Current head of government*: Édouard Ngirente
- *Type of government*: Presidential Republic
- *Literacy rate*:71.2%
- *GDP*: US$ 13.7 billion
- *HDI ranking*: 161

SÃO TOMÉ AND PRÍNCIPE

- *Location*: Central Africa
- *Capital*: São Tomé
- *Area*: 964 sq km
- *Population*: 236,381
- *Language*: Portuguese
- *Dominant religion*: Christianity
- *Time zone*: GMT
- *Currency*: São Tomé and Príncipe Dobra
- *Current head of state*: Carlos Manuel Vila Nova
- *Current head of government*: Patrice Trovoada
- *Type of government*: Semi-Presidential Republic
- *Literacy rate*: 91.7%
- *GDP*: US$ 0.75 billion
- *HDI ranking*: 141

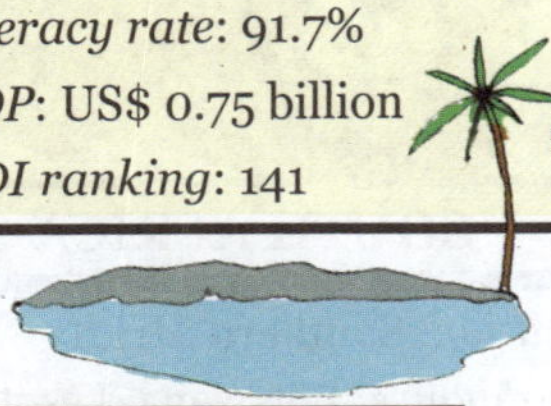

SENEGAL

- *Location*: Western Africa
- *Neighbours*: The Gambia, Guinea, Guinea-Bissau, Mali, Mauritania
- *Capital*: Dakar
- *Area*: 1,96,722 sq km
- *Population*: 18,221,567
- *Languages*: French, Wolof
- *Dominant religion*: Islam
- *Time zone*: GMT
- *Currency*: West African CFA Franc
- *Current head of state*: Bassirou Diomaye Faye
- *Current head of government*: Ousmane Sonko
- *Type of government*: Presidential Republic
- *Literacy rate*: 55.62%
- *GDP*: US$ 35.45 billi
- *HDI ranking*: 169

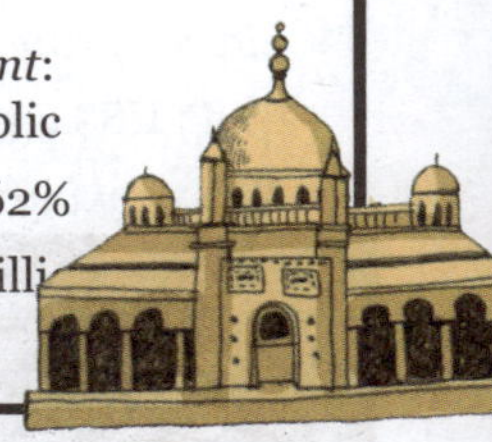

SEYCHELLES

- *Location*: Indian Ocean
- *Capital*: Victoria
- *Area*: 455 sq km
- *Population*: 108,263
- *Languages*: Creole, English, French
- *Dominant religion*: Christianity
- *Time zone*: +4
- *Currency*: Seychellois Rupee
- *Current head of state and government*: Wavel Ramkalawan
- *Type of government*: Presidential Republic
- *Literacy rate*: 95.3%
- *GDP*: US$ 2.2 billion
- *HDI ranking*: 67

SIERRA LEONE

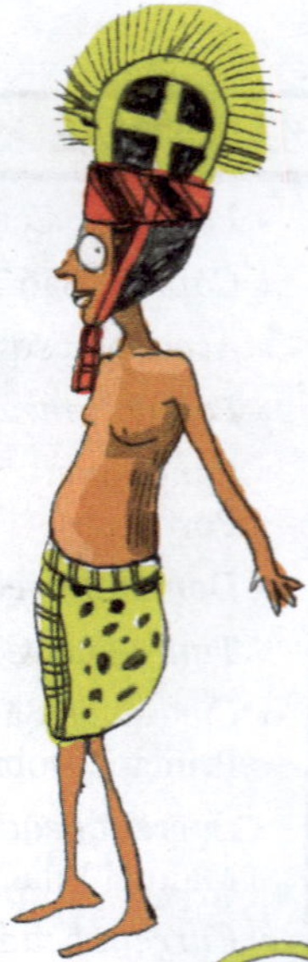

- *Location*: Western Africa
- *Neighbours*: Guinea, Liberia
- *Capital*: Freetown
- *Area*: 71,740 sq km
- *Population*: 8,977,972
- *Languages*: English, Mende, Temne
- *Dominant religions*: Islam, Christianity
- *Time zone*: GMT
- *Currency*: Sierra Leonean Leone
- *Current head of state and government*: Julius Maada Bio
- *Type of government*: Presidential Republic
- *Literacy rate*: 48.4%
- *GDP*: US$ 4.56 billion
- *HDI ranking*: 184

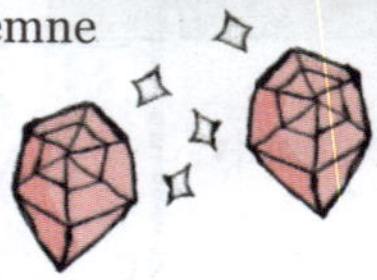

SOMALIA

- *Location*: Eastern Africa
- *Neighbours*: Djibouti, Ethiopia, Kenya
- *Capital*: Mogadishu
- *Area*: 6,37,657 sq km
- *Population*: 18,706,922
- *Languages*: Somali, Arabic
- *Dominant religion*: Islam
- *Time zone*: +3
- *Currency*: Somali Shilling
- *Current head of state*: Hassan Sheikh Mohamud
- *Current head of government*: Hamza Abdi Barre
- *Type of government*: Federal Parliamentary Republic
- *Literacy rate*: 37.8%
- *GDP*: US$ 12.8 billion
- *HDI ranking*: 193

SOUTH AFRICA

- *Location*: Southern Africa
- *Neighbours*: Botswana, Lesotho, Mozambique, Namibia, Eswatini, Zimbabwe
- *Capital*: Pretoria (administrative capital); Cape Town (legislative capital); Bloemfontein (judicial capital)
- *Area*: 12,19,090 sq km
- *Population*: 61,020,221
- *Languages*: English, isiZulu and ten other official languages
- *Dominant religion*: Christianity
- *Time zone*: +2
- *Currency*: South African Rand
- *Current head of state and government*: Cyril Ramaphosa
- *Type of government*: Parliamentary Republic
- *Literacy rate*: 94.6%
- *GDP*: US$ 373.23 billion
- *HDI ranking*: 110

SUDAN

- *Location*: Northeastern Africa
- *Neighbours*: Egypt, Libya, Chad, Ethiopia, Eritrea, Congo, South Sudan, Central African Republic
- *Capital*: Khartoum
- *Area*: 18,61,484 sq km
- *Population*: 49,358,228
- *Languages*: Arabic, English
- *Dominant religion*: Islam
- *Time zone*: +2
- *Currency*: Sudanese Pound
- *Current head of state*: Abdel Fattah al-Burhan
- *Current head of government*: Osman Hussein
- *Type of government*: Presidential Republic
- *Literacy rate*: 58.6%
- *GDP*: US$ 26.87 billion
- *HDI ranking*: 170

SOUTH SUDAN

- *Location*: East Central Africa
- *Neighbours*: Ethiopia, Kenya, Uganda, Central African Republic, DR of the Congo, Sudan
- *Capital*: Juba
- *Area*: 6,44,329 sq km
- *Population*: 11,277,092
- *Languages*: English, Arabic, indigenous languages
- *Dominant religions*: Christianity, indigenous beliefs
- *Time zone*: +3
- *Currency*: South Sudanese Pound
- *Current head of state and government*: Salva Kiir Mayardit
- *Type of government*: Presidential Republic
- *Literacy rate*: 31.9%
- *GDP*: US$ 6.52 billion
- *HDI ranking*: 192

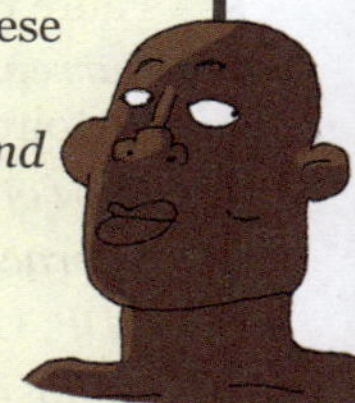

UNITED REPUBLIC OF TANZANIA

- *Location*: Eastern Africa
- *Neighbours*: Burundi, DR of the Congo, Kenya, Malawi, Mozambique, Rwanda, Uganda, Zambia
- *Capital*: Dodoma
- *Area*: 9,47,300 sq km
- *Population*: 69,419,073
- *Languages*: Swahili, English, Arabic
- *Dominant religions*: Islam, indigenous beliefs, Christianity
- *Time zone*: +3
- *Currency*: Tanzanian Shilling
- *Current head of state and government*: Samia Suluhu Hassan
- *Type of government*: Presidential Republic
- *Literacy rate*: 81.8%
- *GDP*: US$ 79.61 billion
- *HDI ranking*: 167

TOGO

- *Location*: Western Africa
- *Neighbours*: Benin, Burkina Faso, Ghana
- *Capital*: Lomé
- *Area*: 56,785 sq km
- *Population*: 9,260,864
- *Languages*: French, Ewe, Mina, Kabye, Dagbani
- *Dominant religions*: Indigenous beliefs, Christianity, Islam
- *Time zone*: GMT
- *Currency*: West African CFA Franc
- *Current head of state*: Faure Essozimna Gnassingbé
- *Current head of government*: Victoire Tomégah Dogbé
- *Type of government*: Presidential Republic
- *Literacy rate*: 66.5%
- *GDP*: US$ 9.83 billion
- *HDI ranking*: 163

TUNISIA

- *Location*: Northern Africa
- *Neighbours*: Libya, Algeria
- *Capital*: Tunis
- *Area*: 1,63,610 sq km
- *Population*: 12,564,689
- *Languages*: Arabic, French, Berber
- *Dominant religion*: Islam
- *Time zone*: +1
- *Currency*: Tunisian Dinar
- *Current head of state*: Kais Saied
- *Current head of government*: Ahmed Hachani
- *Type of government*: Parliamentary Republic
- *Literacy rate*: 81.05%
- *GDP*: US$ 54.71 billion
- *HDI ranking*: 101

UGANDA

- *Location*: East Central Africa
- *Neighbours*: DR of the Congo, Kenya, Rwanda, South Sudan, Tanzania
- *Capital*: Kampala
- *Area*: 2,41,038 sq km
- *Population*: 49,924,252
- *Languages*: English, Ganda, Swahili
- *Dominant religions*: Christianity, Islam
- *Time zone*: +3
- *Currency*: Ugandan Shilling
- *Current head of state*: Yoweri Kaguta Museveni
- *Current head of government*: Robinah Nabbanja
- *Type of government*: Presidential Republic
- *Literacy rate*: 73.81%
- *GDP*: US$ 56.31 billion
- *HDI ranking*: 159

ZAMBIA

- *Location*: Southern Africa
- *Neighbours*: Angola, Botswana, DR of the Congo, Malawi, Mozambique, Namibia, Tanzania, Zimbabwe
- *Capital*: Lusaka
- *Area*: 7,52,618 sq km
- *Population*: 21,134,695
- *Languages*: English, Bembe, Nyanja, Tonga
- *Dominant religion*: Christianity
- *Time zone*: +2
- *Currency*: Zambian Kwacha
- *Current head of state and government*: Hakainde Hichilema
- *Type of government*: Presidential Republic
- *Literacy rate*: 85.1%
- *GDP*: US$ 29.87 billion
- *HDI ranking*: 153

ZIMBABWE

- *Location*: Southern Africa
- *Neighbours*: Zambia, Botswana, Mozambique, South Africa
- *Capital*: Harare
- *Area*: 3,90,757 sq km
- *Population*: 17,020,321
- *Languages*: Shona, Ndebele, English and thirteen other official languages
- *Dominant religions*: Christianity, indigenous faiths
- *Time zone*: +2
- *Currency*: Zimbabwean Dollar
- *Current head of state and government*: Emmerson Dambudzo Mnangagwa
- *Type of government*: Presidential Republic
- *Literacy rate*: 86.8%
- *GDP*: US$ 34.41 billion
- *HDI ranking*: 159

AFGHANISTAN

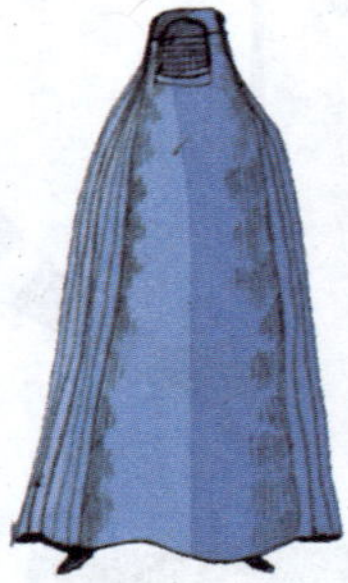

- *Location*: Southern Asia
- *Neighbours*: China, Iran, Pakistan, Tajikistan, Turkmenistan, Uzbekistan
- *Capital*: Kabul
- *Area*: 6,52,230 sq km
- *Population*: 43,372,950
- *Languages*: Pashto, Dari
- *Dominant religion*: Islam
- *Time zone*: +4:30
- *Currency*: Afghan Afghani
- *Current head of state and government*: Taliban Leader Haybatullah Akhundzada
- *Type of government*: Theocratic
- *Literacy rate*: 38.1%
- *GDP*: US$ 14.7 billion
- *HDI ranking*: 182

BAHRAIN

- *Location*: Middle East
- *Neighbours*: Saudi Arabia, Qatar
- *Capital*: Manama
- *Area*: 760 sq km
- *Population*: 1,498,712
- *Languages*: Arabic, English, Farsi
- *Dominant religion*: Islam
- *Time zone*: +3
- *Currency*: Bahraini Dinar
- *Current head of state*: Sheikh Hamad bin Isa Al Khalifa
- *Current head of government*: Salman bin Hamad Al Khalifa
- *Type of government*: Constitutional Monarchy
- *Literacy rate*: 95.7%
- *GDP*: US$ 46.79 billion
- *HDI ranking*: 34

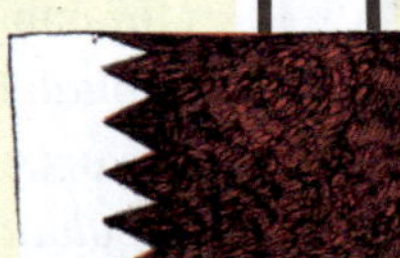

BANGLADESH

- *Location*: Southern Asia
- *Neighbours*: India, Burma
- *Capital*: Dhaka
- *Area*: 1,48,460 sq km
- *Population*: 174,701,211
- *Languages*: Bengali, English
- *Dominant religion*: Islam
- *Time zone*: +6
- *Currency*: Bangladeshi Taka
- *Current head of state*: Mohammad Shahabuddin Chuppi
- *Current head of goverment*: Sheikh Hasina
- *Type of government*: Parliamentary Republic
- *Literacy rate*: 61.4%
- *GDP*: US$ 455.16 billion
- *HDI ranking*: 129

BHUTAN

- *Location*: Southern Asia
- *Neighbours*: India, China
- *Capital*: Thimphu
- *Area*: 38,394 sq km
- *Population*: 792,382
- *Language*: Dzongkha, Sharchopka
- *Dominant religion*: Buddhism
- *Time zone*: +6
- *Currency*: Ngultrum
- *Current head of state*: King Jigme Khesar Namgyel Wangchuck
- *Current head of government*: Tshering Tobgay
- *Type of government*: Constitutional Monarchy
- *Literacy rate*: 63.9%
- *GDP*: US$ 3.11 billion
- *HDI ranking*: 125

BRUNEI DARUSSALAM

- *Location*: Southeastern Asia
- *Neighbours*: Malaysia
- *Capital*: Bandar Seri Begawan
- *Area*: 5,765 sq km
- *Population*: 455,858
- *Languages*: Malay, Chinese
- *Dominant religion*: Islam
- *Time zone*: +8
- *Currency*: Brunei Dollar
- *Current head of state and government*: Sultan Hassanal Bolkiah Mu'izzaddin Waddaulah
- *Type of government*: Absolute Monarchy
- *Literacy rate*: 96.6%
- *GDP*: US$ 15.51 billion
- *HDI ranking*: 55

BURMA (MYANMAR)

- *Location*: Southeastern Asia
- *Neighbours*: India, Bangladesh, China, Laos, Thailand
- *Capital*: Nai Pyi Taw
- *Area*: 6,76,578 sq km
- *Population*: 54,964,694
- *Language*: Burmese
- *Dominant religion*: Buddhism
- *Time zone*: +6:30
- *Currency*: Kyat
- *Current head of state and government*: Min Aung Hlaing
- *Type of government*: Military regime
- *Literacy rate*: 93.09%
- *GDP*: US$ 68.01 billion
- *HDI ranking*: 144

CAMBODIA

- *Location*: Southeastern Asia
- *Neighbours*: Vietnam, Thailand, Laos
- *Capital*: Phnom Penh
- *Area*: 1,81,035 sq km
- *Population*: 17,121,847
- *Language*: Khmer
- *Dominant religion*: Buddhism
- *Time zone*: +7
- *Currency*: Riel
- *Current head of state*: King Norodom Sihamoni
- *Current head of government*: Samdech Moha Bovorthipadi Hun Manet
- *Type of government*: Parliamentary Constitutional Monarchy
- *Literacy rate*: 78.3%
- *GDP*: US$ 45.15 billion
- *HDI ranking*: 148

PEOPLE'S REPUBLIC OF CHINA

- *Location*: Eastern Asia
- *Neighbours*: Mongolia, India, Nepal, Burma, Kazakhstan, Kyrgyzstan, Afghanistan, Pakistan , Bhutan, North Korea, Laos, Russia, Tajikistan, Vietnam
- *Capital*: Beijing
- *Area*: 95,96,960 sq km
- *Population*: 1,425,178,782
- *Languages*: Mandarin, various Chinese dialects
- *Dominant religions*: Atheism (official), Buddhism
- *Time zone*: +8
- *Currency*: Yuan/Renminbi
- *Current head of state*: Xi Jinping
- *Current head of government*: Li Qiang
- *Type of government*: Communist Party-led State
- *Literacy rate*: 96.3%
- *GDP*: US$ 18530 billion
- *HDI ranking*: 75

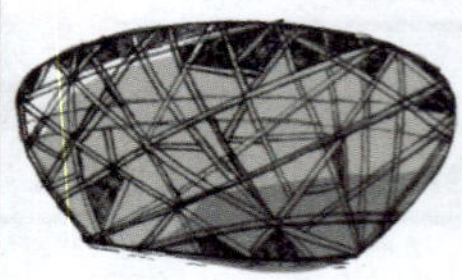

INDIA

- *Location*: Southern Asia
- *Neighbours*: Pakistan, China, Bangladesh, Myanmar, Nepal, Bhutan
- *Capital*: New Delhi
- *Area*: 32,87,263 sq km
- *Population*: 1,441,719,852
- *Languages*: Hindi, English and twenty-one other official languages
- *Dominant religions*: Hinduism, Islam, Sikhism, Christianity
- *Time zone*: +5:30
- *Currency*: Indian Rupee
- *Current head of state*: Droupadi Murmu
- *Current head of government*: Narendra Modi
- *Type of government*: Federal Parliamentary Republic
- *Literacy rate*: 72.2%
- *GDP*: US$ 3940 billion
- *HDI ranking*: 134

INDONESIA

- *Location*: Southeastern Asia
- *Neighbours*: Malaysia, Timor-Leste, Papua New Guinea
- *Capital*: Jakarta
- *Area*: 19,04,569 sq km
- *Population*: 279,798,049
- *Language*: Bahasa Indonesia
- *Dominant religion*: Islam
- *Time zone*: +7
- *Currency*: Indonesian Rupiah
- *Current head of state and government*: Joko Widodo
- *Type of government*: Presidential Republic
- *Literacy rate*: 95.4%
- *GDP*: US$ 1480 billion
- *HDI ranking*: 112

IRAN

- *Location*: Middle East
- *Neighbours*: Iraq, Turkmenistan, Pakistan, Afghanistan, Armenia, Azerbaijan, Turkey
- *Capital*: Tehran
- *Area*: 16,48,195 sq km
- *Population*: 89,809,781
- *Languages*: Persian, Azeri Turkic and Turkic dialects
- *Dominant religion*: Islam
- *Time zone*: +3:30
- *Currency*: Iranian Rial
- *Supreme Leader*: Sayyid Ali Hosseini Khamenei
- *Current head of state*: Ebrahim Raisi
- *Type of government*: Islamic Republic
- *Literacy rate*: 87.1%
- *GDP*: US$ 464.18 billion
- *HDI ranking*: 78

IRAQ

- *Location*: Middle East
- *Neighbours*: Iran, Syria, Saudi Arabia, Jordan, Kuwait, Turkey
- *Capital*: Baghdad
- *Area*: 4,38,317 sq km
- *Population*: : 46,523,657
- *Languages*: Arabic, Kurdish
- *Dominant religion*: Islam
- *Time zone*: +3
- *Currency*: Iraqi Dinar
- *Current head of state*: Abdul Latif Rashid
- *Current head of government*: Mohammed Shia' Al Sudani
- *Type of government*: Federal Parliamentary Republic
- *Literacy rate*: 79.7%
- *GDP*: US$ 265.89 billion
- *HDI ranking*: 128

ISRAEL

- *Location*: Middle East
- *Neighbours*: Egypt, Jordan, Lebanon, Gaza Strip and West Bank
- *Capital*: Jerusalem
- *Area*: 21,937 sq km
- *Population*: 9,311,652
- *Languages*: Hebrew, Arabic, English
- *Dominant religion*: Judaism
- *Time zone*: +2
- *Currency*: Israeli Shekel
- *Current head of state*: Isaac Herzog
- *Current head of government*: Benjamin Netanyahu
- *Type of government*: Parliamentary Democracy
- *Literacy rate*: 97.1%
- *GDP*: US$ 530.66 billion
- *HDI ranking*: 25

JAPAN

- *Location*: Eastern Asia
- *Capital*: Tokyo
- *Neighbours*: South Korea, Russia
- *Area*: 3,77,915 sq km
- *Population*: 122,631,432
- *Language*: Japanese
- *Dominant religions*: Shinto, Buddhism
- *Time zone*: +9
- *Currency*: Japanese Yen
- *Current head of state*: Emperor Naruhito
- *Current head of government*: Fumio Kishida
- *Type of government*: Parliamentary Constitutional Monarchy
- *Literacy rate*: 99%
- *GDP*: US$ 4110 billion
- *HDI ranking*: 24

JORDAN

- *Location*: Middle East
- *Neighbours*: Iraq, Israel, Saudi Arabia, Syria, West Bank
- *Capital*: Amman
- *Area*: 89,342 sq km
- *Population*: 111,384,922
- *Languages*: Arabic, English
- *Dominant religion*: Islam
- *Time zone*: +3
- *Currency*: Jordanian Dinar
- *Current head of state*: King Abdullah II ibn Al-Hussein
- *Current head of government*: Bishr al-Khasawneh
- *Type of government*: Parliamentary Constitutional Monarchy
- *Literacy rate*: 98.01%
- *GDP*: US$ 53.57 billion
- *HDI ranking*: 99

KAZAKHSTAN

- *Location*: Central Asia
- *Neighbours*: China, Kyrgyzstan, Russia, Turkmenistan, Uzbekistan
- *Capital*: Nur-Sultan
- *Area*: 27,24,900 sq km
- *Population*: 19,828,165
- *Languages*: Kazakh, Russian
- *Dominant religions*: Islam, Christianity
- *Time zone*: +6
- *Currency*: Tenge
- *Current head of state*: Kassym-Jomart Tokayev
- *Current head of government*: Oljas Bektenov
- *Type of government*: Presidential Republic
- *Literacy rate*: 99.7%
- *GDP*: US$ 296.74 billion
- *HDI ranking*: 67

KOREA (NORTH)

- *Location*: Eastern Asia
- *Neighbours*: South Korea, China, Russia
- *Capital*: Pyongyang
- *Area*: 1,20,538 sq km
- *Population*: 26,244,582
- *Language*: Korean
- *Dominant religions*: Buddhism, Chondogyo
- *Time zone*: +8:30
- *Currency*: North Korean Won
- *Current head of state and government*: Kim Jong-Un
- *Type of government*: Dictatorship
- *Literacy rate*: 100%

KOREA (SOUTH)

- *Location*: Eastern Asia
- *Neighbour*: North Korea
- *Capital*: Seoul
- *Area*: 99,720 sq km
- *Population*: 51,741,963
- *Language*: Korean
- *Dominant religions*: Christianity, Buddhism
- *Time zone*: +9
- *Currency*: South Korean Won
- *Current head of state and government*: Yoon Suk-yeol
- *Type of government*: Presidential Republic
- *Literacy rate*: 97.9%
- *GDP*: US$ 1760 billion
- *HDI ranking*: 19

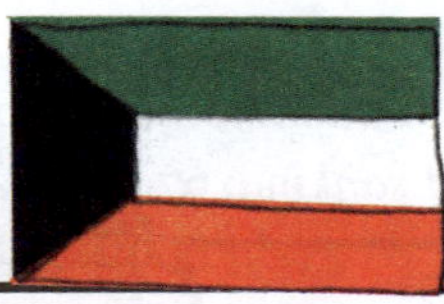

KUWAIT

- *Location*: Middle East
- *Neighbours*: Iraq, Saudi Arabia
- *Capital*: Kuwait City
- *Area*: 17,818 sq km
- *Population*: 4,349,380
- *Languages*: Arabic, English
- *Dominant religion*: Islam
- *Time zone*: +3
- *Currency*: Kuwaiti Dinar
- *Current head of state*: Sheikh Mishal Al-Ahmad Al-Jaber Al-Sabah
- *Current head of government*: Sheikh Ahmad Abdullah Al-Sabah
- *Type of government*: Constitutional Monarchy
- *Literacy rate*: 96.1%
- *GDP*: US$ 160.4 billion
- *HDI ranking*: 49

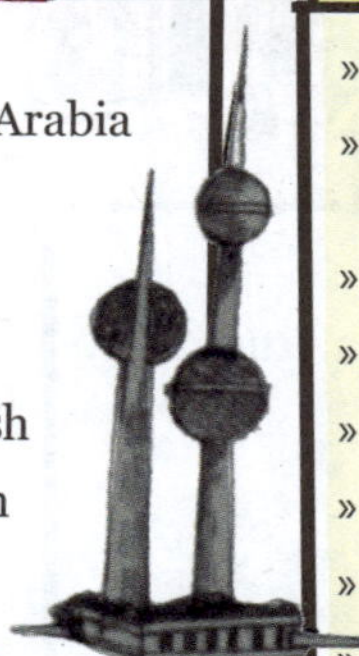

KYRGYZSTAN

- *Location*: Central Asia
- *Neighbours*: Kazakhstan, Tajikistan, China, Uzbekistan
- *Capital*: Bishkek
- *Area*: 1,99,951 sq km
- *Population*: 6,828,888
- *Languages*: Kyrgyz, Russian, Uzbek
- *Dominant religion*: Islam
- *Time zone*: +6
- *Currency*: Kyrgyzstani Som
- *Current head of state*: Sadyr Japarov
- *Current head of government*: Japarov Üsönbek uulu Aqılbek
- *Type of government*: Parliamentary Republic
- *Literacy rate*: 99.5%
- *GDP*: US$ 13.6 billion
- *HDI ranking*: 117

LAOS

- *Location*: Southeastern Asia
- *Neighbours*: Cambodia, China, Thailand, Vietnam, Myanmar
- *Capital*: Vientiane
- *Area*: 2,36,800 sq km
- *Population*: 7,726,194
- *Languages*: Lao, French
- *Dominant religion*: Buddhism
- *Time zone*: +7
- *Currency*: Kip
- *Current head of state*: Thongloun Sisoulith
- *Current head of government*: Sonexay Siphandone
- *Type of government*: Communist State
- *Literacy rate*: 79.87%
- *GDP*: US$ 15.19 billion
- *HDI ranking*: 139

LEBANON

- *Location*: Middle East
- *Neighbours*: Israel, Syria
- *Capital*: Beirut
- *Area*: 10,400 sq km
- *Population*: 5,219,044
- *Languages*: Arabic, French
- *Dominant religions*: Islam, Christianity
- *Time zone*: +2
- *Currency*: Lebanese Pound
- *Current head of state*: Vacant
- *Current head of government*: Najib Mikati
- *Type of government*: Parliamentary Republic
- *Literacy rate*: 94.05%
- *GDP*: US$ 23.13 billion
- *HDI ranking*: 109

MALAYSIA

- *Location*: Southeastern Asia
- *Neighbours*: Indonesia, Singapore, Thailand, Brunei
- *Capital*: Kuala Lumpur
- *Area*: 3,29,847 sq km
- *Population*: 34,671,895
- *Languages*: Bahasa Malaysia, English, Tamil, Cantonese
- *Dominant religions*: Islam, Buddhism
- *Time zone*: +8
- *Currency*: Ringgit
- *Current head of state*: King Sultan Ibrahim ibni Sultan Iskandar (known as Yang di-Pertuan Agong)
- *Current head of government*: Anwar Ibrahim
- *Type of government*: Federal Parliamentary Constitutional Monarchy
- *Literacy rate*: 94.6%
- *GDP*: US$ 445.52 billion
- *HDI ranking*: 63

MALDIVES

- *Location*: Southern Asia
- *Capital*: Malé
- *Area*: 298 sq km
- *Population*: 517,887
- *Languages*: Maldivian Dhivehi, English
- *Dominant religion*: Islam
- *Time zone*: +5
- *Currency*: Rufiyaa
- *Current head of state and government*: Mohamed Muizzu
- *Type of government*: Presidential Republic
- *Literacy rate*: 99.3%
- *GDP*: US$ 7.2 billion
- *HDI ranking*: 87

MONGOLIA

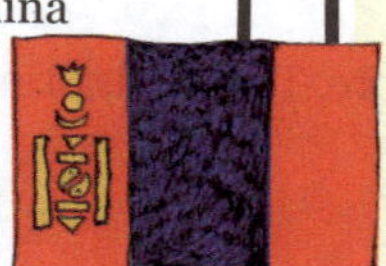

- *Location*: Northern Asia
- *Neighbours*: Russia, China
- *Capital*: Ulaanbaatar
- *Area*: 15,64,116 sq km
- *Population*: 3,493,629
- *Language*: Khalkha
- *Dominant religion*: Buddhism
- *Time zone*: +7, +8
- *Currency*: Tögrög
- *Current head of state*: Ukhnaagiin Khürelsükh
- *Current head of government*: Luvsannamsrain Oyun-Erdene
- *Type of government*: Semi-Presidential Republic
- *Literacy rate*: 98.3%
- *GDP*: US$ 21.94 billion
- *HDI ranking*: 96

NEPAL

- *Location*: Southern Asia
- *Neighbours*: China, India
- *Capital*: Kathmandu
- *Area*: 1,47,181 sq km
- *Population*: 31,240,315
- *Language*: Nepali
- *Dominant religion*: Hinduism
- *Time zone*: +5:45
- *Currency*: Nepalese Rupee
- *Current head of state*: Ram Chandra Poudel
- *Current head of government*: Pushpa Kamal Dahal
- *Type of government*: Federal Parliamentary Republic
- *Literacy rate*: 64.66%
- *GDP*: US$ 44.18 billion
- *HDI ranking*: 146

OMAN

- *Location*: Middle East
- *Neighbours*: Saudi Arabia, UAE, Yemen
- *Capital*: Muscat
- *Area*: 3,09,500 sq km
- *Population*: 4,713.553
- *Language*: Arabic
- *Dominant religion*: Islam
- *Time zone*: +4
- *Currency*: Omani Rial
- *Current head of state and government*: Sultan Haitham bin Tariq al-Said
- *Type of government*: Absolute Monarchy
- *Literacy rate*: 93.9%
- *GDP*: US$ 108.93 billion
- *HDI ranking*: 59

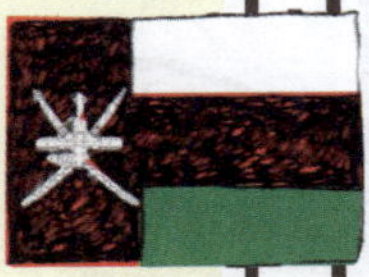

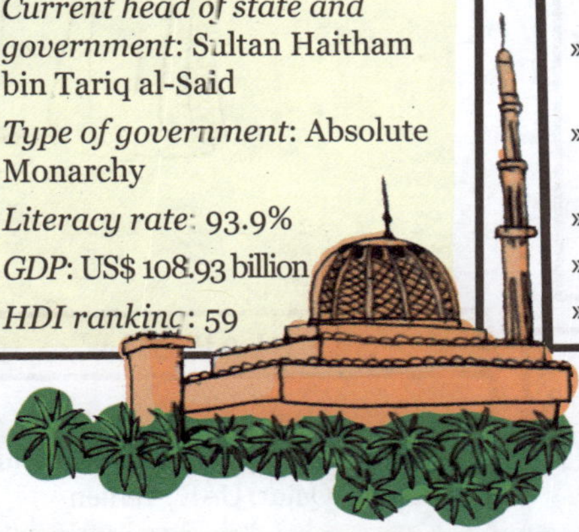

PAKISTAN

- *Location*: Southern Asia
- *Neighbours*: India, Iran, Afghanistan, China
- *Capital*: Islamabad
- *Area*: 7,96,095 sq km
- *Population*: 245,209,815
- *Languages*: Urdu, Punjabi, English
- *Dominant religion*: Islam
- *Time zone*: +5
- *Currency*: Pakistani Rupee
- *Current head of state*: Asif Ali Zardari
- *Current head of government*: Shehbaz Sharif
- *Type of government*: Federal Parliamentary Republic
- *Literacy rate*: 56.4%
- *GDP*: US$ 338.24 billion
- *HDI ranking*: 164

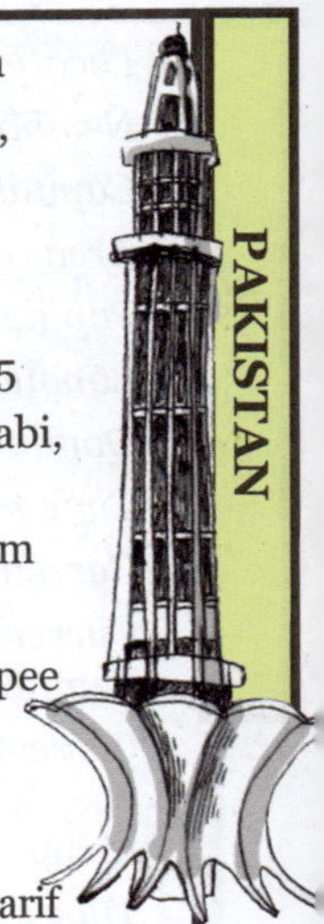

PHILIPPINES

- *Location*: Southeastern Asia
- *Capital*: Manila
- *Area*: 3,00,000 sq km
- *Population*: 119,106,224
- *Languages*: Filipino, English
- *Dominant religion*: Catholicism
- *Time zone*: +8
- *Currency*: Philippines Peso
- *Current head of state and government*: Bongbong Marcos
- *Type of government*: Presidential Republic
- *Literacy rate*: 96.6%
- *GDP*: US$ 471.52 billion
- *HDI ranking*: 113

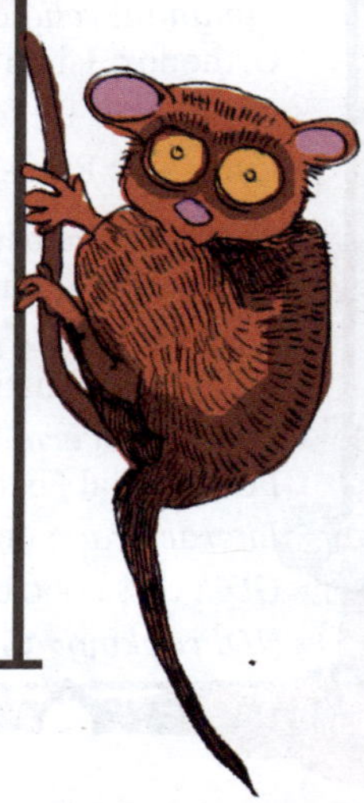

QATAR

- *Location*: Middle East
- *Neighbours*: Saudi Arabia
- *Capital*: Doha
- *Area*: 11,586 sq km
- *Population*: 2,737,061
- *Languages*: Arabic, English
- *Dominant religion*: Islam
- *Time zone*: +3
- *Currency*: Qatari Rial
- *Current head of state*: Sheikh Tamim bin Hamad Al-Thani
- *Current head of government*: Sheikh Mohammed bin Abdulrahman bin Jassim Al Thani
- *Type of government*: Absolute Monarchy
- *Literacy rate*: 97.7%
- *GDP*: US$ 244.69 billion
- *HDI ranking*: 40

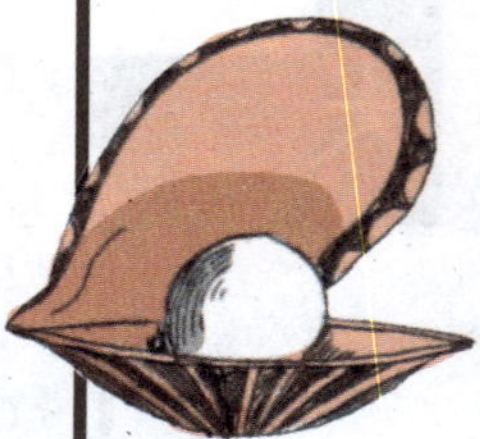

RUSSIAN FEDERATION

- *Location*: Eurasia
- *Neighbours*: Azerbaijan, Belarus, China, Estonia, Finland, Georgia, Kazakhstan, North Korea, Latvia, Lithuania, Mongolia, Norway, Poland, Ukraine
- *Capital*: Moscow
- *Area*: 1,70,98,242 sq km
- *Population*: 143,957,079
- *Language*: Russian
- *Dominant religion*: Russian Orthodox, Islam
- *Time zone*: + 3 to + 12
- *Currency*: Ruble
- *Current head of state*: Vladimir Vladimirovich Putin
- *Current head of government*: Mikhail Mishustin
- *Type of government*: Semi-Presidential Federation
- *Literacy rate*: 99.7%
- *GDP*: US$ 2060 billion
- *HDI ranking*: 56

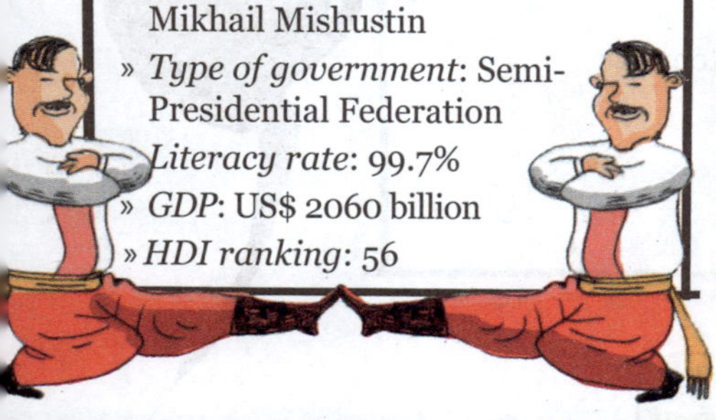

SAUDI ARABIA

- *Location*: Middle East
- *Neighbours*: Iraq, Jordan, Kuwait, Oman, Qatar, UAE , Yemen
- *Capital*: Riyadh
- *Area*: 21,49,690 sq km
- *Population*: 37,473,929
- *Language*: Arabic
- *Dominant religion*: Islam
- *Time zone*: +3
- *Currency*: Saudi Rial
- *Current head of state*: King Salman bin Abdulaziz Al-Saud
- *Current head of government*: Prince Mohammed bin Salman bin Abdulaziz Al Saud
- *Type of government*: Absolute Monarchy
- *Literacy rate*: 94.8%
- *GDP*: US$ 1110 billion
- *HDI ranking*: 40

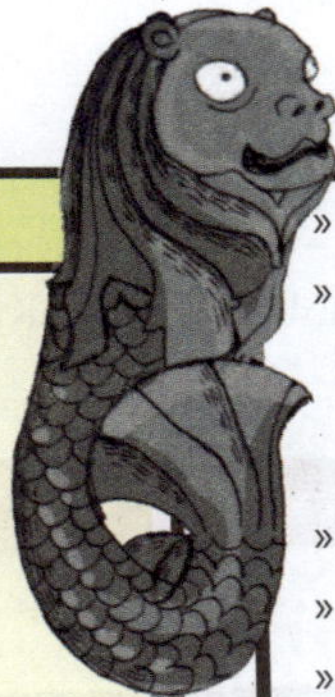

SINGAPORE

- *Location*: Southeastern Asia
- *Neighbours*: Malaysia, Indonesia
- *Capital*: Singapore
- *Area*: 719.2 sq km
- *Population*: 6,052,709
- *Languages*: English, Malay, Mandarin, Tamil
- *Dominant religions*: Buddhism, Islam, Christianity
- *Time zone*: +8
- *Currency*: Singapore Dollar
- *Current head of state*: Tharman Shanmugaratnam
- *Current head of government*: Lawrence Wong
- *Type of government*: Parliamentary Republic
- *Literacy rate*: 96.7%
- *GDP*: US$ 525.23 billion
- *HDI ranking*: 9

SRI LANKA

- *Location*: Southern Asia
- *Capital*: Colombo (commercial capital); Sri Jayewardenepura Kotte (legislative capital)
- *Area*: 65,610 sq km
- *Population*: 21,949,268
- *Languages*: Sinhala, Tamil
- *Dominant religions*: Buddhism, Christianity
- *Time zone*: +5:30
- *Currency*: Sri Lankan Rupee
- *Current head of state and government*: Ranil Wickremesinghe
- *Type of government*: Presidential Republic
- *Literacy rate*: 92.61%
- *GDP*: US$ 84.4 billion
- *HDI ranking*: 78

SYRIA

- *Location*: Middle East
- *Neighbours*: Iraq, Israel, Jordan, Lebanon, Turkey
- *Capital*: Damascus
- *Area*: 1,87,437 sq km
- *Population*: 24,348,053
- *Language*: Arabic
- *Dominant religion*: Islam
- *Time zone*: +2
- *Currency*: Syrian Pound
- *Current head of state*: Bashar al-Assad
- *Current head of government*: Hussein Arnous
- *Type of government*: Presidential Republic
- *Literacy rate*: 86.3%
- *GDP*: US$ 12 billion
- *HDI ranking*: 157

TAJIKISTAN

- *Location*: Central Asia
- *Neighbours*: Afghanistan, China, Uzbekistan, Kyrgyzstan
- *Capital*: Dushanbe
- *Area*: 1,41,400 sq km
- *Population*: 10,331,513
- *Languages*: Tajik, Russian
- *Dominant religion*: Islam
- *Time zone*: +5
- *Currency*: Somoni
- *Current head of state*: Emomali Rahmon
- *Current head of government*: Kokhir Rasulzoda
- *Type of government*: Presidential Republic
- *Literacy rate*: 99.7%
- *GDP*: US$ 12.95 billion
- *HDI ranking*: 126

THAILAND

- *Location*: Southeastern Asia
- *Neighbours*: Cambodia, Laos Vietnam, Malaysia, Myanmar
- *Capital*: Bangkok
- *Area*: 5,13,120 sq km
- *Population*: 71, 697, 030
- *Language*: Thai
- *Dominant religion*: Buddhism
- *Time zone*: +7
- *Currency*: Baht
- *Current head of state*: Maha Vajiralongkorn
- *Current head of government*: Srettha Thavisin
- *Type of government*: Constitutional Monarchy
- *Literacy rate*: 93.9%
- *GDP*: US$ 548.89 billion
- *HDI ranking*: 66

TIMOR-LESTE

- *Location*: Southeastern Asia
- *Neighbour*: Indonesia
- *Capital*: Dili
- *Area*: 14,874 sq km
- *Population*: 1,428,911
- *Languages*: Tetun Prasa, Mambai, Makasai
- *Dominant religion*: Roman Catholicism
- *Time zone*: +9
- *Currency*: US Dollar
- *Current head of state*: José Manuel Ramos-Horta
- *Current head of government*: Xanana Gusmão
- *Type of government*: Semi-Presidential Republic
- *Literacy rate*: 69.9%
- *GDP*: US$ 1.99 billion
- *HDI ranking*: 155

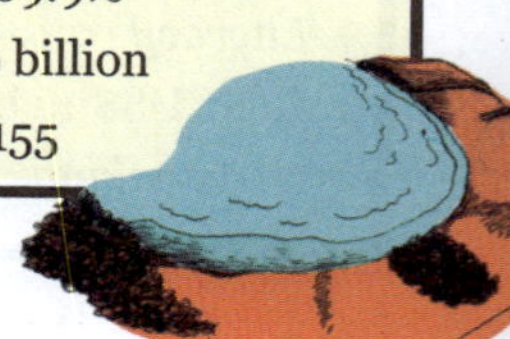

TURKMENISTAN

- *Location*: Central Asia
- *Neighbours*: Iran, Uzbekistan, Kazakhstan, Afghanistan
- *Capital*: Ashgabat
- *Area*: 4,88,100 sq km
- *Population*: 6,598,071
- *Language*: Turkmen
- *Dominant religion*: Islam
- *Time zone*: +5
- *Currency*: Turkmen Manat
- *Current head of state and government*: Serdar Berdimuhamedow
- *Type of government*: Presidential Republic
- *Literacy rate*: 99.6%
- *GDP*: US$ 81.9 billion
- *HDI ranking*: 94

TURKEY

- *Location*: Eurasia
- *Neighbours*: Armenia, Azerbaijan, Bulgaria, Georgia, Greece, Iran, Iraq, Syria
- *Capital*: Ankara
- *Area*: 7,83,562 sq km
- *Population*: 86,227,713
- *Language*: Turkish
- *Dominant religion*: Islam
- *Time zone*: +2
- *Currency*: Lira
- *Current head of state and government*: Recep Tayyip Erdoğan
- *Type of government*: Presidential Republic
- *Literacy rate*: 95.6%
- *GDP*: US$ 1110 billion
- *HDI ranking*: 45

UNITED ARAB EMIRATES

- *Location*: Middle East
- *Neighbours*: Saudi Arabia, Oman
- *Capital*: Abu Dhabi
- *Area*: 83,600 sq km
- *Population*:9,516,871
- *Language*: Arabic
- *Dominant religion*: Islam
- *Time zone*: +4
- *Currency*: UAE Dirham
- *Current head of state*: Sheikh Khalifa Bin Zayed Al Nahyan
- *Current head of government*: Sheikh Mohammed Bin Rashid Al Maktoum
- *Type of government*: Federation of Monarchies
- *Literacy rate*: 92.9%
- *GDP*: US$ 527.8 billion
- *HDI ranking*: 17

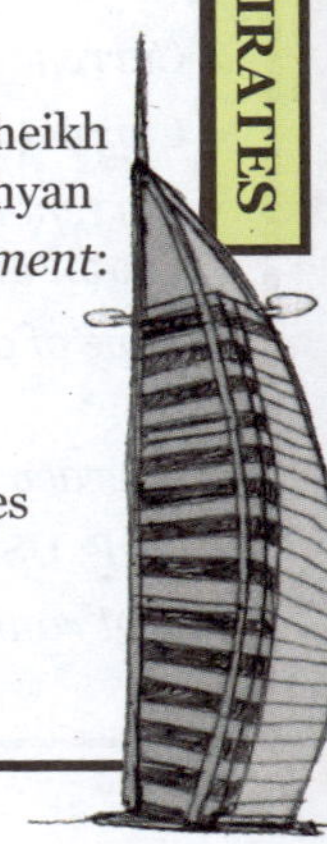

UZBEKISTAN

- *Location*: Central Asia
- *Neighbours*: Kazakhstan, Turmkenistan, Tajikistan, Afghanistan, Kyrgyzstan
- *Capital*: Tashkent
- *Area*: 4,47,400 sq km
- *Population*: 35,673,804
- *Language*: Uzbek
- *Dominant religion*: Islam
- *Time zone*: +5
- *Currency*: Uzbekistan Som
- *Current head of state*: Shavkat Mirziyoyev
- *Current head of government*: Abdulla Aripov
- *Type of government*: Presidential Republic
- *Literacy rate*: 100%
- *GDP*: US$ 97.96 billion
- *HDI ranking*: 106

VIETNAM

- *Location*: Southeastern Asia
- *Neighbours*: Cambodia, Laos, China
- *Capital*: Hanoi
- *Area*: 3,31,210 sq km
- *Population*: 99,497,680
- *Languages*: Vietnamese, English
- *Dominant religions*: Buddhism, Christianity
- *Time zone*: +7
- *Currency*: Dong
- *Current head of state*: Tô Lâm
- *Current head of government*: Pham Minh Chinh
- *Type of government*: Communist State
- *Literacy rate*: 94.5%
- *GDP*: US$ 465.81 billion
- *HDI ranking*: 107

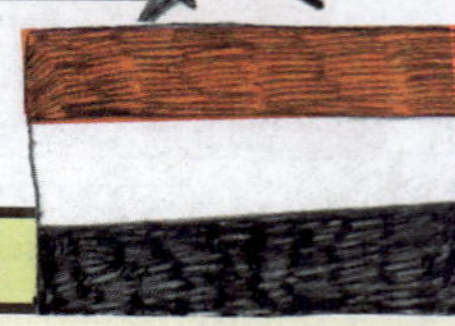

YEMEN

- *Location*: Middle East
- *Neighbours*: Saudi Arabia, Oman
- *Capital*: Sana'a
- *Area*: 5,27,968 sq km
- *Population*: 35,219,853
- *Language*: Arabic
- *Dominant religion*: Islam
- *Time zone*: +3
- *Currency*: Yemeni Rial
- *Current head of state*: Rashad al-Alimi
- *Current head of government*: Ahmed Awad bin Mubarak
- *Type of government*: In transition
- *Literacy rate*: 69.9%
- *GDP*: US$ 16.94 billion
- *HDI ranking*: 186

ALBANIA

- *Location*: Southeastern Europe
- *Neighbours*: North Macedonia, Greece, Montenegro, Kosovo, Italy
- *Capital*: Tirana
- *Area*: 28,748 sq km
- *Population*: 2,826,020
- *Language*: Albanian
- *Dominant religions*: Islam
- *Time zone*: +1
- *Currency*: Lek
- *Current head of state*: Bajram Begaj
- *Current head of government*: Edi Rama
- *Type of government*: Parliamentary Republic
- *Literacy rate*: 97.5%
- *GDP*: US$ 25.43 billion
- *HDI ranking*: 74

ANDORRA

- *Location*: Southwestern Europe
- *Neighbours*: France, Spain
- *Capital*: Andorra la Vella
- *Area*: 468 sq km
- *Population*: 80,341
- *Language*: Catalan
- *Dominant religion*: Roman Catholicism
- *Time zone*: +1
- *Currency*: Euro
- *Current heads of state*: Co-Prince Emmanuel Macron and Co-Prince Archbishop Joan-Enric Vives i Sicília
- *Current head of government*: Xaviar Espot Zamora
- *Type of government*: Parliamentary Democracy
- *Literacy rate*: 100%
- *GDP*: US$ 3.9 billion
- *HDI ranking*: 35

ARMENIA

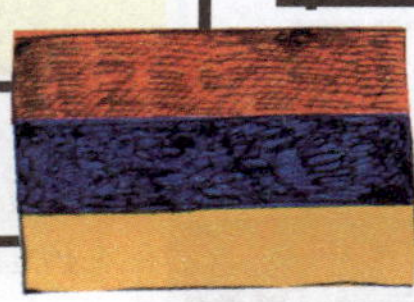

- *Location*: Eurasia
- *Neighbours*: Azerbaijan, Georgia, Iran, Turkey
- *Capital*: Yerevan
- *Area*: 29,743 sq km
- *Population*: 2,777,979
- *Language*: Armenian
- *Dominant religion*: Armenian Apostolic
- *Time zone*: +4
- *Currency*: Dram
- *Current head of state*: Vahagn Khachaturyan
- *Current head of government*: Nikol Pashinyan
- *Type of government*: Parliamentary Democracy
- *Literacy rate*: 99.7%
- *GDP*: US$ 25.4 billion
- *HDI ranking*: 76

AUSTRIA

» *Location*: Central Europe

» *Neighbours*: Czech Republic, Germany, Hungary, Italy, Liechtenstein, Slovakia, Slovenia, Switzerland

» *Capital*: Vienna

» *Area*: 83,871 sq km

» *Population*: 8,977,139

» *Language*: German

» *Dominant religion*: Roman Catholicism

» *Time zone*: +1

» *Currency*: Euro

» *Current head of state*: Alexander Van der Bellen

» *Current head of government*: Karl Nehammer

» *Type of government*: Federal Parliamentary Republic

» *Literacy rate*: 98%

» *GDP*: US$ 540.89 billion

» *HDI ranking*: 22

AZERBAIJAN

» *Location*: Eurasia

» *Neighbours*: Armenia, Georgia, Iran, Russia, Turkey

» *Capital*: Baku

» *Area*: 86,600 sq km

» *Population*: 10,462,904

» *Languages*: Azerbaijani, Russian, Armenian

» *Dominant religion*: Islam

» *Time zone*: +4

» *Currency*: Manat

» *Current head of state*: Ilham Heydar oglu Aliyev

» *Current head of government*: Ali Asadov

» *Type of government*: Presidential Republic

» *Literacy rate*: 99.8%

» *GDP*: US$ 78.75 billion

» *HDI ranking*: 89

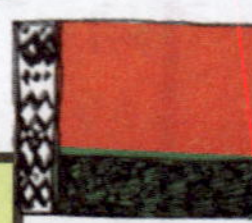

BELARUS

» *Location*: Eastern Europe

» *Neighbours*: Ukraine, Russia, Poland, Lithuania, Latvia

» *Capital*: Minsk

» *Area*: 2,07,600 sq km

» *Population*: 9,455,037

» *Languages*: Belarusian, Russian

» *Dominant religion*: Eastern Orthodox Church

» *Time zone*: +3

» *Currency*: Belarusian Ruble

» *Current head of state*: Aleksandr Grigoryevich Lukashenko

» *Current head of government*: Roman Golovchenko

» *Type of government*: Presidential Republic

» *Literacy rate*: 99.7%

» *GDP*: US$ 69.05 billion

» *HDI ranking*: 69

BELGIUM

- *Location*: Western Europe
- *Neighbours*: Germany, France, Luxembourg, The Netherlands
- *Capital*: Brussels
- *Area*: 30,528 sq km
- *Population*: 11,715,774
- *Languages*: Dutch, French, German
- *Dominant religion*: Roman Catholicism
- *Time zone*: +1
- *Currency*: Euro
- *Current head of state*: King Philippe
- *Current head of government*: Alexander De Croo
- *Type of government*: Federal Parliamentary Democracy under a Constitutional Monarchy
- *Literacy rate*: 99%
- *GDP*: US$ 655.19 billion
- *HDI ranking*: 12

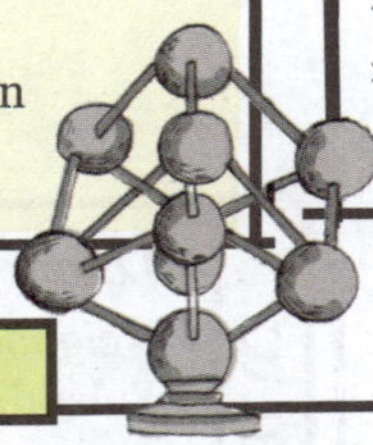

BOSNIA AND HERZEGOVINA

- *Location*: Southeastern Europe
- *Neighbours*: Serbia, Croatia, Montenegro
- *Capital*: Sarajevo
- *Area*: 51,197 sq km
- *Population*: 3,210,847
- *Languages*: Serbian, Croatian, Bosnian
- *Dominant religions*: Christianity, Islam
- *Time zone*: +1
- *Currency*: Convertible Mark
- *Current heads of state*: Denis Bećirović, Zeljka Cvijanovic and Željko Komšić
- *Current head of government*: Borjana Krišto
- *Type of government*: Parliamentary Republic
- *Literacy rate*: 98.4%
- *GDP*: US$ 29.08 billion
- *HDI ranking*: 80

BULGARIA

- *Location*: Southeastern Europe
- *Neighbours*: Greece, North Macedonia, Romania, Serbia, Turkey
- *Capital*: Sofia
- *Area*: 1,10,879 sq km
- *Population*: 6,618,615
- *Language*: Bulgarian
- *Dominant religion*: Eastern Orthodox Church
- *Time zone*: +2
- *Currency*: Lev
- *Current head of state*: Rumen Radev
- *Current head of government*: Dimitar Glavchev
- *Type of government*: Parliamentary Republic
- *Literacy rate*: 98.3%
- *GDP*: US$ 107.93 billion
- *HDI ranking*: 70

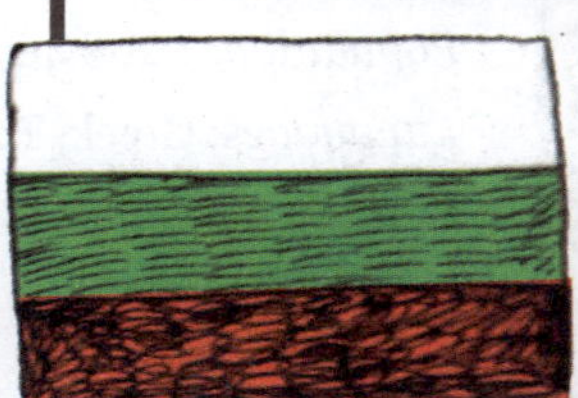

CROATIA

- *Location*: Southeastern Europe
- *Neighbours*: Slovenia, Hungary, Yugoslavia, Bosnia and Herzegovina, Montenegro
- *Capital*: Zagreb
- *Area*: 56,594 sq km
- *Population*: 3,986,627
- *Language*: Croatian
- *Dominant religion*: Roman Catholicism
- *Time zone*: +1
- *Currency*: Kuna
- *Current head of state*: Zoran Milanović
- *Current head of government*: Andrej Plenković
- *Type of government*: Parliamentary Republic
- *Literacy rate*: 99.2%
- *GDP*: US$ 88.08 billion
- *HDI ranking*: 39

CYPRUS

- *Location*: Mediterranean
- *Capital*: Nicosia
- *Area*: 9,251 sq km
- *Population*: 1,268,467
- *Languages*: Greek, Turkish
- *Dominant religion*: Greek Orthodox Church
- *Time zone*: +2
- *Currency*: Euro
- *Current head of state and government*: Nikos Christodoulides
- *Type of government*: Unitary Presidential Republic
- *Literacy rate*: 99.06%
- *GDP*: US$ 34.22 billion
- *HDI ranking*: 29

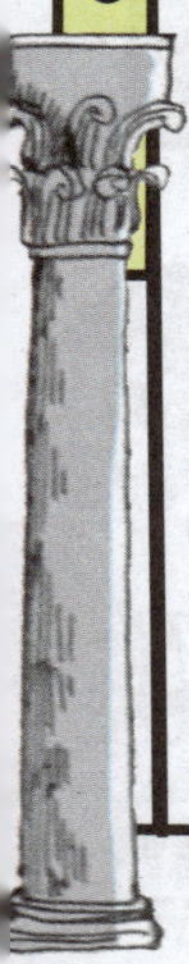

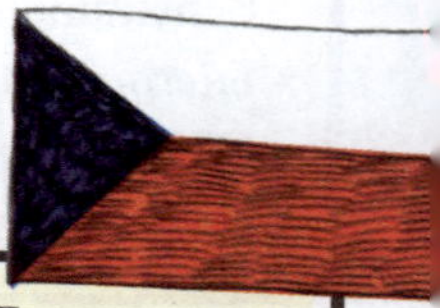

CZECH REPUBLIC

- *Location*: Central Europe
- *Neighbours*: Austria, Germany, Poland, Slovakia
- *Capital*: Prague
- *Area*: 78,867 sq km
- *Population*: 10,503,734
- *Language*: Czech
- *Dominant religion*: Roman Catholicism
- *Time zone*: +1
- *Currency*: Koruna
- *Current head of state*: Petr Pavel
- *Current head of government*: Petr Fiala
- *Type of government*: Parliamentary Republic
- *Literacy rate*: 99%
- *GDP*: US$ 325.88 billion
- *HDI ranking*: 32

DENMARK

- *Location*: Northern Europe
- *Capital*: Copenhagen
- *Area*: 43,094 sq km
- *Population*: 5,939,695
- *Languages*: Danish, English
- *Dominant religion*: Evangelical Lutheran Church
- *Time zone*: +1
- *Currency*: Krone
- *Current head of state*: King Frederik X
- *Current head of government*: Mette Frederiksen
- *Type of government*: Parliamentary Constitutional Monarchy
- *Literacy rate*: 99%
- *GDP*: US$ 409.99 billion
- *HDI ranking*: 5

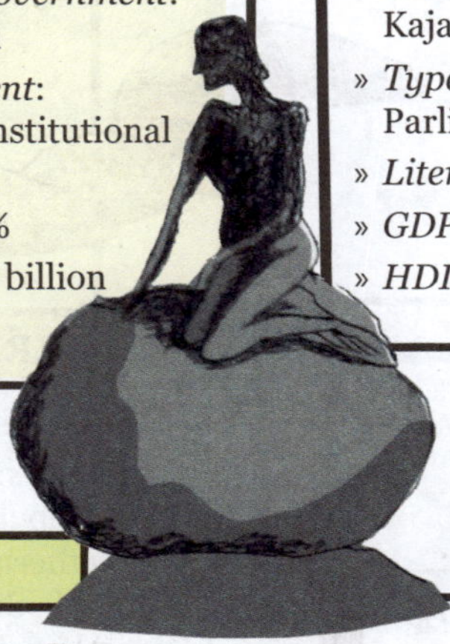

ESTONIA

- *Location*: Eastern Europe
- *Neighbours*: Latvia, Russia
- *Capital*: Tallinn
- *Area*: 45,228 sq km
- *Population*: 1,366,491
- *Languages*: Estonian, Russian
- *Dominant religion*: Orthodox Church of Estonia, Lutheran
- *Time zone*: +2
- *Currency*: Euro
- *Current head of state*: Alar Karis
- *Current head of government*: Kaja Kallas
- *Type of government*: Parliamentary Republic
- *Literacy rate*: 99.8%
- *GDP*: US$ 43.49 billion
- *HDI ranking*: 31

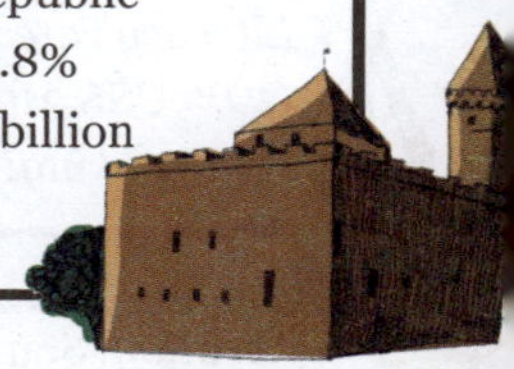

FINLAND

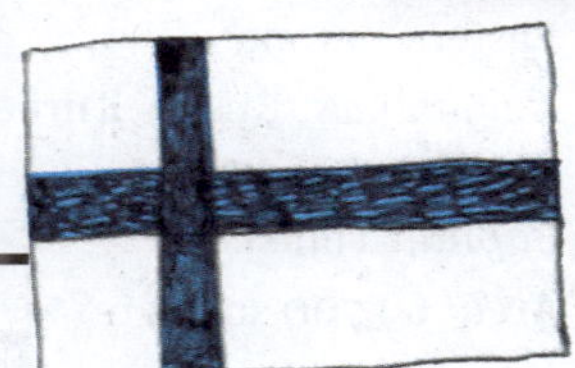

- *Location*: Northern Europe
- *Neighbours*: Russia, Sweden, Norway
- *Capital*: Helsinki
- *Area*: 6,43,801 sq km
- *Population*: 5,549,886
- *Languages*: Finnish, Swedish
- *Dominant religion*: Lutheran
- *Time zone*: +2
- *Currency*: Euro
- *Current head of state*: Alexander Stubb
- *Current head of government*: Petteri Orpo
- *Type of government*: Parliamentary Republic
- *Literacy rate*: 100%
- *GDP*: US$ 308.06 billion
- *HDI ranking*: 12

FRANCE

» *Location*: Western Europe
» *Neighbours*: Germany, Italy, Spain, Belgium, Switzerland, Monaco, Luxembourg, Andorra
» *Capital*: Paris
» *Area*: 6,43,801 sq km
» *Population*: 64,881,830
» *Language*: French
» *Dominant religion*: Roman Catholicism
» *Time zone*: +1
» *Currency*: Euro
» *Current head of state*: Emmanuel Jean-Michel Frédéric Macron
Current head of government: Gabriel Attal
Type of government: Semi-Presidential Republic
» *Literacy rate*: 99%
» *GDP*: US$ 3130 billion
HDI ranking: 28

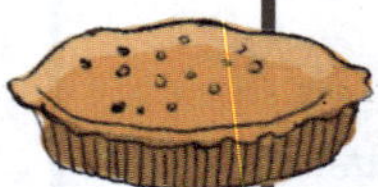

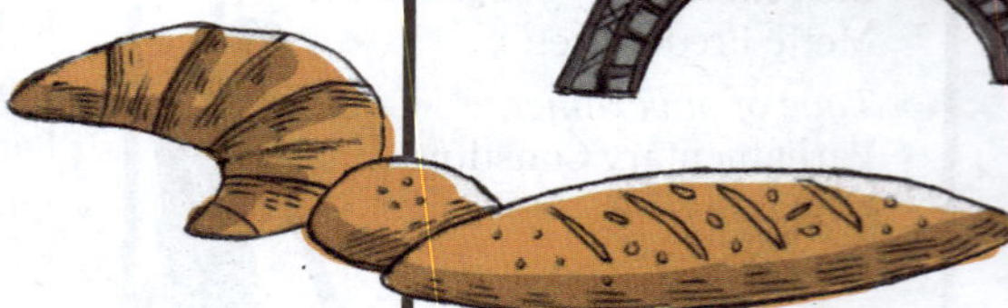

GEORGIA

» *Location*: Southwestern Asia/ Eastern Europe
» *Neighbours*: Russia, Turkey, Azerbaijan, Armenia
» *Capital*: Tbilisi
» *Area*: 69,700 sq km
» *Population*: 3,717,425
» *Languages*: Georgian, Azeri, Armenian
» *Dominant religion*: Orthodox Christian
» *Time zone*: +4
» *Currency*: Lari
» *Current head of state*: Salome Zourabichvili
» *Current head of government*: Irakli Kobakhidze
» *Type of government*: Semi-Presidential
» *Literacy rate*: 99.7%
» *GDP*: US$ 32.87 billion
» *HDI ranking*: 60

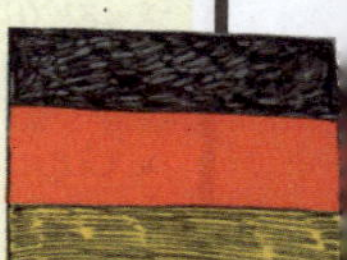

GERMANY

» *Location*: Central Europe
» *Neighbours*: France, Austria, Czech Republic, Poland, The Netherlands, Belgium, Denmark, Switzerland, Luxembourg
Capital: Berlin
Area: 3,57,022 sq km
» *Population*: 84,607,016
» *Language*: German
» *Dominant religion*: Roman Catholicism, Protestantism
» *Time zone*: +1
» *Currency*: Euro
» *Current head of state*: Frank-Walter Steinmeier
» *Current head of government*: Olaf Scholz
» *Type of government*: Federal Parliamentary Republic
» *Literacy rate*: 99%
» *GDP*: US$ 4590 billion
HDI ranking: 7

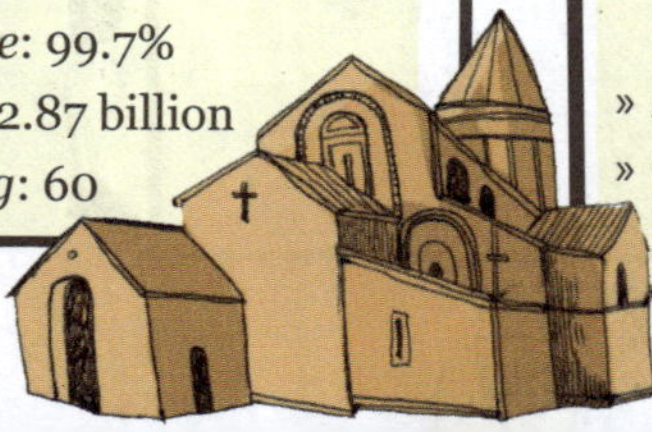

GREECE

- *Location*: Southern Europe
- *Capital*: Athens
- *Neighbours*: Turkey, Bulgaria, North Macedonia, Albania
- *Area*: 1,31,957 sq km
- *Population*: 10,302,720
- *Language*: Greek
- *Dominant religion*: Greek Orthodox Church
- *Time zone*: +2
- *Currency*: Euro
- *Current head of state*: Katerina Sakellaropoulou
- *Current head of government*: Kyriakos Mitsotakis
- *Type of government*: Parliamentary Republic
- *Literacy rate*: 95.2%
- *GDP*: US$ 250.28 billion
- *HDI ranking*: 33

HUNGARY

- *Location*: Central Europe
- *Neighbours*: Slovakia, Romania, Croatia, Austria, Serbia, Turkey, Slovenia, Ukraine
- *Capital*: Budapest
- *Area*: 93,028 sq km
- *Population*: 9,994,993
- *Language*: Hungarian
- *Dominant religion*: Roman Catholicism
- *Time zone*: +1
- *Currency*: Forint
- *Current head of state*: Tamás Sulyok
- *Current head of government*: Viktor Orbán
- *Type of government*: Parliamentary Republic
- *Literacy rate*: 99.3%
- *GDP*: US$ 223.41 billion
- *HDI ranking*: 47

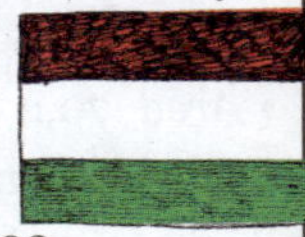

ICELAND

- *Location*: Northern Europe
- *Capital*: Reykjavik
- *Area*: 1,03,000 sq km
- *Population*: 377,689
- *Languages*: Icelandic, English
- *Dominant religion*: Evangelical Lutheran Church of Iceland
- *Time zone*: GMT
- *Currency*: Icelandic Króna
- *Current head of state*: Halla Tómasdóttir
- *Current head of government*: Bjarni Benediktsson
- *Type of government*: Unitary Parliamentary Republic
- *Literacy rate*: 99%
- *GDP*: US$ 33.34 billion
- *HDI ranking*:3

IRELAND

- *Location*: Western Europe
- *Capital*: Dublin
- Neighbouring countries: Northern Ireland, England, Scotland (The UK)
- *Area*: 70,273 sq km
- *Population*: 5,089,478
- *Languages*: Irish, English
- *Dominant religion*: Roman Catholicism
- *Time zone*: +1
- *Currency*: Euro
- *Current head of state*: Michael D Higgins
- *Current head of government*: Simon Harris
- *Type of government*: Parliamentary Republic
- *Literacy rate*: 99%
- *GDP*: US$ 564.02 billon
- *HDI ranking*: 7

ITALY

- *Location*: Southern Europe
- *Neighbours*: France, Austria, Vatican City, San Marino, Slovenia, Switzerland
- *Capital*: Rome
- *Area*: 3,01,340 sq km
- *Population*: 58,697,744
- *Language*: Italian
- *Dominant religion*: Roman Catholicism
- *Time zone*: +1
- *Currency*: Euro
- *Current head of state*: Sergio Mattarella
- *Current head of government*: Giorgia Meloni
- *Type of government*: Parliamentary Republic
- *Literacy rate*: 99.02%
- *GDP*: US$ 2330 billion
- *HDI ranking*: 30

LATVIA

- *Location*: Eastern Europe
- *Neighbours*: Russia, Belarus, Estonia, Lithuania
- *Capital*: Riga
- *Area*: 64,589 sq km
- *Population*: 1,801,246
- *Language*: Latvian
- *Dominant religion*: Lutheran
- *Time zone*: +2
- *Currency*: Euro
- *Current head of state*: Edgars Rinkēvičs
- *Current head of government*: Evika Siliņa
- *Type of government*: Parliamentary Republic
- *Literacy rate*: 99.8%
- *GDP*: US$ 45.47 billion
- *HDI ranking*: 37

LIECHTENSTEIN

- *Location*: Central Europe
- *Neighbours*: Switzerland, Austria
- *Capital*: Vaduz
- *Area*: 160 sq km
- *Population*: 39,822
- *Language*: German
- *Dominant religion*: Roman Catholicism
- *Time zone*: +1
- *Currency*: Swiss Franc
- *Current head of state*: Prince Hans-Adam II
- *Current head of government*: Daniel Risch
- *Type of government*: Constitutional Monarchy
- *Literacy rate*: 100%
- *GDP*: $7.71 billion
- *HDI ranking*: 12

LITHUANIA

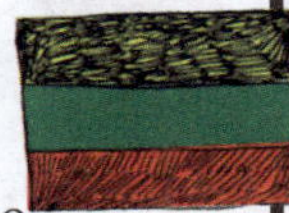

- *Location*: Eastern Europe
- *Neighbours*: Belarus, Poland, Latvia, Russia
- *Capital*: Vilnius
- *Area*: 65,300 sq km
- *Population*: 2,692,798
- *Language*: Lithuanian
- *Dominant religion*: Roman Catholicism
- *Time zone*: +2
- *Currency*: Euro
- *Current head of state*: Gitanas Nauṡda
- *Current head of government*: Ingrida Šimonytė
- *Type of government*: Semi-Presidential Republic
- *Literacy rate*: 99.8%
- *GDP*: US$ 81.17 billion
- *HDI ranking*: 37

LUXEMBOURG

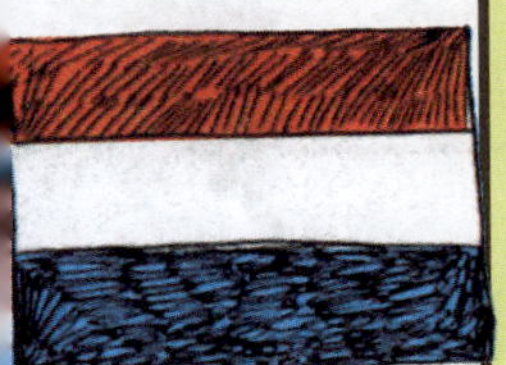

- *Location*: Western Europe
- *Neighbours*: Germany, Belgium, France
- *Capital*: Luxembourg
- *Area*: 2,586 sq km
- *Population*: 671,254
- *Languages*: Luxembourgish, French, German
- *Dominant religion*: Roman Catholicism
- *Time zone*: +1
- *Currency*: Euro
- *Current head of state*: Grand Duke Henri
- *Current head of government*: Luc Frieden
- *Type of government*: Constitutional Monarchy
- *Literacy rate*: 100%
- *GDP*: US$ 88.56 billion
- *HDI ranking*: 20

MALTA

- *Location*: Southern Europe
- *Capital*: Valletta
- *Area*: 316 sq km
- *Population*: 536,740
- *Languages*: Maltese, English
- *Dominant religion*: Roman Catholicism
- *Time zone*: +1
- *Currency*: Euro
- *Current head of state*: Myriam Spiteri Debono
- *Current head of government*: Robert Abela
- *Type of government*: Parliamentary Republic
- *Literacy rate*: 94.07%
- *GDP*: US$ 22.74 billion
- *HDI ranking*: 25

MOLDOVA

- *Location*: Eastern Europe
- *Neighbours*: Ukraine, Romania
- *Capital*: Chisinau
- *Area*: 33,851 sq km
- *Population*: 3,329,865
- *Languages*: Moldovan, Romanian, Russian
- *Dominant religion*: Moldovan Orthodox Church
- *Time zone*: +2
- *Currency*: Moldovan Leu
- *Current head of state*: Maia Sandu
- *Current head of government*: Dorin Recean
- *Type of government*: Parliamentary Republic
- *Literacy rate*: 99.2%
- *GDP*: US$ 18.36 billion
- *HDI ranking*: 86

MONACO

- *Location*: Western Europe
- *Neighbour*: France
- *Capital*: Monaco
- *Area*: 2 sq km
- *Population*: 36,157
- *Languages*: French, English
- *Dominant religion*: Roman Catholicism
- *Time zone*: +1
- *Currency*: Euro
- *Current head of state*: Prince Albert II
- *Current head of government*: Pierre Dartout
- *Type of government*: Constitutional Monarchy
- *Literacy rate*: 99%
- *GDP*: US$ 8.78 billion

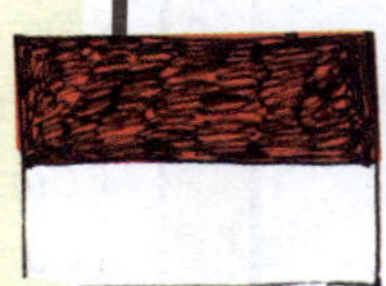

MONTENEGRO

- *Location*: Southeastern Europe
- *Neighbours*: Serbia, Albania, Bosnia and Herzegovinia, Croatia, Kosovo
- *Capital*: Podgorica
- *Area*: 13,812 sq km
- *Population*: 626,102
- *Languages*: Montenegrin, Serbian
- *Dominant religion*: Christian Orthodox
- *Time zone*: +1
- *Currency*: Euro
- *Current head of state*: Jakov Milatović
- *Current head of government*: Milojko Spajić
- *Type of government*: Parliamentary Republic
- *Literacy rate*: 98.7%
- *GDP*: US$ 8.01 billion
- *HDI ranking*: 50

NORTH MACEDONIA

- *Location*: Southeastern Europe
- *Neighbours*: Albania, Bulgaria, Greece, Kosovo, Serbia
- *Capital*: Skopje
- *Area*: 25,713 sq km
- *Population*: 2,082,706
- *Languages*: Macedonian, Albanian
- *Dominant religions*: Macedonian Orthodox, Islam
- *Time zone*: +1
- *Currency*: Macedonian Denar
- *Current head of state*: Gordana Siljanovska-Davkova
- *Current head of government*: Talat Xhaferi
- *Type of government*: Parliamentary Republic
- *Literacy rate*: 97.8%
- *GDP*: US$ 15.87 billion
- *HDI ranking*: 83

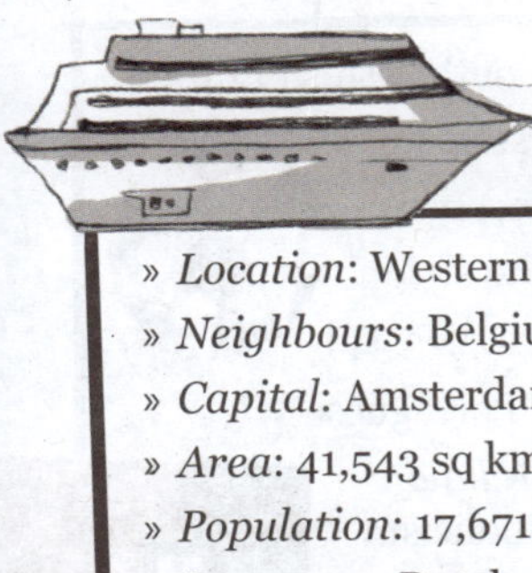

THE NETHERLANDS

- *Location*: Western Europe
- *Neighbours*: Belgium, Germany
- *Capital*: Amsterdam
- *Area*: 41,543 sq km
- *Population*: 17,671,125
- *Language*: Dutch
- *Dominant religion*: Roman Catholicism
- *Time zone*: +1
- *Currency*: Euro
- *Current head of state*: King Willem-Alexander
- *Current head of government*: Mark Rutte
- *Type of government*: Parliamentary Constitutional Monarchy
- *Literacy rate*: 99%
- *GDP*: US$ 1140 billion
- *HDI ranking*: 10

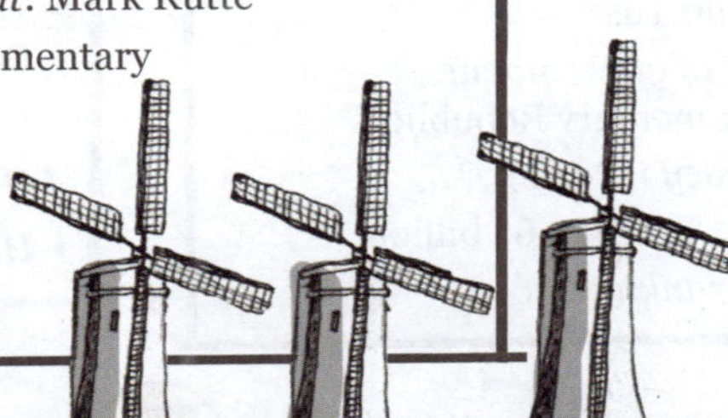

NORWAY

- *Location*: Northern Europe
- *Neighbours*: Finland, Sweden, Russia
- *Capital*: Oslo
- *Area*: 3,23,802 sq km
- *Population*: 5,514,477
- *Languages*: Bokmal Norwegian, Nynorsk Norwegian
- *Dominant religion*: Evangelical Lutheran
- *Time zone*: +1
- *Currency*: Norwegian Krone
- *Current head of state*: King Harald V
- *Current head of government*: Jonas Gahr Støre
- *Type of government*: Parliamentary Constitutional Monarchy
- *Literacy rate*: 100%
- *GDP*: US$ 526.95 billion
- *HDI ranking*: 2

POLAND

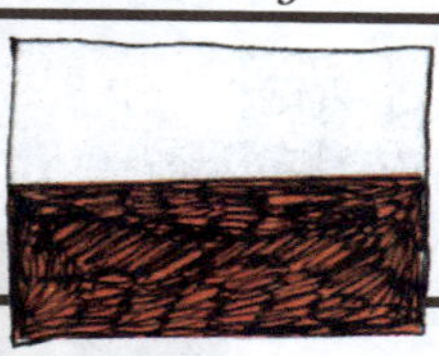

- *Location*: Central Europe
- *Neighbours*: Belarus, Czech Republic, Germany, Lithuania, Russia, Slovakia, Ukraine
- *Capital*: Warsaw
- *Area*: 3,12,685 sq km
- *Population*: 40,262,720
- *Language*: Polish
- *Dominant religion*: Catholicism
- *Time zone*: +1
- *Currency*: Zloty
- *Current head of state*: Andrzej Duda
- *Current head of government*: Donald Tusk
- *Type of government*: Parliamentary Republic
- *Literacy rate*: 99.7%
- *GDP*: US$ 844.62 billion
- *HDI ranking*: 36

PORTUGAL

- *Location*: Southwestern Europe
- *Neighbours*: Spain
- *Capital*: Lisbon
- *Area*: 92,090 sq km
- *Population*: 10,223,349
- *Language*: Portuguese
- *Dominant religion*: Roman Catholicism
- *Time zone*: +1
- *Currency*: Euro
- *Current head of state*: Marcelo Rebelo de Sousa
- *Current head of government*: Luís Montenegro
- *Type of government*: Semi-Presidential Republic
- *Literacy rate*: 95.4%
- *GDP*: US$ 298.95 billion
- *HDI ranking*: 42

ROMANIA

- *Location*: Southeastern Europe
- *Neighbours*: Ukraine, Bulgaria, Hungary, Serbia, Moldova
- *Capital*: Bucharest
- *Area*: 2,38,391 sq km
- *Population*: 19,618,996
- *Languages*: Romanian, Hungarian
- *Dominant religion*: Eastern Orthodox
- *Time zone*: +2
- *Currency*: Leu
- *Current head of state*: Klaus Werner Iohannis
- *Current head of government*: Marcel Ciolacu
- *Type of government*: Semi-Presidential Republic
- *Literacy rate*: 98.7%
- *GDP*: US$ 369.97 billion
- *HDI ranking*: 53

SAN MARINO

- *Location*: Southern Europe
- Neighbour: Italy
- *Capital*: San Marino
- *Area*: 61 sq km
- *Population*: 33,614
- *Language*: Italian
- *Dominant religion*: Roman Catholicism
- *Time zone*: +1
- *Currency*: Euro
- *Current head state and head of government*: Alessandro Rossi and Milena GasperoniI
- *Type of government*: Parliamentary Republic
- *Literacy rate*: 96%
- *GDP*: US$ 2.03 billion
- *HDI Ranking:* 43

SERBIA

- *Location*: Southeastern Europe
- *Neighbours*: Romania, Montenegro, Croatia, Albania, Bulgaria, Hungary, Kosovo, Macedonia, Bosnia and Herzegovina
- *Capital*: Belgrade
- *Area*: 77,474 sq km
- *Population*: 7,097,028
- *Language*: Serbian
- *Dominant religion*: Serbian Orthodox
- *Time zone*: +1
- *Currency*: Serbian Dinar
- *Current head of state*: Aleksandar Vučić
- *Current head of government*: Milos Vucevic
- *Type of government*: Parliamentary Republic
- *Literacy rate*: 98%
- *GDP*: US$ 81.87 billion
- *HDI ranking*: 65

SLOVAKIA

- *Location*: Central Europe
- *Neighbours*: Austria, Czech Republic, Hungary, Poland, Ukraine
- *Capital*: Bratislava
- *Area*: 49,035 sq km
- *Population*: 5,702,832
- *Language*: Slovak
- *Dominant religion*: Roman Catholicism
- *Time zone*: +1
- *Currency*: Euro
- *Current head of state*: Zuzana Čaputová
- *Current head of government*: Robert Fico
- *Type of government*: Parliamentary Republic
- *Literacy rate*: 99.6%
- *GDP*: US$ 140.81 billion
- *HDI ranking*: 45

SLOVENIA

- *Location*: South Central Europe
- *Neighbours*: Austria, Croatia, Hungary, Italy
- *Capital*: Ljubljana
- *Area*: 20,273 sq km
- *Population*: 2,123,949
- *Language*: Slovenian
- *Dominant religion*: Catholicism
- *Time zone*: +1
- *Currency*: Euro
- *Current head of state*: Nataša Pirc Musar
- *Current head of government*: Robert Golob
- *Type of government*: Parlimentary Republic
- *Literacy rate*: 99.7%
- *GDP*: US$ 72.1 billion
- *HDI ranking*: 22

SPAIN

- *Location*: Southwestern Europe
- *Neighbours*: Andorra, Gibraltar, Portugal, Morocco
- *Capital*: Madrid
- *Area*: 5,05,370 sq km
- *Population*: 48,692,804
- *Languages*: Castilian Spanish, Catalan
- *Dominant religion*: Roman Catholicism
- *Time zone*: +1
- *Currency*: Euro
- *Current head of state*: King Felipe VI
- *Current head of government*: Pedro Sánchez
- *Type of government*: Parliamentary Constitutional Monarchy
- *Literacy rate*: 98.1%
- *GDP*: US$ 1650 billion
- *HDI ranking*: 27

SWEDEN

- *Location*: Northern Europe
- *Neighbours*: Finland, Norway
- *Capital*: Stockholm
- *Area*: 4,50,295 sq km
- *Population*: 10,673,669
- *Language*: Swedish
- *Dominant religion*: Church of Sweden (Lutheran)
- *Time zone*: +1
- *Currency*: Swedish Krona
- *Current head of state*: King Carl XVI Gustaf
- *Current head of government*: Ulf Kristersson
- *Type of government*: Parliamentary Constitutional Monarchy
- *Literacy rate*: 99%
- *GDP*: US$ 623.05 billion
- *HDI ranking*: 5

SWITZERLAND

- *Location*: Central Europe
- *Neighbours*: France, Germany, Austria, Italy, Liechtenstein
- *Capital*: Bern
- *Area*: 41,277 sq km
- *Population*: 8,851,431
- *Languages*: German, French, Italian
- *Dominant religion*: Roman Catholicism
- *Time zone*: +1
- *Currency*: Swiss Franc
- *Current head of state and government*: Viola Amherd
- *Type of government*: Confederation (Federal Republic)
- *Literacy rate*: 99%
- *GDP*: US$ 938.46 billion
- *HDI ranking*: 1

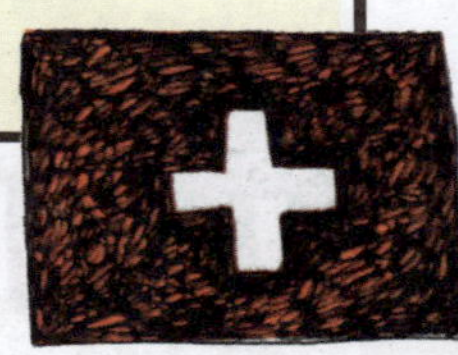

UKRAINE

- *Location*: Eastern Europe
- *Neighbours*: Belarus, Hungary, Moldova, Poland, Romania, Russia, Slovakia
- *Capital*: Kyiv
- *Area*: 6,03,550 sq km
- *Population*: 37,937,821
- *Languages*: Ukranian, Russian
- *Dominant religion*: Ukranian Orthodox Church
- *Time zone*: +2
- *Currency*: Hryvnia
- *Current head of state*: Volodymyr Zelenskyy
- *Current head of government*: Denys Shmyhal
- *Type of government*: Semi-Presidential Republic
- *Literacy rate*: 99.7%
- *GDP*: US$ 188.94 billion
- *HDI ranking*: 100

VATICAN CITY (HOLY SEE)

- *Location*: Southern Europe (a city-state in Rome, Italy)
- Neighbour: Italy
- *Capital*: Vatican City
- *Area*: 0.44 sq km
- *Population*: 764
- *Languages*: Italian, Latin
- *Dominant religion*: Roman Catholicism
- *Time zone*: +1
- *Currency*: Euro
- *Current head of state*: Pope Francis
- *Current head of government*: Fernando Vérgez Alzaga
- *Type of government*: Ecclesiastical Elective Monarchy
- *Literacy rate*: 100%

UNITED KINGDOM

- *Location*: Western Europe
- *Neighbours*: Ireland, France
- *Capital*: London
- *Area*: 2,43,610 sq km
- *Population*: 67,961,439
- *Language*: English
- *Dominant religion*: Christianity
- *Time zone*: GMT
- *Currency*: British Pound
- *Current head of state*: King Charles III
- *Current head of government*: Rishi Sunak
- *Type of government*: Parliamentary Constitutional Monarchy
- *Literacy rate*: 99%
- *GDP*: US$ 3500 billion
- *HDI ranking*: 15

BARBADOS

- *Location*: Caribbean
- *Capital*: Bridgetown
- *Area*: 430 sq km
- *Population*: 282,309
- *Languages*: English, Bajan
- *Dominant religion*: Protestantism
- *Time zone*: -4
- *Currency*: Bajan Dollar
- *Current head of state*: Dame Sandra Prunella Mason
- *Current head of government*: Mia Mottley
- *Type of government*: Parliamentary Democracy under a Constitutional Monarchy
- *Literacy rate*: 99.7%
- *GDP*: US$ 6.86 billion
- *HDI ranking*: 62

ANTIGUA AND BARBUDA

- *Location*: Caribbean
- *Capital*: Saint John's
- *Area*: 442.6 sq km
- *Population*: 94,816
- *Language*: English
- *Dominant religion*: Protestantism
- *Time zone*: -4
- *Currency*: East Caribbean Dollar
- *Current head of state*: King Charles III and Sir Rodney Williams
- *Current head of government*: Gaston Alphonso Browne
- *Type of government*: Parliamentary Democracy under a Constitutional Monarchy
- *Literacy rate*: 98.9%
- *GDP*: US$ 2.13 billion
- *HDI ranking*: 54

BAHAMAS

- *Location*: North Atlantic Ocean
- *Capital*: Nassau
- *Area*: 13,880 sq km
- *Population*: 415,223
- *Languages*: English, Creole
- *Dominant religion*: Protestantism
- *Time zone*: -4
- *Currency*: Bahamian Dollar
- *Current head of state*: King Charles III and Cynthia A. Pratt
- *Current head of government*: Philip Edward Davis
- *Type of government*: Parliamentary Democracy under a Constitutional Monarchy
- *Literacy rate*: 95.6%
- *GDP*: US$ 14.39 billion
- *HDI ranking*: 57

BELIZE

- *Location*: Central America
- *Neighbours*: Guatemala, Mexico
- *Capital*: Belmopan
- *Area*: 22,966 sq km
- *Population*: 416,656
- *Languages*: English, Creole, Spanish
- *Dominant religion*: Roman Catholicism
- *Time zone*: -6
- *Currency*: Belizean Dollar
- *Current head of state*: King Charles III and Dame Froyla Tzalam
- *Current head of government*: Johnny Briceño
- *Type of government*: Parliamentary Democracy under a Constitutional Monarchy
- *Literacy rate*: 82.7%
- *GDP*: US$ 3.3 billion
- *HDI ranking*: 118

CANADA

- *Location*: Northern America
- *Neighbours*: US
- *Capital*: Ottawa
- *Area*: 99,84,670 sq km
- *Population*: 39,107,046
- *Languages*: English, French
- *Dominant religion*: Catholicism
- *Time zone*: -3:30 to -8
- *Currency*: Canadian Dollar
- *Current head of state*: King Charles III and Dame Mary Simon
- *Current head of government*: Justin Pierre James Trudeau
- *Type of government*: Federal Parliamentary Democracy under a Constitutional Monarchy
- *Literacy rate*: 99%
- *GDP*: US$ 2240 billion
- *HDI ranking*: 18

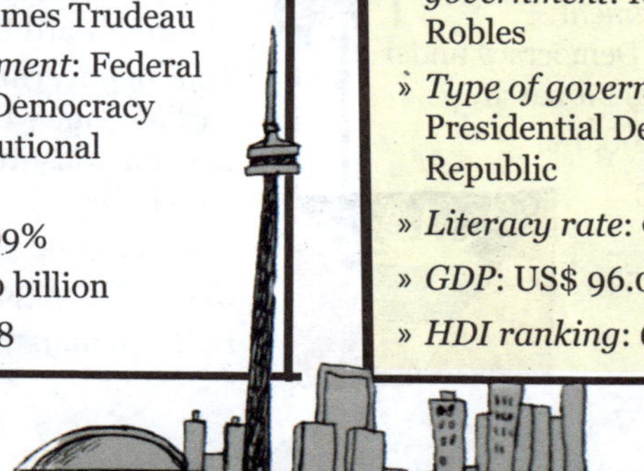

COSTA RICA

- *Location*: Central America
- *Neighbours*: Nicaragua, Panama
- *Capital*: San Jośe
- *Area*: 51,100 sq km
- *Population*: 5,246,714
- *Language*: Spanish
- *Dominant religion*: Roman Catholicism
- *Time zone*: -6
- *Currency*: Costa Rican Colón
- *Current head of state and government*: Rodrigo Chaves Robles
- *Type of government*: Presidential Democratic Republic
- *Literacy rate*: 97.6%
- *GDP*: US$ 96.06 billion
- *HDI ranking*: 64

CUBA

- *Location*: Caribbean
- *Capital*: Havana
- *Area*: 1,10,860 sq km
- *Population*: 11,174,587
- *Language*: Spanish
- *Dominant religion*: Bermudez Christianity
- *Time zone*: -5
- *Currency*: Cuban Preso
- *Current head of state*: Miguel Diaz-Canel
- *Current head of government*: Manuel Marrero Cruz
- *Type of government*: Communist State
- *Literacy rate*: 99.7%
- *GDP*: US$ 107 billion
- *HDI ranking*: 85

DOMINICA

- *Location*: Caribbean
- *Capital*: Roseau
- *Area*: 751 sq km
- *Population*: 73,368
- *Languages*: English, French patois
- *Dominant religion*: Roman Catholicism
- *Time zone*: -4
- *Currency*: East Caribbean Dollar
- *Current head of state*: Sylvanie Burton
- *Current head of government*: Roosevelt Skerrit
- *Type of government*: Parliamentary Republic
- *Literacy rate*: 94%
- *GDP*: US$ 0.71 billion
- *HDI ranking*: 97

DOMINICAN REPUBLIC

- *Location*: Caribbean
- *Capital*: Santo Domingo
- *Area*: 48,670 sq km
- *Population*: 11,434,005
- *Language*: Spanish
- *Dominant religion*: Roman Catholicism
- *Time zone*: -4
- *Currency*: Dominican Peso
- *Current head of state and government*: Luis Abinader
- *Type of government*: Presidential Democratic Republic
- *Literacy rate*: 92.4%
- *GDP*: US$ 127.36 billion
- *HDI ranking*: 82

EL SALVADOR

- *Location*: Central America
- *Neighbours*: Honduras, Guatemala
- *Capital*: San Salvador
- *Area*: 21,041 sq km
- *Population*: 6,396,289
- *Language*: Spanish
- *Dominant religion*: Roman Catholicism
- *Time zone*: -6
- *Currency*: US Dollar
- *Current head of state and government*: Nayib Armando Bukele Ortez
- *Type of government*: Presidential Republic
- *Literacy rate*: 87.6%
- *GDP*: US$ 35.33 billion
- *HDI ranking*: 127

GRENADA

- *Location*: Caribbean
- *Capital*: St George's
- *Area*: 344 sq km
- *Population*: 126,887
- *Language*: English
- *Dominant religion*: Protestantism
- *Time zone*: -4
- *Currency*: East Caribbean Dollar
- *Current head of state*: King Charles III and Dame Cécile La Grenade
- *Current head of government*: Dickon Mitchell
- *Type of government*: Parliamentary Democracy under a Constitutional Monarchy
- *Literacy rate*: 96%
- *GDP*: US$ 1.41 billion
- *HDI ranking*: 73

GUATEMALA

- *Location*: Central America
- *Neighbours*: Mexico, Belize, Honduras, El Salvador
- *Capital*: Guatemala City
- *Area*: 1,08,889 sq km
- *Population*: 18,358,430
- *Languages*: Spanish, indigenous languages
- *Dominant religions*: Christianity, indigenous faiths
- *Time zone*: -6
- *Currency*: Quetzal
- *Current head of state and government*: Bernardo Arévalo
- *Type of government*: Presidential Republic
- *Literacy rate*: 79.07%
- *GDP*: US$ 110.04 billion
- *HDI ranking*: 136

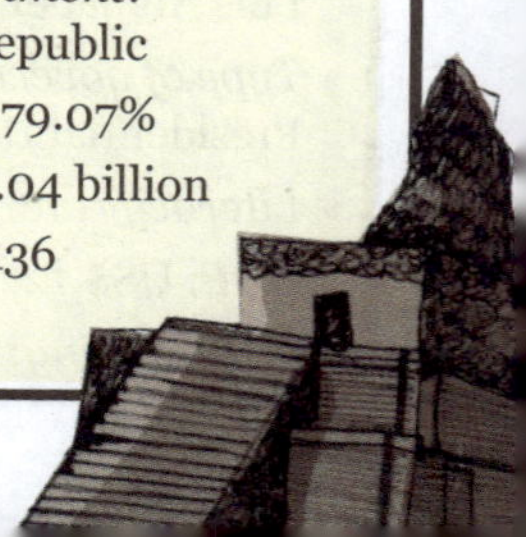

HAITI

- *Location*: Caribbean
- *Neighbour*: Dominican Republic
- *Capital*: Port-au-Prince
- *Area*: 27,750 sq km
- *Population*: 11,867,030
- *Languages*: French, Creole
- *Dominant religion*: Roman Catholicism
- *Time zone*: -5
- *Currency*: Gourde
- *Current head of state*: Vacant (Transitional Presidential Council)
- *Current head of government*: Garry Conille
- *Type of government*: Semi-Presidential Republic
- *Literacy rate*: 60.6%
- *GDP*: US$ 24.05 billion
- *HDI ranking*: 158

HONDURAS

- *Location*: Central America
- *Neighbours*: Guatemala, El Salvador, Nicaragua
- *Capital*: Tegucigalpa
- *Area*: 1,12,090 sq km
- *Population*: 10,759,406
- *Language*: Spanish
- *Dominant religion*: Roman Catholicism
- *Time zone*: -6
- *Currency*: Lempira
- *Current head of state and government*: Xiomara Castro
- *Type of government*: Presidential Republic
- *Literacy rate*: 88.4%
- *GDP*: US$ 37.35 billion
- *HDI ranking*: 138

JAMAICA

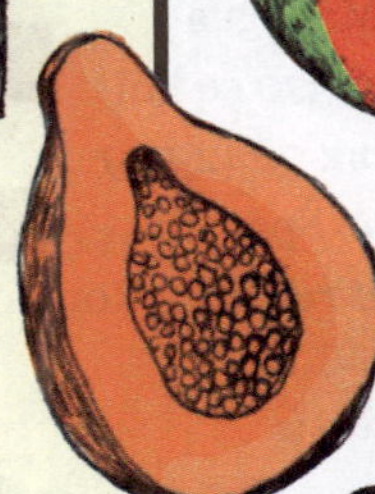

- *Location*: Caribbean
- *Capital*: Kingston
- *Area*: 10,991 sq km
- *Population*: 2,824,738
- *Languages*: English, Jamaican Patois
- *Dominant religion*: Protestantism
- *Time zone*: -5
- *Currency*: Jamaican Dollar
- *Current head of state*: King Charles III and Sir Patrick Allen
- *Current head of government*: Andrew Holness
- *Type of government*: Parliamentary Democracy under a Constitutional Monarchy
- *Literacy rate*: 88.5%
- *GDP*: US$ 20.1 billion
- *HDI ranking*: 115

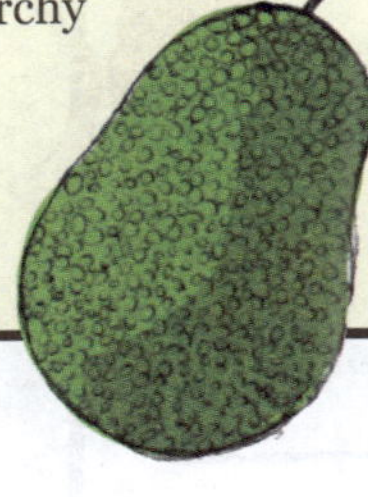

MEXICO

- *Location*: Northern America
- *Neighbours*: US, Belize, Guatemala
- *Capital*: Mexico City
- *Area*: 19,64,375 sq km
- *Population*: 129,388,467
- *Language*: Spanish
- *Dominant religion*: Roman Catholicism
- *Time zone*: -6
- *Currency*: Mexican Peso
- *Current head of state and government*: Andrés Manuel López Obrador
- *Type of government*: Federal Presidential Republic
- *Literacy rate*: 94.5%
- *GDP*: US$ 2020 billion
- *HDI ranking*: 77

NICARAGUA

- *Location*: Central America
- *Neighbours*: Honduras, Costa Rica
- *Capital*: Managua
- *Area*: 1,30,370 sq km
- *Population*: 7,142,529
- *Language*: Spanish
- *Dominant religion*: Roman Catholicism
- *Time zone*: -6
- *Currency*: Nicaraguan Córdoba
- *Current head of state and government*: José Daniel Ortega Saavedra
- *Type of government*: Presidential Republic
- *Literacy rate*: 82.4%
- *GDP*: US$ 18.83 billion
- *HDI ranking*: 130

PANAMA

- *Location*: Central America
- *Neighbours*: Costa Rica, Colombia
- *Capital*: Panama City
- *Area*: 75,420 sq km
- *Population*: 4,527,961
- *Language*: Spanish
- *Dominant religion*: Roman Catholicism
- *Time zone*: -5
- *Currency*: Balboa
- *Current head of state and government*: Laurentino Cortizo
- *Type of government*: Presidential Republic
- *Literacy rate*: 95.04%
- *GDP*: US$ 87.35 billion
- *HDI ranking*: 57

ST KITTS AND NEVIS

- *Location*: Caribbean
- *Capital*: Basseterre
- *Area*: 261 sq km
- *Population*: 55,133
- *Language*: English
- *Dominant religion*: Protestantism
- *Time zone*: -4
- *Currency*: East Caribbean Dollar
- *Current head of state*: King Charles III and Sir Marcella Liburd
- *Current head of government*: Terrance Drew
- *Type of government*: Parliamentary Democracy under a Constitutional Monarchy
- *Literacy rate*: 97.8%
- *GDP*: US$ 1.13 billion
- *HDI ranking*: 51

ST LUCIA

- *Location*: Caribbean
- *Capital*: Castries
- *Area*: 616 sq km
- *Population*: 180,771
- *Language*: English
- *Dominant religion*: Roman Catholicism
- *Time zone*: -4
- *Currency*: East Caribbean Dollar
- *Current head of state*: King Charles III and Cyril Errol Melchiades Charles
- *Current head of government*: Philip J Pierre
- *Type of government*: Parliamentary Democracy under a Constitutional Monarchy
- *Literacy rate*: 90.1%
- *GDP*: US$ 2.58 billion
- *HDI ranking*: 108

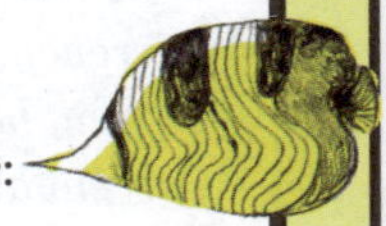

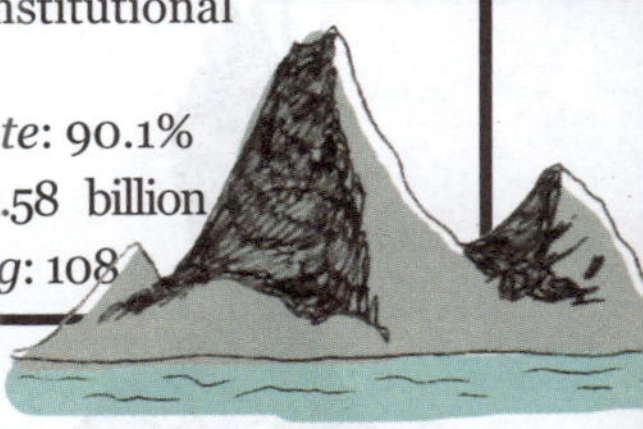

ST VINCENT AND THE GRENADINES

- *Location*: Caribbean
- *Capital*: Kingstown
- *Area*: 389 sq km
- *Population*: 100,647
- *Language*: English
- *Dominant religion*: Protestantism
- *Time zone*: -4
- *Currency*: East Caribbean Dollar
- *Current head of state*: King Charles III and Dame Susan Dougan
- *Current head of government*: Ralph Everard Gonsalves
- *Type of government*: Parliamentary Democracy under a Constitutional Monarchy
- *Literacy rate*: : 95.6%
- *GDP*: US$ 1.13 billion
- *HDI ranking*: 81

TRINIDAD AND TOBAGO

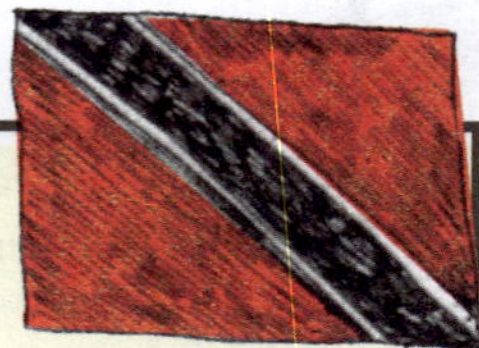

- *Location*: Caribbean
- *Capital*: Port of Spain
- *Area*: 5,128 sq km
- *Population*: 1,538,200
- *Languages*: English, Caribbean Hindustani
- *Dominant religions*: Protestantism, Roman Catholicism
- *Time zone*: -4
- *Currency*: Trinidad and Tobago Dollar
- *Current head of state*: Christine Kangaloo
- *Current head of government*: Keith Christopher Rowley
- *Type of government*: Parliamentary Republic
- *Literacy rate*: 98.9%
- *GDP*: US$ 28.37 billion
- *HDI ranking*: 60

UNITED STATES

- *Location*: North America
- *Neighbours*: Canada, Mexico
- *Capital*: Washington DC
- *Area*: 98,33,517 sq km
- *Population*: 341,705,280
- *Language*: English
- *Dominant religion*: Protestantism
- *Time zone*: -5 to -9
- *Currency*: US Dollar
- *Current head of state and government*: Joseph (Joe) Biden
- *Type of government*: Federal Republic
- *Literacy rate*: 99%
- *GDP*: US$ 28780 billion
- *HDI ranking*: 20

AUSTRALIA

» *Location*: Oceania
» *Capital*: Canberra
» *Area*: 77,41,220 sq km
» *Population*: 26,699,482
» *Language*: English
» *Dominant religion*: Protestantism
» *Time zone*: +8 to +10:30
» *Currency*: Australian Dollar
» *Current head of state*: King Charles III and David Hurley
» *Current head of government*: Anthony Albanese
» *Type of government*: Federal Parliamentary Democracy under a Constitutional Monarchy
» *Literacy rate*: 99%
» *GDP*: US$ 1790 billion
» *HDI ranking*: 10

FIJI

» *Location*: Oceania
» *Capital*: Suva
» *Area*: 18,274 sq km
» *Population*: 951,611
» *Languages*: English, Fijian, Fiji Hindi
» *Dominant religion*: Protestantism
» *Time zone*: +12
» *Currency*: Fijian Dollar
» *Current head of state*: Wiliame Katonivere
» *Current head of government*: Sitiveni Rabuka
» *Type of government*: Parliamentary Republic
» *Literacy rate*: 93.7%
» *GDP*: US$ 5.8 billion
» *HDI ranking*: 104

KIRIBATI

» *Location*: Oceania
» *Capital*: Tarawa
» *Area*: 811 sq km
» *Population*: 135,763
» *Languages*: English, I Kiribati
» *Dominant religion*: Roman Catholicism
» *Time zone*: +12 to +14
» *Currency*: Australian Dollar
» *Current head of state and government*: Taneti Maamau
» *Type of government*: Presidential Republic
» *GDP*: US$ 0.31 billion
» *HDI ranking*: 137

MARSHALL ISLANDS

- *Location*: Oceania
- *Capital*: Majuro
- *Area*: 181 sq km
- *Population*: 42,415
- *Languages*: Marshallese, English
- *Dominant religion*: Protestantism
- *Time zone*: +12
- *Currency*: US Dollar
- *Current head of state and government*: Hilda C. Heine
- *Type of government*: Presidential Republic in Free Association with the US
- *Literacy rate*: 98.27%
- *GDP*: US$ 0.31 billion
- *HDI ranking*: 102

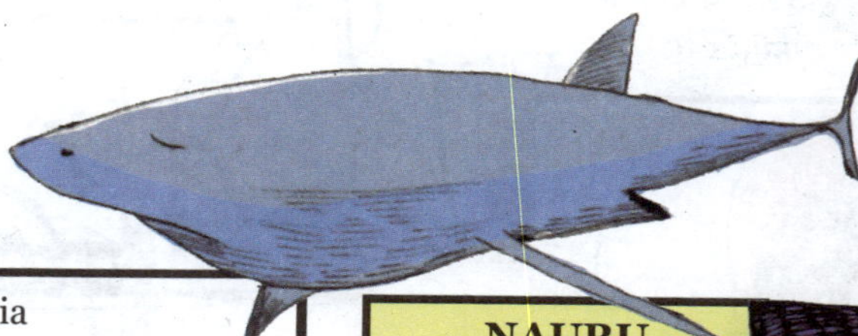

MICRONESIA (FEDERATED STATES OF)

- *Location*: Oceania
- *Capital*: Palikir
- *Area*: 702 sq km
- *Population*: 116,300
- *Language*: English
- *Dominant religion*: Roman Catholicism
- *Time zone*: +10, +11
- *Currency*: US Dollar
- *Current head of state and government*: Wesley Simina
- *Type of government*: Federal Republic in Free Association with the US
- *Literacy rate*: 89%
- *GDP*: US$ 0.48 billion
- *HDI ranking*: 135

NAURU

- *Location*: Oceania
- *Capital*: Yaren
- *Area*: 21 sq km
- *Population*: 12,884
- *Languages*: Nauruan, English
- *Dominant religion*: Protestantism
- *Time zone*: +12
- *Currency*: Australian Dollar
- *Current head of state and government*: David W.R Adeang
- *Type of government*: Parliamentary Republic
- *GDP*: US$ 0.16 billion
- *HDI ranking:* 122

NEW ZEALAND

- *Location*: Oceania
- *Capital*: Wellington
- *Area*: 2,68,838 sq km
- *Population*: 5,269,939
- *Languages*: English, Maori
- *Dominant religion*: Christianity
- *Time zone*: +12
- *Currency*: New Zealand Dollar
- *Current head of state*: Queen King Charles III and Dame Cindy Kiro
- *Current head of government*: Christopher Luxon
- *Type of government*: Parliamentary Democracy under a Constitutional Monarchy
- *Literacy rate*: 99%
- *GDP*: US$ 257.63 billion
- *HDI ranking*: 13

PALAU

- *Location*: Oceania
- *Capital*: Ngerulmud
- *Area*: 459 sq km
- *Population*: 21,864
- *Languages*: Palauan, English
- *Dominant religion*: Roman Catholicism
- *Time zone*: +9
- *Currency*: US Dollar
- *Current head of state and government*: Surangel S Whipps Jr.
- *Type of government*: Presidential Republic in Free Association with the US
- *Literacy rate*: 96.6%
- *GDP*: US$ 0.31 billion
- *HDI ranking*: 71

PAPUA NEW GUINEA

- *Location*: Oceania
- Neighbour: Indonesia
- *Capital*: Port Moresby
- *Area*: 4,62,840 sq km
- *Population*: 10,515,788
- *Languages*: Tok Pisin, English, Hiri Motu
- *Dominant religion*: Roman Catholicism
- *Time zone*: +10
- *Currency*: Kina
- *Current head of state*: King Charles III and Bob Dadae
- *Current head of government*: James Marape
- *Type of government*: Parliamentary Democracy under a Constitutional Monarchy
- *Literacy rate*: 63.4%
- *GDP*: US$ 31.72 billion
- *HDI ranking*: 154

SAMOA

- *Location*: Oceania
- *Capital*: Apia
- *Area*: 2,831 sq km
- *Population*: 228,966
- *Languages*: Samoan, English
- *Dominant religion*: Protestantism
- *Time zone*: +13
- *Currency*: Tālā
- *Current head of state*: Afioga Tuimalealiìfano Va'aleto'a Eti Sualauvi II
- *Current head of government*: Fiame Naomi Mata'afa
- *Type of government*: Parliamentary Republic
- *Literacy rate*: 99.1%
- *GDP*: US$ 1.02 billion
- *HDI ranking*: 116

SOLOMON ISLANDS

- *Location*: Oceania
- *Capital*: Honiara
- *Area*: 28,896 sq km
- *Population*: 756,673
- *Languages*: Melanesian Pidgin, English
- *Dominant religion*: Protestantism
- *Time zone*: +11
- *Currency*: Solomon Island Dollar
- *Current head of state*: King Charles III and Reverend David Vunagi
- *Current head of government*: Jeremiah Manele
- *Type of government*: Parliamentary Democracy under a Constitutional Monarchy
- *Literacy rate*: 84.1%
- *GDP*: US$ 1.71 billion
- *HDI ranking*: 156

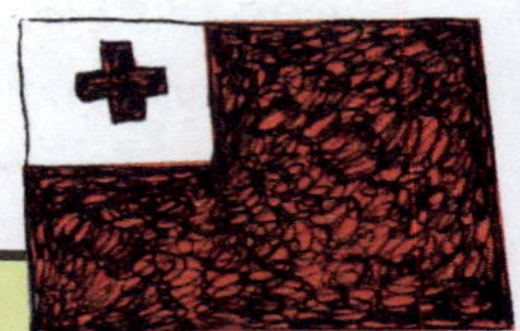

TONGA

- *Location*: Oceania
- *Capital*: Nuku'alofa
- *Area*: 747 sq km
- *Population*: 108,683
- *Languages*: Tongan, English
- *Dominant religion*: Protestantism
- *Time zone*: +13
- *Currency*: Pa'anga
- *Current head of state*: King Tupou VI
- *Current head of government*: Siaosi Sovaleni
- *Type of government*: Constitutional Monarchy
- *Literacy rate*: 99.4%
- *GDP*: US$ 0.58 billion
- *HDI ranking*: 98

TUVALU

- *Location*: Oceania
- *Capital*: Funafuti
- *Area*: 26 sq km
- *Population*: 11,478
- *Languages*: Tuvaluan, English
- *Dominant religion*: Church of Tuvalu
- *Time zone*: +12
- *Currency*: Tuvaluan Dollar
- *Current head of state*: King Charles III and Tofiga Vaevalu Falani
- *Current head of government*: Feleti Teo
- *Type of government*: Parliamentary Democracy under a Constitutional Monarchy
- *GDP*: US$ 0.07 billion
- HDI ranking: 132

VANUATU

- *Location*: Oceania
- *Capital*: Port Vila
- *Area*: 12,189 sq km
- *Population*: 342,325
- *Languages*: Bislama, English
- *Dominant religion*: Protestantism
- *Time zone*: +11
- *Currency*: Vanuatu Vatu
- *Current head of state*: Nikenike Vurobaravu
- *Current head of government*: Charlot Salwai
- *Type of government*: Parliamentary Republic
- *Literacy rate*: 89.1%
- *GDP*: US$ 1.29 billion
- *HDI ranking*: 140

ARGENTINA

» *Location*: Southern South America
» *Neighbours*: Chile, Paraguay, Uruguay, Bolivia, Brazil
» *Capital*: Buenos Aires
» *Area*: 27,80,400 sq km
» *Population*: 46,057,866
» *Language*: Spanish
» *Dominant religion*: Roman Catholicism
» *Time zone*: -3
» *Currency*: Peso
» *Current head of state and government*: Javier Gerardo Milei
» *Type of government*: Federal Presidential Republic
» *Literacy rate*: 98.09%
» *GDP*: US$ 604.26 billion
» *HDI ranking*: 48

BOLIVIA

» *Location*: Central South America
» *Neighbours*: Peru, Chile, Argentina, Paraguay, Brazil
» *Capitals*: Sucre and La Paz
» *Area*: 10,98,581 sq km
» *Population*: 12,567,336
» *Languages*: Spanish, Quehcua, Aymara, Guarani
» *Dominant religion*: Roman Catholicism
» *Time zone*: -4
» *Currency*: Boliviano
» *Current head of state and government*: Luis Arce
» *Type of government*: Presidential Republic
» *Literacy rate*: 95.1%
» *GDP*: US$ 49.33 billion
» *HDI ranking*: 120

BRAZIL

Location: Eastern South America
» *Neighbours*: Peru, Bolivia, Ecuador, Paraguay, Colombia, Venezuela, Guyana, Suriname, Argentina, French Guiana, Uruguay
» *Capital*: Brasília
» *Area*: 85,15,770 sq km
» *Population*: 217,637,297
» *Language*: Portuguese
» *Dominant religion*: Roman Catholicism
» *Time zone*: -2 to -5
» *Currency*: Real
» *Current head of state and government*: Luiz Inácio Lula da Silva
» *Type of government*: Federal Presidential Republic
» *Literacy rate*: 92.5%
» *GDP*: US$ 2330 billion
» *HDI ranking*: 89

CHILE

- *Location*: Southern South America
- *Neighbours*: Argentina, Peru, Bolivia
- *Capital*: Santiago
- *Area*: 7,56,102 sq km
- *Population*: 19,658,839
- *Language*: Spanish
- *Dominant religion*: Roman Catholicism
- *Time zone*: -4
- *Currency*: Chilean Peso
- *Current head of state and government*: Gabriel Boric
- *Type of government*: Presidential Republic
- *Literacy rate*: 96.6%
- *GDP*: US$ 333.76 billion
- *HDI ranking*: 44

COLOMBIA

- *Location*: Northern South America
- *Neighbours*: Brazil, Ecuador, Panama, Peru, Venezuela
- *Capital*: Bogotá
- *Area*: 11,38,910 sq km
- *Population*: 52,340,774
- *Language*: Spanish
- *Dominant religion*: Roman Catholicism
- *Time zone*: -5
- *Currency*: Columbian Peso
- *Current head of state and government*: Gustavo Petro
- *Type of government*: Presidential Republic
- *Literacy rate*: 94.5%
- *GDP*: US$ 386.08 billion
- *HDI ranking*: 91

ECUADOR

- *Location*: Western South America
- *Neighbours*: Peru, Colombia
- *Capital*: Quito
- *Area*: 2,83,561 sq km
- *Population*: 18,377,367
- *Language*: Spanish
- *Dominant religion*: Roman Catholicism
- *Time zone*: -5
- *Currency*: US Dollar
- *Current head of state and government*: Daniel Noboa
- *Type of government*: Presidential Republic
- *Literacy rate*: 94.52%
- *GDP*: US$ 121.59 billion
- *HDI ranking*: 83

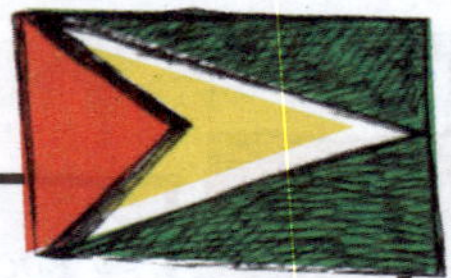

GUYANA

- *Location*: Northern South America
- *Neighbours*: Suriname, Brazil, Venezuela
- *Capital*: Georgetown
- *Area*: 2,14,969 sq km
- *Population*: 819,594
- *Languages*: English, local dialects
- *Dominant religions*: Christianity, Hinduism
- *Time zone*: -4
- *Currency*: Guyanese Dollar
- *Current head of state and government*: Mohamed Irfaan Ali
- *Current head of government*: Mark Phillips
- *Type of government*:Parliamentary Republic
- *Literacy rate*: 87.5%
- *GDP*: US$ 21.18 billion
- *HDI ranking*: 95

PARAGUAY

- *Location*: Central South America
- *Neighbours*: Bolivia, Brazil, Argentina
- *Capital*: Asunción
- *Area*: 4,06,752 sq km
- *Population*: 6,947,270
- *Languages*: Spanish, Guarani
- *Dominant religion*: Roman Catholicism
- *Time zone*: -4
- *Currency*: Guarani
- *Current head of state and government*: Santiago Peña
- *Type of government*: Presidential Republic
- *Literacy rate*: 95.5%
- *GDP*: US$ 45.82 billion
- *HDI ranking*: 102

PERU

- *Location*: Western South America
- *Neighbours*: Ecuador, Bolivia, Colombia, Brazil, Chile
- *Capital*: Lima
- *Area*: 12,85,216 sq km
- *Population*: 34,683,444
- *Languages*: Spanish, Quechua Aymara
- *Dominant religion*: Roman Catholicism
- *Time zone*: -5
- *Currency*: Sol
- *Current head of state and government*: Dina Ercilia Boluarte Zegarra
- *Type of government*: Presidential Republic
- *Literacy rate*: : 94.3%
- *GDP*: US$ 282.46 billion
- *HDI ranking*: 87

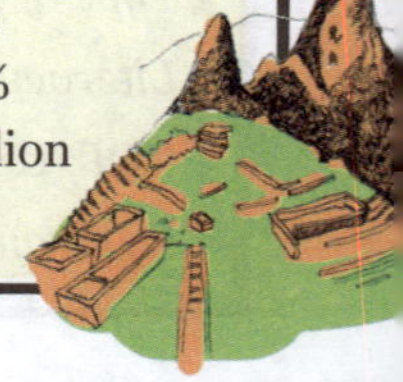

SURINAME

- *Location*: Northern South America
- *Neighbours*: French Guiana, Guyana, Brazil
- *Capital*: Paramaribo
- *Area*: 1,63,820 sq km
- *Population*: 628,785
- *Language*: Dutch
- *Dominant religions*: Hinduism, Protestantism
- *Time zone*: -3
- *Currency*: Surinamese Dollar
- *Current head of state and government*: Chandrikapersad 'Chan' Santokhi
- *Type of government*: Presidential Republic
- *Literacy rate*: 95.5%
- *GDP*: US$ 4.34 billion
- *HDI ranking*: 124

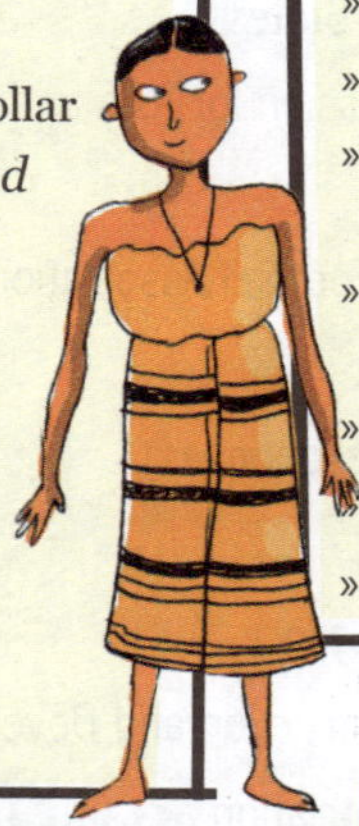

URUGUAY

- *Location*: Southern South America
- *Neighbours*: Brazil, Argentina
- *Capital*: Montevideo
- *Area*: 1,76,215 sq km
- *Population*: 3,423,316
- *Languages*: Spanish
- *Dominant religion*: Roman Catholicism
- *Time zone*: -3
- *Currency*: Uruguayan Peso
- *Current head of state and government*: Luis Lacalle Pou
- *Type of government*: Presidential Republic
- *Literacy rate*: 98.4%
- *GDP*: US$ 82.61 billion
- *HDI ranking*: 52

VENEZUELA

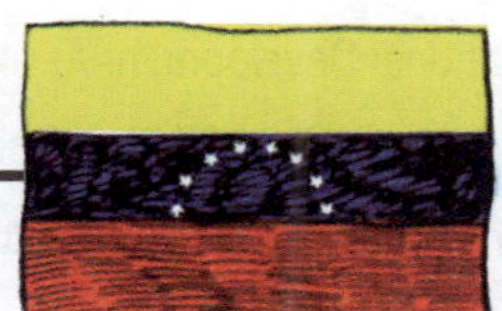

- *Location*: Northern South America
- *Neighbours*: Colombia, Brazil, Guyana
- *Capital*: Caracas
- *Area*: 9,12,050 sq km
- *Population*: 29,395,334
- *Languages*: Spanish, indigenous languages
- *Dominant religion*: Roman Catholicism
- *Time zone*: -4
- *Currency*: Bolivar
- *Current head of state*: Nicolás Maduro Moros
- *Type of government*: Federal Presidential Republic
- *Literacy rate*: 95.4%
- *GDP*: US$ 102.33 billion
- *HDI ranking*: 119

INTERNATIONAL ORGANIZATIONS

AL - Arab League

OACPS - Organization of African, Caribbean and Pacific States

APEC - Asia-Pacific Economic Co-operation

ADB - Asian Development Bank

ASEAN - Association of Southeast Asian Nations

AI - Amnesty International

AU - African Union

CIS - Commonwealth of Independent States

ESCAP - Economic and Social Commission for Asia and the Pacific

EC - European Commission

FIFA - Fédération Internationale de Football Association

G7 - Group of Seven (countries)

G20 - Group of Twenty (developing economies)

GCC - Gulf Cooperation Council

IAEA - International Atomic Energy Agency

IBRD - International Bank for Reconstruction and Development

IDA - International Development Association

INTERPOL - International Criminal Police Organization

IFAD - International Fund for Agricultural Development

IFC - International Finance Corporation

IFRC - International Federation of Red Cross and Red Crescent Societies

IMF - International Monetary Fund

IMO - International Maritime Organization

UNITED NATIONS

UN - United Nations

UN General Assembly

UN Security Council

Economic and Social Council

UN Trusteeship Council

International Court of Justice

United Nations Secretariat

MORE INTERNATIONAL ORGANIZATIONS

INMARSAT - International Maritime Satellite Organization

IOC - International Olympic Committee

ISO - International Organization for Standardisation

ITU - International Telecommunication Union

INTELSAT - International Telecommunications Satellite Organization

MERCOSUR - Trading and Political bloc in Latin America comprising Brazil, Argentina, Uruguay, Venezuela and Paraguay

NAM - Non-Aligned Movement

NATO - North Atlantic Treaty Organization

OAS - Organization of American States

OECD - Organization for Economic Co-operation and Development

OPEC - Organization of the Petroleum Exporting Countries

SAARC - South Asian Association for Regional Cooperation

WIPO - World Intellectual Property Organization

WMO - World Meteorological Organization

WTO - World Trade Organization

WWF - World Wide Fund for Nature

UN SPECIALISED AGENCIES

WHO - World Health Organization

UNESCO - United Nations Educational, Scientific and Cultural Organization

UNICEF - United Nations International Children's Emergency Fund

UNIDO - United Nations Industrial Development Organization

UNDP - United Nations Development Programme

UNHCR - United Nations High Commissioner for Refugees

FAO - Food and Agriculture Organization

UNHRC - United Nations Human Rights Council

IMPORTANT OFFICE HOLDERS

President of the World Bank: Ajay Banga

Secretary-General of the United Nations: António Guterres

Secretary General of Amnesty International: Dr Agnès Callamard

Director-General of UNESCO: Audrey Azoulay

Executive Director of UNICEF: Catherine Russell

Director-General of WHO: Tedros Adhanom Ghebreyesus

ILO Director-General: Gilbert F. Houngbo

President of the International Court of Justice: Judge Nawaf Salam

President of the International Olympic Committee: Thomas Bach

President of the Fédération Internationale de Football Association: Gianni Infantino

President of the United Nations Human Rights Council (UNHRC): Omar Zniber

Secretary General of the South Asian Association for Regional Cooperation: Golam Sarwar

President of the European Commission: Ursula von der Leyen

Director-General of the WTO: Ngozi Okonjo-Iweala

UAE AND QATAR ANNOUNCE RESTORATION OF DIPLOMATIC RELATIONS

In a significant move to strengthen the bilateral relationship between Qatar and the United Arab Emirates (UAE), the two countries announced a restoration of diplomatic representation on 19 June 2023. This decision marked the resumption of operations at the Embassy of the State of Qatar in Abu Dhabi and its consulate in Dubai, and the Embassy of the United Arab Emirates in Doha. This restoration was based on the Al-Ula agreement and reflected the interest of both nations in enhancing their diplomatic ties. The move was seen as an embodiment of the will of the leaderships of the two countries and a consolidation of joint Arab action.

UN SECURITY COUNCIL VOTES TO END PEACEKEEPING MISSION IN MALI

On 30 June 2023, the UN Security Council unanimously approved the complete withdrawal of the UN peacekeeping forces in Mali, marking the end of the decade-old UN Multidimensional Integrated Stabilization Mission in Mali (MINUSMA). The decision was made to transfer security responsibilities to the country's transitional government.

WILDFIRES RAGE IN GREECE AND HAWAII

In the summer of 2023, two popular tourist destinations, Greece and Hawaii, were ravaged by devastating wildfires. In Greece, the fires forced tens of thousands of people to evacuate from islands, including Rhodes and Corfu. The fires, fuelled by a long spell of extreme heat, destroyed many homes and businesses. Similarly, in Hawaii, the fast-spreading wildfires caused significant damage on the island of Maui, leading to the largest natural disaster in Hawaii's state history. The fires resulted in a significant rise in the death toll and left hundreds of people missing.

PRESIDENT MOHAMED BAZOUM OF NIGER TOPPLED IN A COUP D'ÉTAT

On 26 July 2023, a coup d'état occurred in Niger when the country's presidential guard detained President Mohamed Bazoum. The Presidential Guard commander, General Abdourahamane Tchiani, proclaimed himself the leader of a new military junta. The junta announced plans to prosecute the deposed president for high treason and undermining national security. The coup was met with international condemnation, with many countries and organizations calling for the immediate restoration of democratic governance.

EARTHQUAKE IN MOROCCO CLAIMS THOUSANDS OF LIVES

On 8 September 2023, a severe earthquake struck the Marrakesh-Safi region in Morocco. The 6.8-magnitude earthquake resulted in the deaths of more than 2,900 people and injured over 5,500. It caused heavy damage to parts of the ancient section of Marrakech and devastated several remote settlements in the Atlas Mountains. This was one of the deadliest earthquakes in Morocco's history and highlighted the country's vulnerability to seismic events.

AFRICAN UNION BECOMES 21ST PERMANENT MEMBER OF G20

On 9 September 2023, a historic announcement was made that the African Union would become the twenty-first permanent member of the G20. This decision marked a significant step in strengthening global relations and was broadly welcomed for giving the continent an important voice on key global issues. The inclusion of the African Union in the G20 was seen as a recognition of Africa's growing economic and political influence on the global stage.

QUEEN MARGRETHE II OF DENMARK STEPS DOWN FROM THRONE AFTER FIFTY-TWO YEARS

On 31 December 2023, Queen Margrethe II of Denmark announced her abdication, effective 14 January 2024, after fifty-two years on the throne. Her eldest son, Crown Prince Frederik, succeeded her on the throne. The abdication marked the end of an era in Danish history and the beginning of a new chapter under the leadership of King Frederik X.

AZERBAIJAN LAUNCHES MILITARY OFFENSIVE AGAINST BREAKAWAY STATE

Between 19 and 20 September 2023, Azerbaijan launched a large-scale military offensive against the self-declared breakaway state of Artsakh. The offensive was seen as a violation of the ceasefire agreement signed after the Second Nagorno-Karabakh War in 2020. The international community expressed deep concern over the escalation of violence and called for an immediate end to hostilities.

ARCHAEOLOGISTS DISCOVER WORLD'S OLDEST WOODEN STRUCTURE IN ZAMBIA

In September 2023, archaeologists in Zambia uncovered a wooden structure dating back about 476,000 years to the Early Stone Age or Pleistocene Epoch. This represents the earliest known use of wood in construction by human ancestors. The discovery provides valuable insights into the technological capabilities and lifestyle of early humans.

FIRST GLOBAL AI SAFETY SUMMIT HELD IN THE UNITED KINGDOM

The United Kingdom hosted the first global AI Safety Summit in November 2023. The summit brought together leading AI nations, technology companies, researchers, and civil society groups to turbocharge action on the safe and responsible development of frontier AI around the world. The summit highlighted the importance of international cooperation in ensuring the safe and ethical use of AI.

FIVE NEW COUNTRIES BECOME MEMBERS OF THE BRICS

In August 2023, Argentina, Egypt, Ethiopia, Iran, Saudi Arabia, and the United Arab Emirates were invited to become full members of BRICS. Their membership took effect on 1 January 2024. However, Argentina formally rejected the offer after a change in leadership. The expansion of BRICS was seen as a reflection of the growing economic and political influence of these countries.

RUSSIA LAUNCHES BIGGEST AIR ATTACK ON UKRAINE SINCE INVASION

On 29 December 2023, Russia launched the biggest air attack on Ukraine since the beginning of its full-scale invasion. The attack involved an unprecedented number of drones and missiles fired at targets across the country, killing at least thirty-one people and injuring more than 160 others. The international community condemned the attack and called for an immediate end to the violence.

IRAN LAUNCHES ATTACK IN PAKISTAN'S BALUCHISTAN PROVINCE

On 16 January 2024, Iran carried out a series of missile and drone strikes within Pakistan's Balochistan province. Iran claimed that it had targeted the Iranian Baloch militant group Jaish ul-Adl. The strikes marked a significant escalation in tensions between Iran and Pakistan.

PUTIN ELECTED AS PRESIDENT OF RUSSIA FOR THE FIFTH TIME

On 18 March 2024, incumbent Vladimir Putin was re-elected for a fifth term in the 2024 Russian presidential election. Putin won with 87 per cent of the vote, the highest percentage in a presidential election in post-Soviet Russia. The election was marked by allegations of voter suppression and fraud.

G7 COUNTRIES AGREE TO PHASE OUT COAL POWER BY 2030-35

The G7 countries agreed to phase out unabated coal power by 2030-35. This decision is part of their commitment to combat climate change and transition to renewable energy sources. The agreement was hailed as a major step forward in the global fight against climate change.

ISRAEL-GAZA CONFLICT WORSENS AFTER HAMAS ATTACK

On 7 October 2023, the Israeli-Palestinian conflict escalated dramatically when the Palestinian group Hamas launched a surprise attack on Israel, marking the beginning of a new war. The operation, named Operation Al-Aqsa Flood, was the most ambitious and complex that Hamas had ever undertaken. The attack began at dawn during the Jewish holiday of Simchat Torah, with Hamas firing a barrage of rockets into southern Israel. The initial barrage involved around 5,000 rockets, with sirens heard as far away as Tel Aviv and Beersheba. The rocket attack served as a cover for an unprecedented multipronged infiltration of fighters. Hamas fighters breached the security barriers separating Gaza and Israel in multiple places. The fighters targeted several military installations around the frontier, including the Beit Hanoon border crossing, the Zikim base, and the Gaza division headquarters at Reim.

The Israeli military responded with air strikes on Gaza, causing significant casualties. However, the presence of Israeli hostages in Gaza complicated the situation and made the planning of a ground operation more challenging. In Gaza, an Israeli airstrike on a UN-run school in the Nuseirat refugee camp killed at least forty people. The Israeli military claimed that the school was being used by Hamas militants. The war sparked international condemnation and calls for an immediate end to the violence. However, it also highlighted the deep-seated issues and tensions that continue to fuel the Israeli-Palestinian conflict. As the war raged on, the world watched in anticipation of what would come next.

GOOD NEWS

THREE AFRICAN NATIONS ROLL OUT MALARIA VACCINE IN A BREAKTHROUGH MOMENT

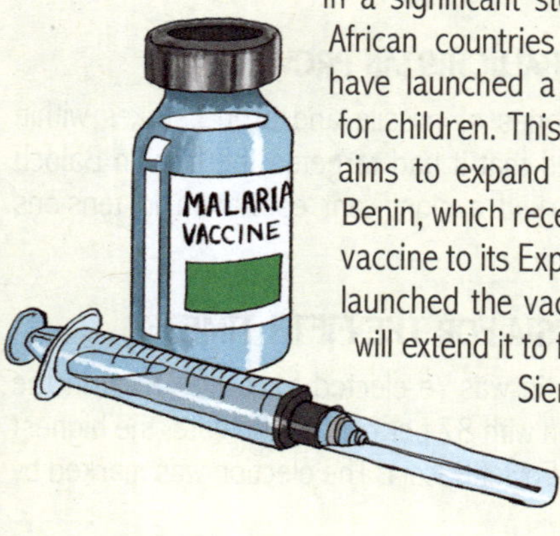

In a significant step towards malaria prevention, three West African countries — Benin, Liberia, and Sierra Leone — have launched a large-scale rollout of the malaria vaccine for children. This initiative, announced on World Malaria Day, aims to expand vaccine deployment in the African region. Benin, which received 215,900 doses, has added the malaria vaccine to its Expanded Programme on Immunization. Liberia launched the vaccine in the southern Rivercess County and will extend it to five other counties with high malaria burden. Sierra Leone initiated the rollout with the first doses administered to children at a health centre in Western Area Rural. A pilot program in Ghana, Kenya, and Malawi reached over 2 million children from 2019 to 2023, showing a significant reduction in malaria illness and a 13 per cent drop in overall child mortality. This initiative marks a major step forward in the fight against malaria, offering hope for millions of children across these nations.

NEW EXPERIMENT BRINGS WORLD CLOSER TO DREAM OF LIMITLESS CLEAN ENERGY

A new world record has been set at the UK-based Joint European Torus (JET) laboratory, bringing the world a step closer to the dream of limitless, clean power through nuclear fusion. The process, which powers stars, works by heating and forcing tiny particles together to make a heavier one, releasing useful energy. If successfully scaled up, it could produce endless amounts of clean energy without carbon emissions, and unlike wind and solar energy, would not be at the mercy of weather conditions. The experiments produced 69 megajoules of energy over five seconds, triple what was achieved in similar tests back in 1997. Although this is only enough energy for four to five hot baths, it is a significant step forward. The result came from the lab's final experiment after more than forty years of fusion research. The JET facility, constructed in Culham in Oxford in the late 1970s, was the world's most advanced experimental fusion reactor until the end of last year. This result instils greater confidence in the development of fusion energy.

HEARING AIDS FOUND TO SLOW COGNITIVE DECLINE IN OLDER ADULTS

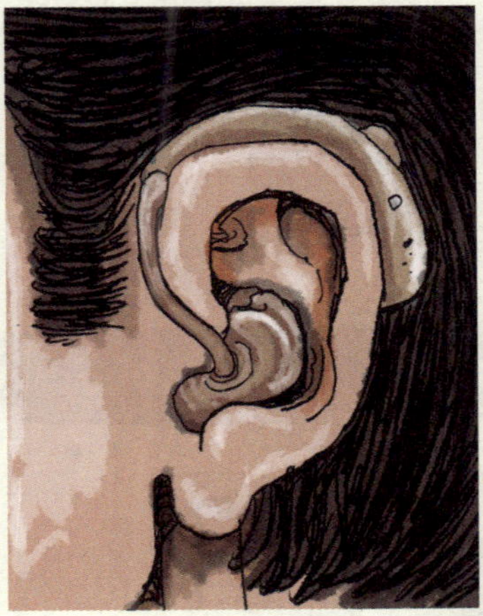

A groundbreaking study has found that hearing aids can significantly slow cognitive decline in older adults at high risk of dementia. The study, led by Dr Frank Lin from Johns Hopkins University, involved nearly 1,000 adults aged seventy to eighty-four with substantial hearing loss. Participants were randomly assigned to receive either hearing aids or a health education program. Over three years, those who received hearing aids reported substantial improvement in communication abilities. While the overall rate of cognitive decline was similar in both groups, among those at higher risk of dementia, the use of hearing aids reduced the rate of cognitive decline by nearly 50 per cent. This research underscores the potential of treating hearing loss as a safe way to lower the risk of dementia in vulnerable populations.

By **NAMIT HANS**

4500 BC
Sumerian civilization in Mesopotamia (present-day Iraq) established in this period.

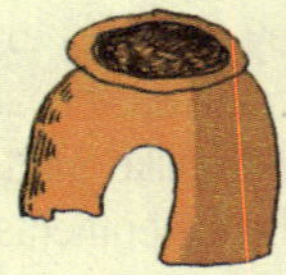

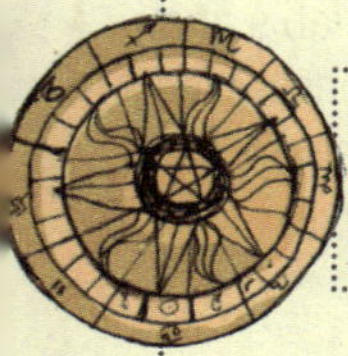

2700 BC
Egyptians create 365-day calendar with the new year beginning in June.

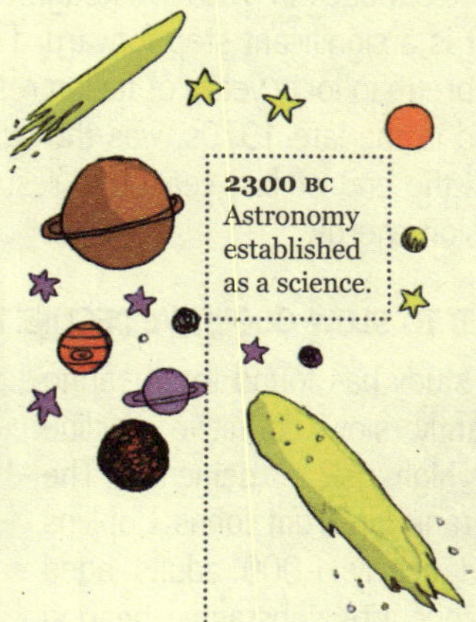

2300 BC
Astronomy established as a science.

2000–1200 BC
Iron Age begins with the discovery of iron. Iron replaces bronze in implements and weapons.

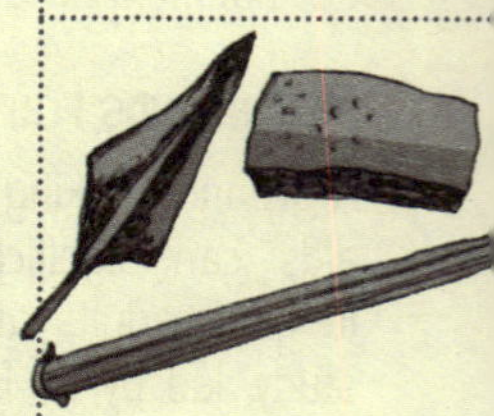

3500 BC
Wheel used for the first time.

000 BC — 3500 BC — 2500 BC — 2000 BC — 1800 BC

3100 BC
Work begins on Stonehenge.

2500 BC
City of Mohenjo-Daro established in the Indus Valley.

2700-2300 BC
Pyramids built in Egypt.

2000 BC
The Bronze Age reaches Europe.

1500 BC
Rise of the Ganges civilization in northern India. The Rig Veda, the oldest book in Sanskrit or any Indo-European language, compiled around this time.

753 BC
Rome is founded by Romulus. Twelve birds circled overhead during the founding ceremony and legend had it that the city would survive for twelve centuries.

509 BC
Founding of the Roman Republic. The great architecture of Rome can be traced back to this period.

776 BC
First Olympics held in Olympia, Greece.

438 BC
Parthenon in Athens completed after nearly forty years of work.

430 BC
Democritus theorizes that matter is composed of tiny grains called 'atomos' that cannot be subdivided.

1500 BC
The Maya civilization established.

1120 BC
Magnetic compass is invented.

400–200 BC
Hindu epics, the Mahabharata and the Ramayana, composed.

44 BC
Julius Caesar assassinated by Brutus and other conspirators.

6-4 BC
Jesus is born.

1500 BC — 1000 BC — 500 BC — 250 BC — 0 BC

1184 BC Trojan war ends.

347 BC
Death of Greek philosopher Plato.

55 BC
Julius Caesar invades Britain, having already captured Gaul, what is now modern France.

1100 BC
Phoenicians develop alphabetic script.

586 BC
Fall of Jerusalem to the Babylonians.

1000 BC
The Chinese develop gunpowder.

220 BC
Building of the Great Wall of China commences.

850 BC
Iliad and *Odyssey* composed by Homer.

623 BC
Gautama Buddha, founder of Buddhism, born in India.

268 BC
Ashoka is crowned.

1500 BC
Birth of Zoroaster, the founder of Zoroastrianism, in Media, Iran.

650 BC
Earliest coins appear.

336 BC
Accession of Alexander the Great at the age of twenty-two to the throne of Macedon in southeastern Europe.

Not to scale

1300 AD
Gunpowder used for warfare in England after being introduced to Europe in 1242.

1 AD
Since the scholars who designed the new calendar did not have the concept of zero, the new Gregorian calendar is calculated to start at Year 1.

1285 AD
Spectacles for the far-sighted are invented in Italy.

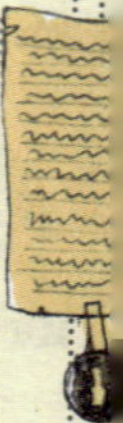

1215 AD
King John of England seals the Magna Carta, giving more power to the Barons. Mongols under Genghis Khan conquer Beijing.

500 AD
Persians use windmills to power irrigation pumps.

64 AD
Great Fire of Rome lasts for six days. Emperor Nero does nothing to stop it.

1096–99 AD
First Crusade.

1140 AD
Angkor Wat, a huge temple complex, built in Cambodia.

570 AD
Birth of Prophet Mohammad, the founder of Islam, in Mecca.

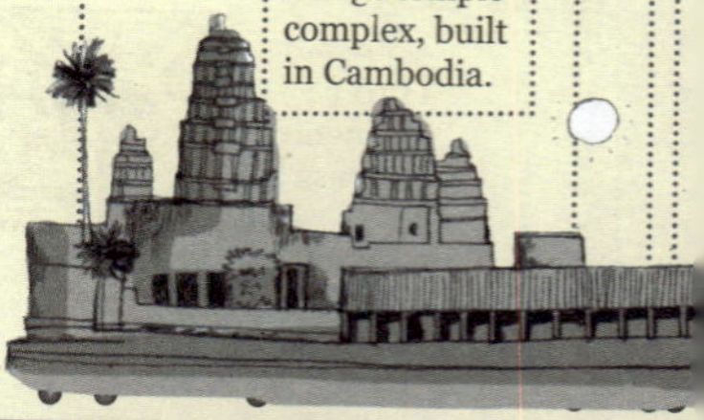

0 AD ---------- 500 AD ---------- 1000 AD ---------- 1200 AD

70 AD
Romans under Titus destroy Jerusalem; 1.5 million Jews die. Gold taken from the temple finances the Colosseum in Rome.

1024 AD
The Chinese start issuing paper money.

1069 AD
Oxford University founded in Oxford, England.

68–69 AD
Civil War in Rome after Emperor Nero dies.

754 AD
Beginning of the state of the Vatican City.

1187 AD
Ships begin to use the magnetic compass.

50 AD
Buddhism reaches China.

1271 AD
Marco Polo starts on his trip to China. He returns to Venice in 1295.

30D
Crucifixion of Jesus Christ.

1315 AD
Great Famine of 1315–17.

1337 AD
Beginning of the 100 Years' War between England and France, resolved only in 1453.

1619 AD
Johannes Kepler finally solves the mystery of the motion of the planets.

1347–50 AD
The Great Plague, popularly called Black Death, ravages Europe.

1588 AD
The Spanish Armada is defeated by an English naval force.

1431 AD
Joan of Arc, who is credited with leading the French to victory over the English, is burnt at the stake for allegedly practising witchcraft.

1564 AD
Birth of poet and playwright William Shakespeare in England.

1438 AD
The Inca Empire established in Peru.

1558 AD
Commencement of the Elizabethan era in England.

1498 AD
Vasco da Gama reaches India. He becomes the first European to travel to India by sea.

1350 AD — 1500 AD — 1550 AD — 1700 AD

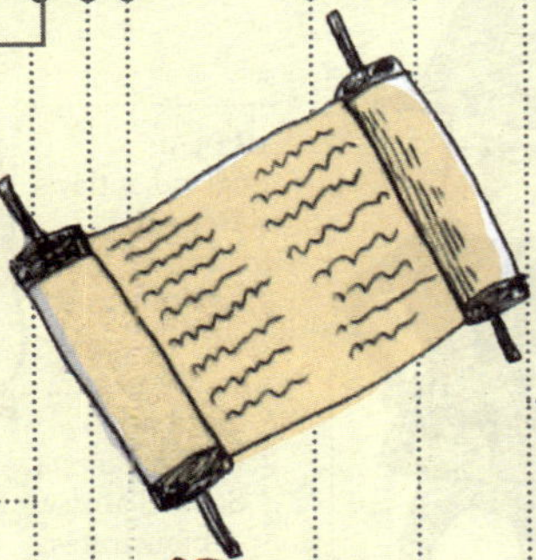

1455 AD
First Bible printed after the invention of the printing press by German goldsmith Johannes Gutenberg.

1556 AD
Earthquake in China kills 8,30,000.

1689 AD
Constitutional Monarchy established in England.

1534 AD
King Henry VIII breaks apart from the Roman Catholic Church and appoints himself as the head of the English Church.

1666 AD
London engulfed by the Great Fire.

1455–85 AD
The civil wars, or the Wars of the Roses, in England.

1488 AD
Bartholomew Diaz rounds the Cape of Good Hope.

1519 AD
Ferdinand Magellan starts what would be the first circumnavigation of the globe.

1503 AD
Mona Lisa painted by Leonardo da Vinci.

1492 AD
Christopher Columbus lands on the Americas. He dies in 1506 believing he had landed in Asia.

1750 AD

1770 AD
Captain James Cook discovers Australia.

1776 AD
US Declaration of Independence is signed on 4 July. American colonies declare themselves independent of Great Britain.

1783 AD
First manned hot-air balloon flight in Paris by Jean Francoise Pilatre de Rozier and Marquis D'Arlands.

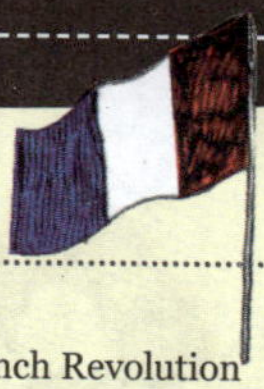

1789 AD
On July 14, the French Revolution begins with the storming of the Bastille to free prisoners and end monarchy. Oddly enough, the Bastille was empty of any real prisoners.

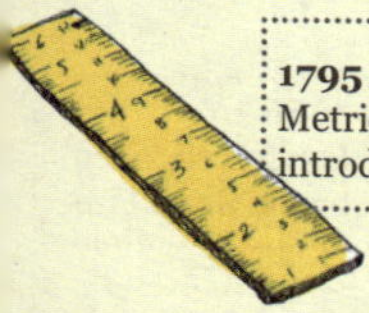

1795 AD
Metric system of measurement introduced in France.

1800 AD

1801 AD
Joseph-Marie Jacquard invents a loom that uses punched cards to create designs in fabric.

1804 AD
Napoleon Bonaparte crowned Emperor of France.

1805 AD
Battle of Trafalgar; British fleet under the command of Horatio Nelson defeats a combined Spanish French fleet.

1812 AD
On September 14, Napoleon takes Moscow, but it is a hollow victory. The city is burned to the ground, yet the Tsar does not surrender. Napoleon and the French army retreat.

1815 AD
Napolean is finally defeated after many attempts in the Battle of Waterloo.

1816 AD
The year without a summer. Mount Tambora erupts and throws up so much dust in the air that it causes 10 inches of snow to fall in June in New England (US). Crops fail and famines are widespread.

1833 AD
England outlaws slavery and frees more than 7,80,000 slaves.

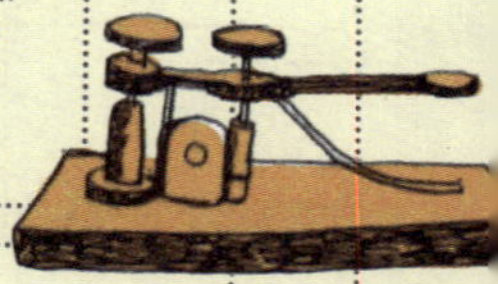

1838 AD
On January 24, Samuel Morse demonstrates the telegraph machine.

1839–1842 AD
The First Opium War: Hong Kong becomes a British colony.

1840 AD

1840 AD
The *Nemesis*, built by a Scottish shipbuilder, becomes the first ironclad to round the Cape of Good Hope.

1845–52 AD
The Great Hunger (aka the Potato Famine) in Ireland. Over 1.5 million die of starvation and disease while Ireland continues to export grain to England to pay rents.

1905 AD
While working as a patent clerk, Albert Einstein publishes his theory of relativity and also states energy equals matter (e = mc²). This is his 'miracle year'.

1898 AD
Spanish-American War starts. Reports of atrocities by the Spaniards against Cubans compels the US to intervene.

1837–1901 AD
Victoria is Queen of the United Kingdom.

1879 AD
The light bulb is invented by Thomas Edison.

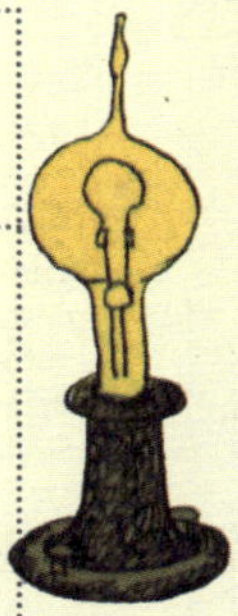

1876 AD
Telephone invented by Alexander Graham Bell.

1848 AD
Karl Marx and Friedrich Engels publish the *Communist Manifesto*.

1860 AD — 1875 AD — 1900 AD

1895 AD
In France, the Lumiere Brothers showcase films for the first time in the history of the world.

1859 AD
Charles Darwin publishes *On the Origin of Species*.

1903 AD
Orville and Wilbur Wright invent, build and fly the first aircraft.

1896 AD
The first modern Olympic Games are held in Athens, Greece.

1856 AD
Louis Pasteur shows that disease is spread by tiny organisms. Modern germ theory born.

1869 AD
Suez Canal opens.

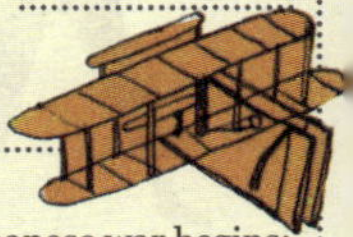

1904 AD
Russo-Japanese war begins: Russians underestimate the modern Japanese fleet, which a year later destroys most of the already depleted Russian navy.

1866 AD
Prussia invades Austria.

1854 AD
Lord Cardigan leads the British cavalry against the Russians in what would become known as 'The Charge of the Light Brigade'.

1861–65 AD
American Civil War; President Lincoln bans slavery; some states attempt to break the Union.

1912–13 AD
The Balkan Wars. Two short wars, fought over the possession of the European territories by the Ottoman Empire.

1914 AD
First World War, commonly known today as World War I, begins. Germany declares war on France and begins the war.

1912 AD
The *Titanic*, which was touted to be the largest luxury liner to sail the open seas sinks with over 1,500 passengers.

1917 AD
The US enters World War I against Germany. Around ten million military personnel die in the war.

1917 AD
The Russian Revolution destroys the Tsarist autocracy and leads to the creation of the Soviet Union.

1944 AD
On 6 June 1944, a date known ever since as D-Day, a mighty armada crosses from England to Normandy, France, and breaks the Nazi grip on western Europe which marks the end of Hitler's Third Reich.

1945 AD
On August 6 an atomic bomb drops on Hiroshima, Japan, killing an estimated 80,000 civilians. On August 9 another bomb is dropped on Nagasaki. On August 14, Japan surrenders and World War II is officially over. The UNO is established.

1910 AD — 1930 AD — 1945 AD — 1950 AD

1916 AD
Easter Rising in Ireland.

1918 AD
At the 11th hour of the 11th day of the 11th month, World War I is officially over.

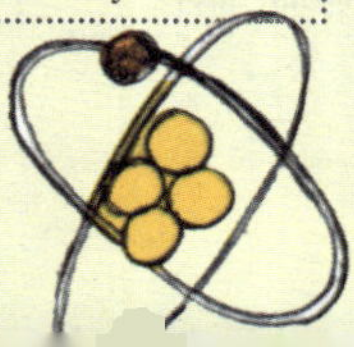

1919 AD
Ernest Rutherford splits an atom for the first time.

1928 AD
British bacteriologist, Sir Alexander Fleming, after many years of research on antibiotics, discovers penicillin.

1930 AD
Planet Pluto is discovered.

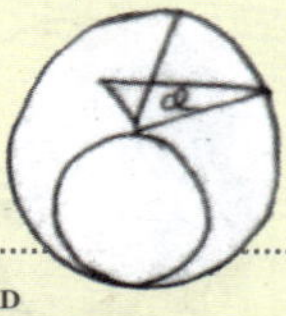

1942 AD
At the University of Chicago, Enrico Fermi conducts the first nuclear reaction and thereby demonstrates the controlled release of nuclear energy.

1939 AD
Hitler invades Poland on September 1. The British Commonwealth and France declare war on Germany, starting World War II.

1938 AD
Adolf Hitler, Chancellor of Germany, launches 'Kristallnacht', a night of terror visited upon the Jews by the Nazis. Hundreds of Jews are killed and the glass from synagogues and businesses is shattered onto the streets.

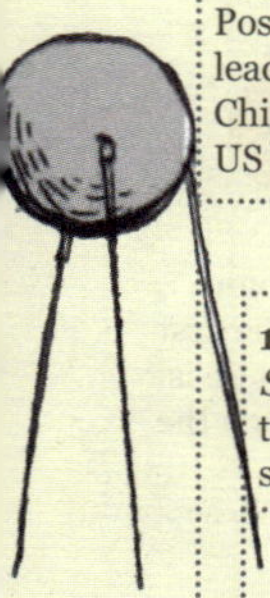

1950–53 AD
Post-World War II division of Korea leads to the Korean War in which China supports North Korea and the US lends support to South Korea.

1957 AD
Sputnik I becomes the first man-made satellite.

1960 AD
On January 23, Jacques Piccard and Don Walsh travel to the bottom of the Marina Trench, the lowest point on the earth, in the Bathsyscaphe Trieste. Oddly, no one has ever gone back a second time.

1961 AD
On April 11, Yuri A Gagarin becomes the first human to reach space.

1991 AD
The Soviet Union dissolves, and with it the Cold War.

2001 AD
On September 11, terrorists attack the World Trade Centre in New York and the Pentagon in Washington DC by flying planes into their targets.

2003 AD
US and British forces invade Iraq. Saddam Hussein is caught, and eventually executed in 2006.

2009 AD
Barack Hussein Obama becomes the first African-American president in the history of the US. He wins the Nobel Peace Prize.

2010 AD
Volcanic eruptions under a glacier in Iceland cause the biggest disruption of international air traffic in recent times.

2011 AD
Osama bin Laden, the mastermind behind the 11 September 2001, terror attack in the US is killed near Islamabad.

1950 AD ---- 1975 AD ---- 2000 AD ---- 2011 AD

1965–73 AD
Vietnam War.

1969 AD
On July 20, Neil Armstrong lands on the surface of the moon.

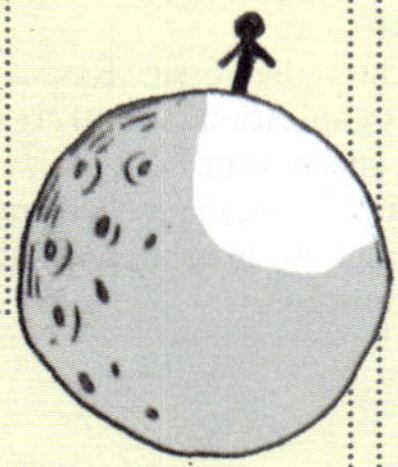

1982 AD
Falklands War fought between Argentina and the United Kingdom over the disputed Falkland Islands, South Georgia and South Sandwich Islands.

1989 AD
In November, the Berlin Wall that divided West Berlin from East Berlin is torn down. Berlin united for the first time since World War II.

1990 AD
First Gulf War begins when the US attacks Iraq in response to Iraq's invasion of Kuwait.

1990 AD
Apartheid ends in South Africa. Nelson Mandela becomes the president of South Africa in the country's first free elections in 1994.

1994 AD
Rwanda is engulfed in a huge and bloody civil war.

2004 AD
A huge earthquake near Indonesia on Christmas Day causes a tsunami in the Indian Ocean that kills thousands in Indonesia, Thailand, Sri Lanka, India and other countries.

2007 AD
Benazir Bhutto, the exiled former Pakistani prime minister, assassinated after her return to Pakistan.

2008 AD
Nepal abolishes monarchy. King Gyanendra vacates the Royal Palace and Nepal becomes a democracy.

2013 AD
A near-earth asteroid entered the earth's atmosphere, bursting over Chelyabinsk in Russia, producing many fragmentary meteorites, a powerful shock wave and damaging more than 7,200 buildings.

2013 AD
US scientists successfully created a cloned human embryo, using the same technique used for developing the cloned sheep in 1996.

2015 AD
Scientists have found water on Mars, the first indication that there is possibility of life on the red planet.

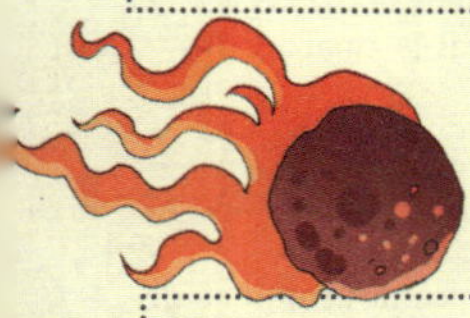

2012 AD
Higgs boson, the particle that is said to give matter mass, is found by scientists at CERN, the European laboratory for particle physics.

2012 AD
Mars rover *Curiosity* finds landforms that point towards flowing liquid. Has there been life on Mars?

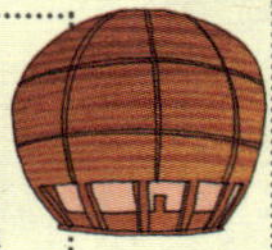

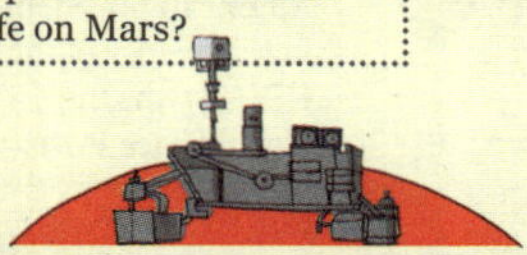

2014 AD
Malaysian Airlines flight MH370, carrying 239 people on board, disappeared over the South China Sea and MH17 was shot down over war-torn eastern Ukraine, killing all 298 on board.

2018 AD
NASA launched a spacecraft named the *Parker Solar Probe* on a daring mission to 'touch' the Sun. It will try to answer several questions about our nearest star.

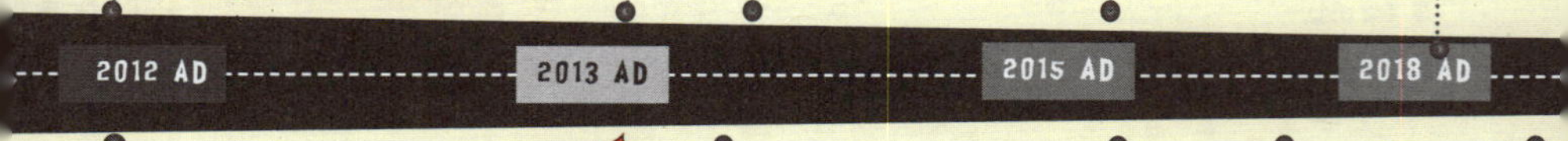

2011–2012 AD
Arab Spring:
Pro-democracy protests overthrow military governments in Egypt and Yemen. In Bahrain and Syria, they challenge the monarchy and the establishment.

2016 AD
In a historic referendum, the United Kingdom voted to leave the European Union.

2017 AD
The Indian Space Research Organization (ISRO) created a space record after it successfully launched 104 satellites in orbit, in a single launch.

2012 AD
Indian American Sunita Williams takes the longest space walk for a woman.

2014 AD
The Ebola Virus, one of the most virulent viral diseases known to mankind, was detected in Guinea. The virus causes haemorrhagic fever and has resulted in over 11,325 deaths so far.

2019 AD
Numerous fires spread throughout the Amazon rainforest causing worldwide concern.

2020 AD
Covid-19 pandemic gripped the world since early December 2019.

2023 AD
Israel-Hamas war begins, leading to heavy casualties in Palestine.

2020 AD — 2022 AD — 2024 AD

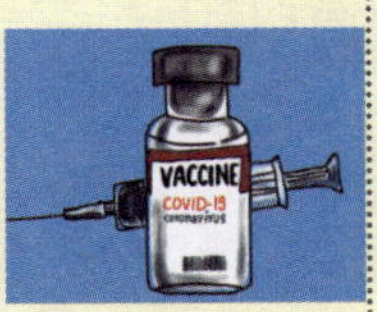

2021 AD
United Kingdom becomes the first country in the world to begin mass vaccination campaign with Pfizer-BioNTech Covid-19 vaccine.

2022 AD
Russia launches full-scale war on Ukraine.

2024 AD
A 7.6 earthquake struck Japan on 1 January 2024, causing major damage and over 200 deaths.

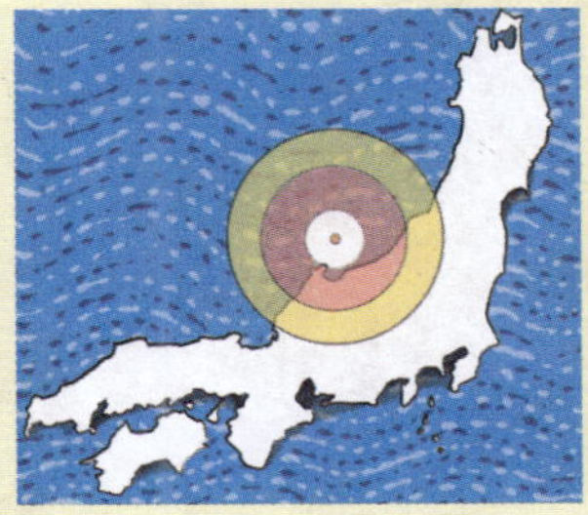

TOP 10

- ☑ WONDERS OF THE WORLD
- ☑ TOP TEN LISTS OF THE BIGGEST, LONGEST, TALLEST AND MUCH MORE

Seven natural wonders of the world

Grand Canyon, Colorado River, Arizona
Rio de Janeiro Harbour, Brazil
Great Barrier Reef, Australia
Parícutin Volcano, Michoaćan, Mexico
Mount Everest, on the border of Tibet and Nepal
Victoria Falls, borders of Zambia and Zimbabwe
Northern Lights (Aurora Borealis), especially from northern Canada and Alaska

Ten man-made wonders of the world

Pyramids of Giza, Egypt
Great Wall of China, China
Taj Mahal, India
Machu Picchu, Peru
Temples of Bali, Indonesia
Angkor Wat, Cambodia
Forbidden City, China
Bagan Temples and Pagodas, Burma
Karnak Temple, Egypt
Teotihuacan, Mexico

Ten famous monuments in India

Taj Mahal, Uttar Pradesh
Qutub Minar, Delhi
Gateway of India, Maharashtra
Gwalior Fort, Madhya Pradesh
Statue of Unity, Gujarat
Khajuraho, Madhya Pradesh
Sanchi Stupa, Madhya Pradesh
Sun Temple, Odisha
Charminar, Hyderabad
Meenakshi Amman Temple, Tamil Nadu

Longest mountain ranges

Andes, South America - 7,242 km
Southern Great Escarpment, Africa - 5000 km
Rocky Mountains, North America - 4,800 km
Great Dividing Range, Australia - 3,621 km
Trans Antarctic, Antarctica - 3,541 km
Appalachian Mountains, North America - 3,200 km
Brazilian East Coast Range, South America - 2600 km
Himalayas/Karakoram/Hindu Kush, Asia - 2,500 km
Tien Shan, Asia - 2,500 km
Urals, Eurasia - 2,500 km

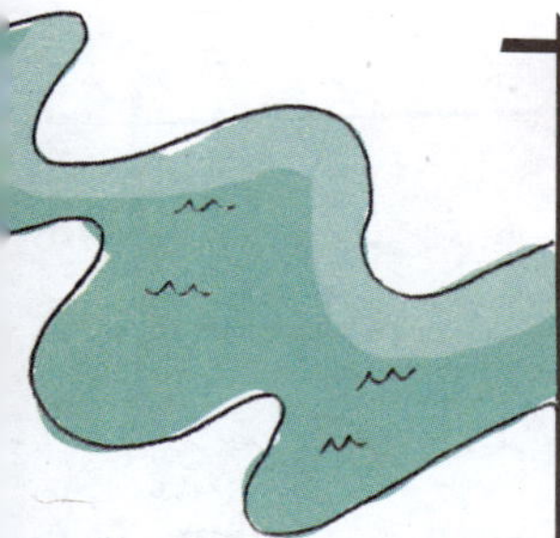

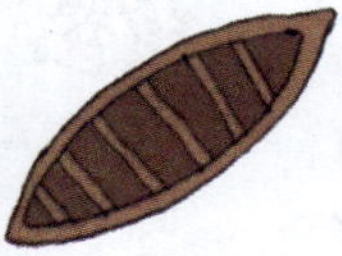

Longest rivers

Nile, Africa - 6,649 km
Amazon, South America - 6,437 km
Yangtze, Asia - 6,300 km
Huang He, Asia - 5,463 km
Parana, South America - 4,879 km
Zaire, Africa - 4,700 km
Irtysh, Asia - 4,248 km
Mississippi, North America - 3,781 km
Ob, Russia - 3,650 km
Yenisei, Asia - 3,487 km

Highest waterfalls

Angel, Churún River, Venezuela - Drop: 979 m
Tugela, Tugela River, South Africa - Drop: 948 m
Mattenbachfälle, Switzerland - Drop: 930 m
Tres Hermanas, Cutevirini River, Peru - Drop: 914 m
Olo'upena Falls, Hawaii - Drop: 900 m
Yumbilla Falls, Peru - Drop: 896 m
Skorga, Skorga (stream), Norway - 875 m
Vinnufallet, Vinnu River, Norway - Drop: 860 m
Pu'uka'oku Falls, Hawaii - Drop: 840 m
James Bruce Falls, Canada - Drop: 840 m

Largest islands

Greenland - 2,166,088 sq km
New Guinea - 8,21,400 sq km
Borneo - 7,48,168 sq km
Madagascar - 5,87,295 sq km
Baffin Island, Canada - 5,07,451 sq km
Sumatra, Indonesia - 4,43,066 sq km
Honshu, Japan - 2,27,898 sq km
Victoria Island, Canada - 2,17,291 sq km
Great Britain - 2,09,331 sq km
Ellesmere Island, Canada - 1,96,236 sq km

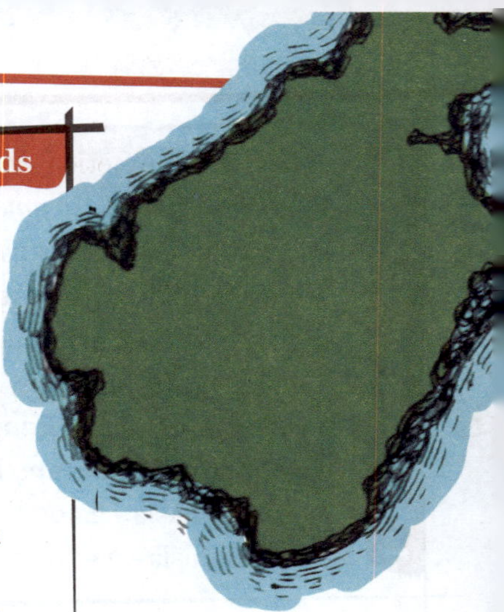

Largest freshwater lakes

Superior, Canada/US
Victoria, Kenya/Tanzania/Uganda
Huron, Canada/US
Michigan, US
Tanganyika, Burundi/Tanzania/
Democratic Republic of the Congo/Zambia
Baikal, Russia
Great Bear, Canada
Malawi, Tanzania/Mozambique/Malawi
Great Slave, Canada
Erie, Canada/US

Biggest deserts

Antarctic Desert, Antarctica - 14.2 million sq km
Arctic Desert, Alaska/Canada/Greenland/Iceland/
Norway/Sweden/Finland/Russia - 13.9 million sq km
Sahara Desert, North Africa - 9.1 million sq km
Arabian Desert, Southwest Asia - 2.6 million sq km
Gobi Desert, Central Asia - 1.3 million sq km
Kalahari Desert, Southern Africa - 0.93 million sq km
Patagonia Desert, South America - 0.67 million sq km
Great Victoria Desert, Australia - 0.64 million sq km
Syrian Desert, Middle East - 0.50 million sq km
Great Basin Desert, US - 0.49 million sq km

Largest oceans and seas

Pacific Ocean
Atlantic Ocean
Indian Ocean
Antarctic Ocean
Arctic Ocean
Coral Sea
Arabian Sea
South China Sea
Caribbean Sea
Mediterranean Sea

Most deadly volcanoes

Year of their most famous eruption

Laki, Iceland - 1783
Mount Vesuvius, Italy - 79 AD, 1631
Mount Tambora, Indonesia - 1815
Krakatoa, Indonesia - 1883
Mount Pelée, Martinique - 1902
Nevado del Ruiz, Colombia - 1985
Unzen, Japan - 1792
Kelut, Indonesia - 1919
Galunggung, Indonesia - 1882
Papandayan, Indonesia - 1772

Hottest places

Location	*Highest Temperature*
Death Valley, USA	56.7°C
Kebili, Tunisia	55°C
Ahvaz, Iran	54°C
Tirat Tsvi, Israel	54°C
Mitribah, Kuwait	53.9°C
Basra, Iraq	53.9°C
Turbat, Pakistan	53.7°C
Mohenjodaro, Pakistan	53.5°C
Mexicali, Mexico	52°C
Jeddah, Saudi Arabia	52°C

Coldest places

Location	*Lowest Temperature*
Dome Fuji Ridge, East Antarctic Plateau	–93.2°C
Russia's Vostok Research Station, Antarctica	–89.2°C
Amundsen-Scott South Pole Station, Antarctica	–82.8°C
Dome Argus, Antarctic Plateau	–82.5°C
Denali, Alaska	–73.8°C
Verkhoyansk, Russia	–69.8°C
Klinck Research Station, Greenland	–69.4°C
Oymyakon, Russia	–67.8°C
North Ice, Greenland	–66.1°C
Snag, Canada	–62.7°C

Wettest places

Location	*Total Rainfall*
Mawsynram, Meghalaya, India	11,871 mm
Cherrapunji, Meghalaya, India	11,777 mm
Tutunendo, Colombia, South America	11,770 mm
Cropp River, New Zealand	11,516 mm
San Antonio de Ureca, Bioko Island, Equatorial Guinea	10,450 mm
Debundscha, Cameroon, Africa	10,299 mm
Big Bog, Maui, Hawaii	10,272 mm
Mt Waialeale, Kauai, Hawaii	9,763 mm
Kukui, Maui, Hawaii	9,293 mm
Emei Shan, Sichuan Province, China	8,169 mm

Places with the lowest population densities

People per square km

Greenland - 0.1
Falkland Islands (Malvinas) - 0.3
Mongolia - 2.2
Western Sahara - 2.2
Namibia - 3.2
Australia - 3.5
Iceland - 3.7
French Guiana - 3.9
Suriname - 4
Libya - 4

Places with the highest population densities

People per square km

Macao SAR - 21,608.7
Monaco - 17,360.4
Singapore - 8,430
Hong Kong - 7,139.7
Gibraltar - 3,274.3
Bahrain - 1,897.1
Maldives - 1,726.3
Malta - 1,677.3
Bangladesh - 1,342.1
Sint Maarten - 1,303.8

Richest countries

GDP (current US$ in billions)

United States - 28,783 billion
China - 18,536 billion
Germany - 4,590 billion
Japan - 4,112 billion
India - 3,942 billion
United Kingdom - 3,502 billion
France - 3,132 billion
Brazil - 2,333 billion
Italy - 2,332 billion
Canada - 2,242 billion

Most populous cities

Tokyo - 37,115,035
Delhi - 33,807,403
Shanghai - 29,867,918
Dhaka - 23,935,652
Sao Paulo - 22,806,704
Cairo - 22,623,874
Mexico City - 22,505,315
Beijing - 22,189,082
Mumbai - 21,673,149
Osaka - 18,967,459

Countries with the lowest HDI*

Somalia - 0.380
South Sudan - 0.381
Central African Republic - 0.387
Niger - 0.394 (tie)
Chad - 0.394 (tie)
Mali - 0.410
Burundi - 0.420
Yemen- 0.424
Burkina Faso - 0.438
Sierra Leone - 0.458

***HDI = Human Development Index**

Tallest buildings

Burj Khalifa, Dubai, UAE - 2,717 ft, 163 storeys

Merdeka 118, Kuala Lumpur, Malaysia - 2,227 ft, 118 storeys

Shanghai Tower, Shanghai, China - 2,073 ft, 128 storeys

Makkah Royal Clock, Mecca, Saudi Arabia - 1,972 ft, 120 storeys

Ping An Finance Centre, Shenzhen, China - 1,965 ft, 115 storeys

Lotte World Tower, Seoul, South Korea - 1,819 ft, 123 storeys

One World Trade Center, New York City, US - 1,776 ft, 94 storeys

Tianjin CTF Finance Centre, Tianjin, China - 1,740 ft, 98 storeys

CTF Finance Centre, Guangzhou, China - 1,739 ft, 111 storeys

CITIC Tower, Beijing, China - 1,731 ft, 109 storeys

Longest bridges

Danyang-Kunshan Grand Bridge, China 1,64,800 m

Changhua-Kaohsiung Viaduct, Taiwan 1,57,317 m

Cangde Grand Bridge, China 1,15,900 m

Tianjin Grand Bridge, China 1,13,700 m

Weinan Weihe Grand Bridge, China 79,732 m

Hong Kong-Zhuhai-Macao Bridge, Hong Kong 55,717 m

Bang Na Expressway, Thailand 54,000 m

Beijing Grand Bridge, China 48,153 m

Wuhan Metro Bridge, China 37, 000 m

Lake Pontchartrain Causeway, US 38,398 m

Countries with the highest HDI

Switzerland - 0.967
Norway - 0.966
Iceland - 0.959
Hong Kong - 0.956
Denmark - 0.952 (tie)
Sweden - 0.952 (tie)
Germany - 0.950 (tie)
Ireland - 0.950 (tie)
Singapore - 0.949
Australia - 0.946 (tie)

Languages

English - 1.5 billion speakers
Mandarin - 1.1 billion speakers
Hindi - 609.5 million speakers
Spanish - 559.1 million speakers
French - 309.8 million speakers
Standard Arabic - 274 million speakers
Bengali - 272.8 million
Portuguese - 263.6 million speakers
Russian - 255 million
Urdu - 231.7 million

SCIENCE

- ☑ Space Round-up
- ☑ Science And Technology
- ☑ Gadgets
- ☑ The Internet

ROCKS FROM SPACE

In 2023 and 2024, missions explored different asteroids, some returning with samples. NASA's OSIRIS-REx mission, launched in 2016, brought samples from asteroid Bennu in the asteroid belt back to Earth in September 2023. Analysing the material making up this asteroid will give scientists information about organic molecules that support life. Now renamed OSIRIS-APEX, it is on its way to asteroid Apophis, expected to arrive in 2029.

NASA also launched the Psyche mission in October 2023, aiming to land on the metallic asteroid Psyche in early 2029.

The Lucy mission, currently flying through the asteroid belt, flew past its first target in November, the asteroid Dinkinesh. Images from the spacecraft showed that the asteroid's moon was a contact binary, or two rocks directly in contact stuck together.

LUNAR HITS AND MISSES

Space agencies across the world are attempting to reach the moon faster than before, thanks to more affordable launches in recent times. The past year saw numerous launches, resulting in both successes and failures.

Japan became the fifth country to soft-land (not crash, but safely land with control) on the moon after the country's space agency, JAXA, launched the Smart Lander for Investigating Moon (SLIM) in September. It entered the lunar orbit in December and landed on the moon in January 2024. There were also two small rovers, one of which ran out of power after completing its mission in a few days.

Not everyone was successful. Russia's Luna-25 lander, developed by the space agency Roscosmos, planned to land near the lunar South Pole in August but crashed. The American company Astrobotic Technology launched its lunar lander called Peregrine in January 2024. However, a fuel leak prevented the spacecraft from landing on the moon, and it returned to Earth where it burned up in the atmosphere.

However, 2024 did see the first successful moon landing by a private company. Intuitive Machines' Nova-C lander, called Odysseus (IM-1) in partnership with NASA, successfully landed in February 2024. The lander is believed to have performed a 'rough' soft landing where it landed at an unplanned 30-degree angle, but the mission was declared successful.

China's Chang'e-6 became the third lander (after Chang'e-5 and Chang'e-4) to touch down on the far side of the moon that we cannot see from Earth. It subsequently collected samples and returned them to Earth as well, while its lander continues to perform experiments on the lunar surface.

END OF A MARTIAN HELICOPTER

NASA's Ingenuity mission, the first powered helicopter on another body outside Earth, came to an end after three years in January 2024, after its last flight on Mars. The mission was originally scheduled to fly just five flights, but it flew a whopping seventy-two, going up from 3 metres to 5 metres in height. The helicopter was a part of the Perseverance rover mission, which continues to function as a powerful Martian surface laboratory.

SCIENCE SATELLITES

India began the first day of 2024 by launching its XPoSat space observatory.

The European Space Agency, Germany's Max Planck Institute for Extraterrestrial Physics, and the Chinese Academy of Sciences launched a collaborative X-ray space telescope called the Einstein Probe in January. The main objective of the satellite is to study high-energy astrophysics. It will study black holes, the merging of extremely dense objects called neutron stars, and monitor the entire sky for sources of X-ray emissions.

NASA launched a powerful Earth observation satellite called Plankton, Aerosol, Cloud, ocean Ecosystem (PACE) that will study climate phenomenon—the effects of climate change on phytoplankton that cover the surface of water bodies, the carbon cycle, aerosols and particles that float around in the atmosphere, clouds and what affects them, marine ecosystems, and so on.

SPACE DEBRIS HURTING SATELLITES

The increasing number of satellites being sent up to space has given rise to an increase in junk or debris in orbit. These include discarded rocket parts during launch, satellites that do not function, nuts and bolts along with other small parts lost by astronauts, and even flecks of paint that are larger than 10 centimetres in width. These pose a risk to satellites as any collision with a piece of junk at high speeds can lead to much larger explosions, and a chain reaction.

The last year saw two space debris events that destroyed satellites. Russia's communications satellite, Kosmos 2143, and a remnant from Europe's VV02 Vega rocket were both impacted by space debris, fully breaking them up. The latter is now the target of the upcoming ClearSpace-1 active space debris removal mission.

AURORA IN INDIA

In May 2024, the Sun unleashed a large solar flare with lots of material, called a coronal mass ejection. This led to a very powerful stream of charged particles moving from the Sun towards Earth, bombarding our ionosphere. This led to majestic and unprecedented displays of aurorae, which are usually confined to the earth's poles. Northern lights (Aurora Borealis) and Sothern lights (Aurora Australis) were seen at latitudes much closer to the equator, being visible as low as Ladakh in India.

CHANDRYAAN-3

India created history by becoming the first country to land in the South Pole region of the moon in August 2023, and the fourth space agency to land on the moon after Russia, USA, and China. The Chandrayaan-3 mission entered into orbit around the moon, before landing on the moon. It consisted of the Vikram lander and the Pragyan rover on the moon, along with instruments on the Propulsion Module which was the engine structure responsible for maneuvering Chandrayaan-3 into orbit.

The mission was designed to last one lunar day or fourteen earth days. During the equally long lunar night, the lack of sun leads to a loss of power for the solar panels of the mission. Both the lander and rover stopped responding to commands from Earth by the end of September.

XPOSAT

On New Year's Day, ISRO launched the XPoSat satellite, which will study cosmic X-rays. It will study the fifty brightest sources of electromagnetic radiation in the universe, such as the centre of galaxies, black holes, supernovae (explosion of stars), and so on.

The satellite is one of India's most sophisticated space observatories, and will also function in tandem with NASA's X-ray Polarimetry Explorer (IXPE) satellite. The telescope was developed by Raman Research Institute and U R Rao Satellite Centre.

ADITYA-L1

In September 2023, ISRO launched India's first space mission to study the sun, called Aditya-L1. The mission is named so because the satellite is located at a moving point in space called Lagrange Point 1 (L1). It is one of five 'Lagrangian Points' in any two-body system like the Earth and Sun, where gravitational forces can balance out in such a way that a satellite can simply orbit empty space.

Here, Aditya orbits an empty space in what is called a halo orbit.

The mission will study the Sun's outer layers and understand how heat transfer occurs. It has already provided data during a total solar eclipse and a powerful geomagnetic storm.

NEWSPACE INDIA

New Space—private space startups—have been making major strides in the space industry after industry collaborations with ISRO began.

Agnikul Cosmos is developing its own 3D-printed small launch vehicle, the Agnibaan, which can carry small satellites to lower orbits at low costs. The first test flight was carried out successfully in May. The company also inaugurated India's first private launchpad within the Satish Dhawan Space Center at Sriharikota, which will function with the support of ISRO.

GAGANYAAN ASTRONAUTS

India announced the names of the four shortlisted candidates who are training to fly on the Gaganyaan mission. Group Captains Prasanth Balakrishnan Nair, Angad Prathap, and Ajit Krishnan, and backup pilot Wing Commander Shubhanshu Shukla, are veteran Air Force pilots with extensive flying experience. The four men entered the shortlist after an initial spaceflight technical training—medical examination, space training, and selection—in Russia. The candidates have also been receiving training at a new astronaut training facility in Bengaluru. Three of them will fly to an orbit of 400 kilometres for a three-day mission by 2025-26.

GOOD NEWS

HUMAN RECORDS IN SPACE

In May 2024, Chinese astronauts Jing Haipeng and Zhu Yangzhu set a spacewalk record at eight hours. In February, Russian cosmonaut Oleg Kononenko completed more than 878 days in space in total, setting a record for the most time in space. In June, he became the first person to spend 1,000 days in space. Alper Gezeravci became the first Turkish astronaut in January although he flew on the Axiom Mission 3 private space mission to the International Space Station. Maryna Vasileuskaya became the first Belarusian woman to fly to space.

Sunita Williams became the first woman to pilot a spacecraft on its first crewed flight—the Boeing Starliner—to space. The spacecraft aims to transport humans to and from the International Space Station.

SOLAR SAIL

The company Rocket Lab launched a new NASA solar sail—a physical sail that looks like those that belong on old ships—that is propelled forward by charged particles from the sun and solar energy. The Advanced Composite Solar Sail System uses a combination of materials and new deployable structures. Such experimental designs will help refine space travel in a way that avoids heavily polluting and expensive rocket fuel.

By **SANDHYA RAMESH**

MRNA GETS A DESERVED WIN

In a rare instance, the Nobel committee awarded the 2023 Nobel Prize in Physiology or Medicine to Katalin Karikó and Drew Weissman in October for their discoveries that enabled the development of mRNA vaccines. These vaccines were used for the first time during COVID-19, ushering in an era of easily programmable vaccines for various diseases. But getting here had been no easy task. Karikó, in particular, endured years of professional disrespect because the University of Pennsylvania, where she worked, deemed her work not important enough to promote her. Finally, the silent weight she carried for years is rewarded with not just the most prestigious prize in science, but also with the rapid pace of mRNA vaccine development technology.

CHIPLETS

In electronics technology, it is common for the number of transistors placed inside a chip to keep doubling every two years because our technology is growing at such a rapid pace. This trend is often known as Moore's Law. The speed at which our chips and circuits are getting smaller, more compact, and efficient, is expected to stop after a while because they can only be made so small. But this year, chip manufacturers have begun making 'chiplets', a new generation of very small chips that function like different parts of a system, and can be linked together in various patterns. This will make manufacturing less expensive, and enable our technology to continue getting smaller, lighter, and more efficient.

BEAMING SOLAR POWER TO EARTH

In a first, US scientists and engineers were able to beam solar energy from space to Earth through the Space Solar Power Project. It involved a group of solar panels that gather the Sun's energy from space. The mission successfully transmitted this energy wirelessly to Earth through microwaves. Such advances sound almost sci-fi-like but will be the future of solar power, which is expected to become an industry by itself in Earth's orbit.

RESURRECTING A ZOMBIE WORM

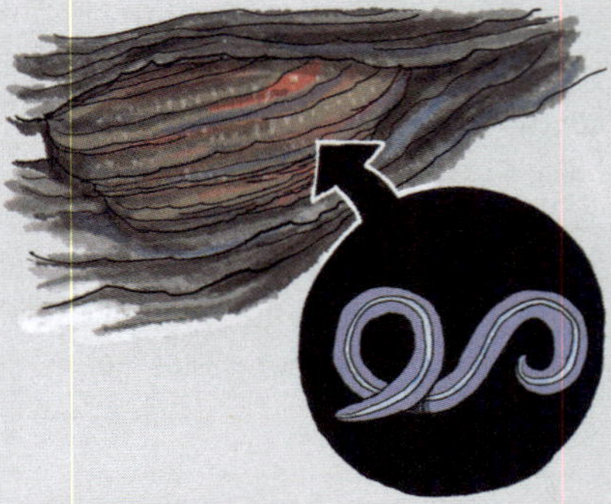

In July, Russian and German researchers announced that they had managed to resurrect a 46,000-year-old ancient worm called a nematode (scientific name: *Panagrolaimus kolymaensis*). This worm had been frozen in ice and had entered a dormant state called cryptobiosis, where very simple organisms can simply pause their functioning and go into extended hibernation. They do this to survive extremely harsh conditions like freezing or drought.

A HAPPY CLONED MONKEY

In January, scientists from the Chinese Academy of Sciences announced that they had successfully cloned a rhesus monkey two years ago and it continues to be healthy and happy. This is the first case of a successfully cloned monkey and is significant because the rhesus monkey's physiology or internal body makeup is quite similar to that of humans. This breakthrough can lead to effective drug developments and new research into animal behavior.

INDIAN NEANDERTHAL ANCESTRY

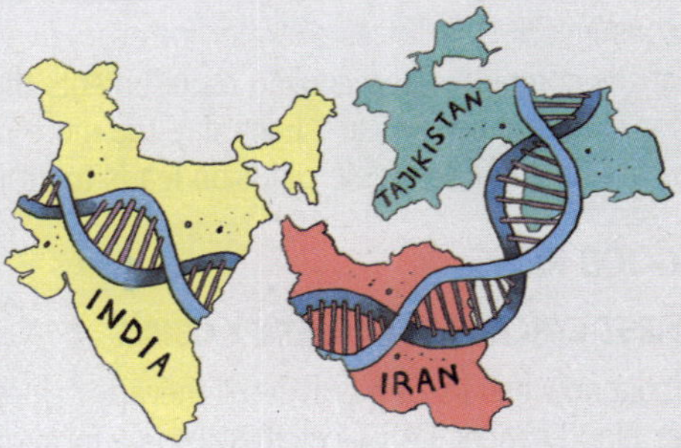

In March, a large study of genetic material belonging to present-day and ancient people from the Indian subcontinent revealed that the Indian genome is closer to Iranian farmers and Central Asia steppe herders (modern-day Tajikistan), than to people from Africa. But most interestingly, the study found that Neanderthals and Denisovans—ancient hominins or species that were cousins to Homo sapiens—make up nearly 2 per cent of our genetic material. How this happened is now a sudden mystery, as archaeologists have not yet found any fossil remains of either Neanderthals (*Homo neanderthalensis*) or Denisovans (*Homo denisova*) in India.

XENOTRANSPLANTATIONS

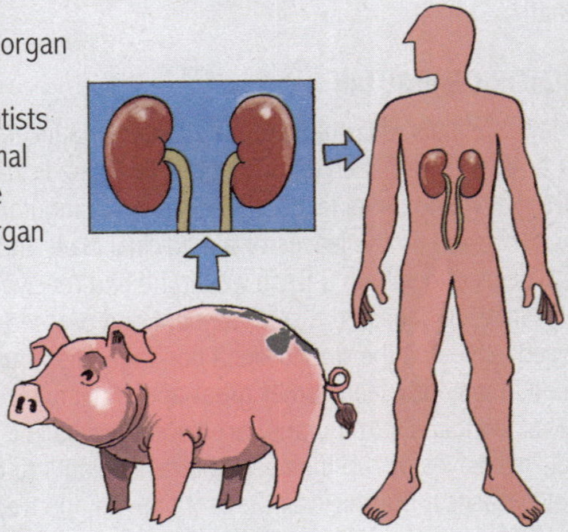

The process of transplanting an organ from one species into another is called xenotransplantation. Scientists are now trying to transplant animal organs into humans because the world is suffering from a huge organ shortage for transplants. Pigs are particularly helpful as they grow quickly and have organ sizes similar to humans. They can be genetically modified so that when their organs are placed inside humans, the human immune system does not attack them as foreign objects. This year, American scientists performed the first full transplantation of a genetically modified pig kidney into a man, whose kidneys functioned fully well as expected. Unfortunately, as with previous partial experiments, he too died a couple of months later. However, his death was unrelated to the kidneys, which were perfectly healthy when he died, which spells great news for medicine.

WATER GUZZLING AI

The world of AI has taken hold of the internet, with more and more corporations like Google, Facebook (Meta), and X (formerly Twitter) rolling out AI in all their products. These advances have given rise to numerous AI images, videos, and text online, which has already begun wreaking havoc and hilarity on the internet. However, there is a darker side to this currently non-functional technology. AI chatbots like ChatGPT consume 500 millilitres of water for every five to fifty prompts they answer because of the computing and cooling requirements these algorithms have. This is even more for AI that generates art. Each day, the mere process of humans across the world using ChatGPT or Stable Diffusion leads to millions of litres of water loss globally.

GOOD NEWS

FIRST CANCER IMMUNOTHERAPY CLINIC

India now has its own CAR T-cell therapy centre at IIT-Bombay to treat various types of blood cancer. CAR T-cell therapy is a form of immunotherapy, where the body's immune system cells are genetically edited to detect cancer cells and destroy them. Cancer has the ability to hide from immune system cells called T-cells that scan the body for foreign bodies or tumours; this is why our body cannot cure cancer on its own. However, with new advances in genetic engineering, researchers can now take a group of T-cells and edit them so that those T-cells can identify a specific mutation in cells that causes various types of blood cancer. When cancer occurs, the body's immune system then jumps into action and fights it off just like a cold. How awesome is that!

DOCTOR ORANGUTAN

In May, scientists who studied orangutans announced that for the first time, they had seen an orangutan using medicinal leaves to treat a wound on its face. The Sumatran orangutan, named Rakus, chewed on the leaves of a medicinal plant and then used its juice to rub on a fresh wound he had received on his face. He ingested a small amount and pressed the chewed leaves on the wound like a bandage. His wound healed in a month. Many other great apes (chimpanzees, gorillas, bonobos, orangutans) are known to swallow medicinal leaves or rub themselves against plants to get rid of parasites. But this was the first time an ape treated an actual wound topically or on the skin using medicinal leaves and their juice.

By **SANDHYA RAMESH**

EAR ENHANCERS

Earphones designs have come a long way over the last few years as newer engineering models attempt to transfer sound into the ear without damaging it or compromising safety.

Audio pioneers, Sony and Bose, have both come out with open-ear earphones, where high-quality sound is delivered through vibrations on the bone and earlobe without blocking the ear canal through noise cancellation and allowing in ambient noise.

Bose's new Open Ear Earphones loop like a U around the earlobe in a completely unfamiliar look, while Sony's new ring-pattern LinkBuds look like two discs that fit in the ear. While the Bose has single-click buttons, the LinkBuds just require tapping on a person's own face somewhere near the ear for a single-click function.

Speaking of earbuds, some AI is being put to good use for in-ear translation. Timekettle's Translation Earbuds come in a range of models, all of which are designed to help in short-term situations where earbuds can translate while a person talks during conversations. The company states that higher-end, more expensive models can help up to six people have simultaneous conversations in six different languages, where the earbuds translate and interpret between forty languages including Hindi, Telugu, and Tamil.

HEALTH MONITORING GADGETS

As tech gets smaller, wearable tech gets better! Many companies have released health monitoring sensors and devices that can be worn on the body to monitor health parameters throughout the day.

Nix, known for its biosensors, has released a new one for monitoring hydration. Looking like a bulky 3D patch that can be placed on one's bicep, the sensor monitors and analyses sweat in real time, providing feedback about dehydration and electrolyte levels in the body. The gadget promises to be nifty for athletes more than anyone else.

MEDICAL DEVICES

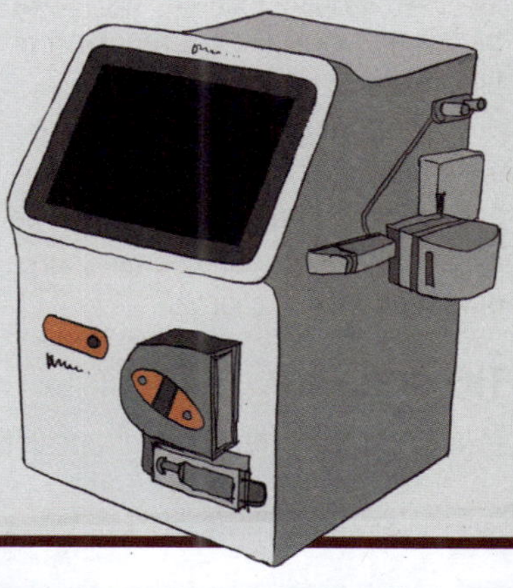

An allergy lifesaving device called Omniject by the company Alerje is an epinephrine auto-injector that attaches to the back of a phone case. The phone attachment case is temperature controlled, and for those with severe allergies, it can be a lifesaving treatment—literally at hand. The device also includes software to alert the patient's support circle if a dose is discharged.

Exorenal has created a portable dialysis machine called xKidney which can be used at home and taken for travelling. It contains disposable compartments and a lightweight unit, avoiding the need for regular clinical visits for dialysis.

NEW KIND OF STOVE

Invisacook is the first induction cooker that goes underneath a counter and comes with cookware that can just be placed on the counter to cook. Cooking with induction is considered more environmentally friendly as it does not utilize petroleum or natural gas.

WORLD'S MOST POWERFUL CAMERA

Canon's Ultra-High Sensitivity Camera MS-500 is the world's highest resolution camera with a sensor containing the world's highest pixel count. The powerful camera functions very well in low light and nighttime conditions, and can capture images several kilometres away in the dark. The camera, however, is first expected to be used by the military and government before anyone else.

NEW TYPE OF PORTABLE BATTERY

Chinese company Oppo continues the country's trend of consumer electronic innovation and has designed a lightweight tracking device that can not only collect power from ambient sources like heat and light but also transmit information like location and temperature. The product, called ZeroPower Tag, is expected to provide theoretically indefinite power as it can never run out.

UNIQUE SOLAR INNOVATION

The ancient town of Pompeii that got buried under Mt. Vesuvisus's eruption in 79 AD today hosts solar tiles on its roofs that are invisible. The Italian company Dyaqua manufactures solar panels that look just like regular roof tiles made of terracotta or brick.

The company Jackery has built a small car that runs on solar power and looks like a tiny Martian bot. The tiny bot, called the Jackery Solar Mars Bot, functions as a portable power source, enough to power an apartment for two to three days with one full charge.

THE GOOD CUP

To address the problem of disposable paper cups actually not being made of paper and clogging up landfills, Choose Planet A developed its Good Cup, which is glued together with a water-based coating. It is leakproof, can be recycled, and is actually biodegradable.

SALIVA PREGNANCY KIT

The only existing pregnancy tests are conducted by measuring hormones in women's urine samples. Such tests date back to at least three thousand years, when women used various types of natural tests for pregnancy. But the biotech company Salignostics has introduced the first-ever saliva-based test called the Salistick, which is expected to be much more convenient to use.

DIGITAL HANDBAG PHONE

The company Honor has introduced its Honor V flip phone, which is the first of its kind foldable phone that doubles as a wallet. In fact, it contains a clip-on strap that makes the phone wearable over the shoulder, with wallpapers lighting up the external displays, making it look like a digital, glittery handbag.

PHOTOGRAPHY AND VISUALS

The pioneering consumer drone company DJI has introduced the DJI Avata, designed to provide a completely immersive experience of first-person flying with a headset connected to a drone. The motion controller accompanying the drone mimics flying as if in the driver's seat, providing a simulated but real flying experience. The DJI Avata 2 has followed suit.

By **SANDHYA RAMESH**

AMAZON VILLAGES GET CONNECTED

Elon Musk's satellite Internet service provider Starlink has provided high-speed Internet access to remote villages in the Amazon rainforest in Brazil. This has helped residents a lot in their daily lives by enabling them to access news, weather forecasts, and stay connected with friends and family who have moved elsewhere. However, for such remote communities, the Internet also has its pitfalls, as young people get addicted to social media and other unsavoury websites. For the time being, the villagers bravely attempt to deal with such adversities and focus on the many benefits the Internet provides.

AN AI-DRIVEN INTERNET

AI has been in the news for over a year now, with AI art, ChatGPT and similar applications coming in very handy for those who cannot draw or write. But there's more to it! Google has implemented AI-generated responses to its users' search queries, something that many find annoying. Popular social media platform Facebook also implemented its Meta AI tool as an assistant. For good or bad, AI has become a buzzword of sorts, with its haters and backers. Some believe it should be controlled or restricted, while others think it opens up whole new possibilities in both business and creative fields. Small businesses and individual entrepreneurs are especially likely to benefit from it as it saves time and spares them from having to spend more on hiring employees. Not all is perfect yet as Google learnt recently after it had to tweak its AI tools that were generating wrong outputs. Such things are bound to happen with new technology. In its early days, AI art generated many deformed figures with extra limbs. That is history now.

Machine learning and deep learning are two subsets of generative AI. Machine learning involves training algorithms with datasets to produce models that can perform complex tasks. Deep learning is based on multiple neural networks that mimic the human brain and can work without human intervention. Both related fields can become very useful in the near future. Also related to this is adaptive AI, which enables faster and more efficient decision-making.

JIO TO LAUNCH SATELLITE INTERNET IN INDIA

Orbit Connect, a joint venture between Reliance's Jio Platforms and Luxembourg-based SES, has received clearance to launch satellite Internet in India after the Indian National Space Promotion and Authorisation Centre (IN-SPACe) gave its approval to provide gigabit fibre Internet. SES is a satellite telecommunications network provider that supplies video and data connectivity to broadcasters globally. Amazon.com's Kuiper and Elon Musk's Starlink are also trying to enter the satellite communication services segment in India. Inmarsat and Eutelsat-Bharti Enterprises' OneWeb have already received approvals. Starlink recently received approval to provide Internet services in Sri Lanka. The satellite Internet race is truly heating up!

OUT OF TOUCH

In not-so-good news, India has the dubious distinction of being the country with the leading number of Internet shutdowns. According to *Access Now*, a digital rights non-profit organization, out of 1,458 Internet shutdowns across the world since 2016, India has accounted for 773 or 53 per cent of them. In 2023 alone, there were 116 instances of Internet shutdown in the country out of 283 worldwide, which amounts to 41 per cent. This makes India the top country in the world for Internet shutdowns for the sixth year in a row. Apart from digital rights, this has a high cost on the economy as well. Other countries with high

rates of Internet shutdowns are Myanmar, Iran, and Pakistan. Palestine and Ukraine, both of which are going through conflict, have also faced Internet shutdowns. But those have been externally imposed, unlike in countries like India where it is the government itself that enforces the shutdown.

It's not that there are no ways around it. In cases where entire Internet services are unavailable, users try to circumvent the blockage by using satellite connections or mesh networks. When individual websites are blocked, those can more easily be accessed through Tor services or VPNs.

WHO ARE YOU TALKING TO?

Internet users in India are quite familiar with bots. A lot of interaction on social media platforms is driven by bots that mimic human communication almost flawlessly, thereby spreading propaganda and misinformation. Cybersecurity specialists Imperva Thales has announced that almost half of the global Internet traffic in 2023 was executed by automated bots and the number has been increasing, while human-generated traffic has been going down. Bad or malicious bots constituted 32 per cent of the Internet traffic in 2023, a rise of 2 per cent from 2022. The recent rise in AI has partly been responsible for the increasing infestation of bots. Malicious bots can cause API (application programming interface) attacks, account takeover attacks, and other automated threats. It is feared that a time will come in the near future when automated bots will surpass human Internet traffic, making the Internet truly soulless and 'artificial intelligence' driven.

QUANTUM LEAPS IN DATA PROCESSING

Quantum computing has been the next big thing for a while now. Quantum computers use quantum mechanics-driven hardware that can solve problems much faster than traditional computers. Quantum computing uses quantum bits or qubits that allow subatomic particles to exist in more than one (multidimensional) state. As a result, the power of a quantum computer can grow exponentially rather than linearly as in traditional computers. It will prove to be immensely helpful in AI and machine learning, data processing, finance, healthcare, and military intelligence.

By **SOURAV DUTTA**

ENVIRONMENT

☑ ENVIRONMENT NEWS

2023 WAS THE HOTTEST YEAR, 2024 COULD BE HOTTER

The global temperature record has been tumbling in recent years. According to the UN's World Meteorological Organization, 2023 was the hottest year since records began in 1850. New research in the leading journal *Nature* suggests it was possibly the northern hemisphere's hottest year in almost 2,000 years. Scientists studied tree rings from nine northern sites to find this out. Tree rings can show how climate changes each year. Trees that depend heavily on temperature in the growing season grow wider rings in warm years and narrower rings in cold years.

June to August 2023 was the hottest three-month period ever recorded, with the first week of July being the hottest week ever. Temperatures exceeded 50°C in Death Valley, USA, and Northwest China, and 40°C in Europe in July. These high temperatures led to extreme weather events like heatwaves, floods, droughts, and wildfires worldwide. Over 45 million acres burned in Canada's worst wildfire season, and a fire in Maui became the deadliest US wildfire in over a century.

22 July 2024, was the hottest day on record, according to a NASA analysis of global daily temperature data. July 21 and 23 of this year also exceeded the previous daily record, set in July 2023. This unprecedented heat is partly due to El Niño, a natural weather pattern that could occur every two to seven years. It is associated with the warming of sea surface temperatures in the Pacific, and the latest El Niño was one of the strongest on record, peaking in January 2024. El Niño can exacerbate the effects of greenhouse gases, which trap the sun's heat in the atmosphere. These gases are produced primarily by human activities such as burning coal, gas and oil to produce energy, which is used to generate electricity, power transportation and more.

ASIA WAS THE WORLD'S MOST DISASTER-HIT REGION IN 2023

According to a World Meteorological Organization (WMO) report, Asia was the most disaster-prone region in 2023, with seventy-nine weather, climate, and water-related hazards. Over 80 per cent of these were floods and storms, which caused the most deaths and economic losses, impacting over 9 million people. Asia is also warming faster than the global average, and this trend has nearly doubled since the 1961-1990 period.

Northern China experienced heavy floods and storms in July, with Beijing recording the most rain in 140 years. Meanwhile, southwestern China suffered from a long drought with lesser-than-usual rain almost every month. India also faced floods and severe droughts, with heatwaves in April and June causing over 100 deaths from heatstroke.

Climate services help reduce disaster risk by providing information on past, present, and future climate to aid in the preparation and management of climate-related events. About 80 per cent of WMO members in the region offer these services, but less than 50 per cent provide detailed climate projections needed for better planning.

Early Warning Systems (EWS) are a cost-effective way to reduce the impact of disasters and potentially save lives, livelihoods, and ecosystems. A warning given twenty-four hours in advance can reduce damage by 30 per cent.

BENGALURU WATER CRISIS AND KASHMIR'S DRY WINTER

Bengaluru, known as India's Silicon Valley, faced a severe water crisis at the end of 2023, which continued into early 2024 due to lower-than-normal rainfall. The crisis also affected other parts of Karnataka and adjoining areas of Telangana and

Maharashtra. Karnataka received 18 per cent less rainfall than usual, the least since 2015. The state relies on monsoon rains to replenish reservoirs and groundwater, but reduced rainfall led to significantly lower water levels. Additionally, unregulated construction and loss of green spaces and lakes in Bengaluru worsened the problem. In Jammu and Kashmir and Ladakh, last winter was the warmest and driest in forty-three years. Snowfall is critical in the region to sustain lives and livelihoods. Less snowfall adversely impacts drinking water supply, agricultural yield, hydroelectric power generation and tourism. December received 79 per cent less rainfall than usual, and January had almost no rain. This decrease in snow and rain is due to fewer western disturbance events, which are rain-bearing wind systems that travel from beyond Afghanistan and Iran, picking up moisture from as far as the Mediterranean Sea and even the Atlantic Ocean. Climate change is also making the region warmer.

INDIA AMENDS FOREST (CONSERVATION) ACT, 1980

The Forest (Conservation) Amendment Act, 2023, effective from 1 December 2023, redefines what a 'forest' is in Indian law. Now, only land notified as 'forest' under the Indian Forest Act 1927 or recorded as 'forests' on or after 25 October 1980, will be considered forests.

This revision starkly contrasts the old law, which applied to any forest land. The amendment allows land not officially classified as 'forests' to be used for commercial activities. It also removes the need for forest clearance permissions and the informed consent of the local community for using these lands.

Further, it exempts 'strategic linear projects of national importance'—like roads and highways—from seeking forest clearance permissions if they are within 100 kilometres of the national border, potentially impacting sensitive areas like the Himalayas and northeastern regions and reducing the rights of indigenous communities.

Significantly affected areas include 40 per cent of the Aravalli range and 95 per cent of the Niyamgiri hills, home to the Dongria Kondhs, a Particularly Vulnerable Tribal Group. The amendment also allows non-forest activities, such as zoos and eco-tourism, on forest lands.

GOOD NEWS

COP 28 MARKS A SHIFT AWAY FROM FOSSIL FUELS

In December 2023, Dubai, UAE, hosted 197 countries and the European Union for the 28th Conference of Parties (COP28), the annual UN climate summit. The historic agreement to 'transition away from fossil fuels,' marked the first time 'fossil fuels' were mentioned in a COP agreement. This is a significant step towards meeting the Paris Agreement (COP21) goal of keeping global warming around 1.5°C above pre-industrial levels. However, many experts pointed out that more needed to be done, calling for a complete phase-out of fossil fuels.

The choice of Dubai, an oil and gas-rich country, and the appointment of Sultan Al Jaber, head of the Abu Dhabi National Oil Company, as COP28 president sparked controversy. Despite this, the summit began on a positive note with an agreement to operationalize the loss and damage fund to help vulnerable communities and developing countries that have suffered major climate-related disasters. Countries pledged $700 million, but this was much less than the $400 billion needed annually.

The summit also completed the first Global Stocktake, evaluating each country's progress in reducing emissions to meet the Paris Agreement goals. The assessment showed that the world was falling behind, and the 1.5°C limit was at risk. The next assessment will be at COP33, which India has proposed to host.

UN ADOPTS HISTORIC HIGH SEAS TREATY

The United Nations adopted a landmark High Seas Treaty to protect marine life in international waters in 2023. The Biodiversity Beyond National Jurisdiction (BBNJ) agreement aims to protect the parts of the ocean that are not owned by any country, which make up two-thirds of the world's oceans. Until now, only about 1 per cent of these high seas were protected, a blaring gap in ocean protection.

The ocean is vital for life on Earth. It produces 50 per cent of our oxygen, absorbs 25 per cent of carbon dioxide emissions, and captures 90 per cent of the excess heat from these emissions. However, greenhouse gases are warming and acidifying the ocean, harming marine life and its ability to absorb carbon dioxide.

The treaty will help create protected areas in the ocean to safeguard fish, plants, and other vulnerable species, manage ocean resources sustainably and reduce pollution from toxic chemicals and plastic waste. It includes rules to make polluters pay for the damage they cause and methods to solve disputes.

Additionally, the treaty offers guidance on building resilient ocean ecosystems to combat climate change and ocean acidification. It also respects the rights and traditional knowledge of indigenous peoples and local communities and supports the fair sharing of benefits from ocean resources.

G20 NEW DELHI LEADERS' DECLARATION SPOTLIGHTS CLIMATE CHANGE

Climate change was a major focus at the G20 summit in New Delhi in September 2023. The New Delhi Leaders' Declaration included the Green Development Pact for a sustainable future. G20 leaders committed to robust, environmentally friendly, and inclusive economic growth, aiming for net-zero emissions by around 2050 and tripling global renewable energy capacity by 2030.

Leaders stressed the importance of fully implementing the Paris Agreement and addressed the contentious issue of climate finance, where developing countries have been asking richer nations to help pay for climate action since the rich countries' past emissions caused much of the climate problem. It emphasized that both public and private funds, as well as more loans from development banks, were needed. India highlighted that the Global South, where billions of people lived, needed trillions of dollars for clean energy and to achieve Sustainable Development Goals (SDGs).

The declaration noted that developing countries need $5.8-5.9 trillion before 2030 to reduce emissions and another $4 trillion annually for clean energy to reach net-zero emissions by 2050.

A BIRD AND RIGHTS AGAINST THE ADVERSE CLIMATE CHANGE EFFECTS

For the first time, the Supreme Court of India recognized that protecting people from the adverse effects of climate change is a fundamental right in the Constitution (Articles 14 and 21). The case was about protecting the Great Indian Bustard (GIB), a critically endangered bird that often collides with high-tension power lines in its habitat in Rajasthan and Gujarat.

In 2021, the Supreme Court ordered that overhead power lines over 99,000 square kilometres covering parts of Gujarat and Rajasthan be moved underground to protect the GIB. However, the region has high renewable energy potential and laying high-tension cables underground could make solar power projects too expensive. Therefore, the government requested a modification, stating that it would impact India's efforts to reduce greenhouse gas emissions.

In the 2024 judgement, the court recognized the need to balance using renewable energy with protecting the GIB. It withdrew the blanket order for underground cables and instead appointed an expert committee to find the best way to protect the GIB. The court also highlighted that promoting renewable energy is important for providing clean and affordable energy to all, especially in rural and underserved areas. It helps reduce poverty, improve quality of life and fosters inclusive growth and development across the nation.

By **MILAN JACOB GEORGE**

ENTERTAINMENT

- ☑ Cinema
- ☑ Art
- ☑ Theatre
- ☑ Indian Dance and Music
- ☑ Music
- ☑ Television
- ☑ Books

It was the year of comebacks. From Shah Rukh Khan's dream run at the box office after a long gap to Mamootty's year of experimenting, to India shining bright at the Cannes Film Festival, there were multiple reasons to celebrate Indian cinema this past year. The year also witnessed a historic writer's and actor's strike in Hollywood, which crippled the economy and the film industry for a few months and delayed major releases. From *12th Fail* doing well to *Animal* dividing audiences and critics alike, here's all that happened in the world of entertainment.

KING KHAN IS BACK WITH A BANG!

Just when the world was writing his career off, Shah Rukh Khan scripted his historic comeback to films in 2023 in a way that no one could have possibly imagined. After a spate of box office duds, Khan stepped away from the arc lights in 2018 but in 2023 the Bollywood superstar came back on the big screen with a bang with not one or two, but three blockbusters that not only created history at the domestic box office but also created a defining impact globally. Khan started the year with the spy thriller *Pathaan*, then followed it up with a vigilante film *Jawan*, and ended the year with *Dunki* which talked of the immigrant crisis around the world. Within the realms of commercial cinema, Khan brought out important societal issues through his films, played the spy who did not take sides, and steered away from jingoism even though his films had nationalist themes. Khan's fans were already longing to see the star on screen for a long time, and he made sure that he came back with a bang.

PUSHING BOUNDARIES, ONE FILM AT A TIME

Bona fide superstar of Malayalam cinema, Mammootty has played varied roles in his long career. In 2023, he pushed the boundaries and played a silent homosexual man undergoing divorce after two decades of marriage. *Kaathal – The Core* was helmed by Jeo Baby and had the veteran star in top form. The actor also shined in two other critically acclaimed films: *Nanpakal Nerathu Mayakkam* and *Kannur Squad*. One was a situational comedy while the other was an action thriller, but both had Mammootty delivering stellar performances. The man who ruled Malayalam cinema for over four decades has been experimenting with roles at an age when most actors play safe or retire. That's not all! The actor also had *Bramayugam* at the beginning of 2024, which may have courted controversy before release, but the horror-thriller had Mamooootty in a never-before-seen avatar. It was truly a special year for the actor, and from the looks of it, he has a few more surprises up his sleeves left.

MAMMOTH SUCCESSES AT THE BOX OFFICE

The pandemic had brought the film industry — much like other industries — to an all-time slump. Audiences no longer wanted to visit the theatre to watch a movie and the content on OTT seemed far more appealing for its freshness. However, 2023 changed the tide for the Hindi film industry. Right at the beginning of the year, Shah Rukh Khan's long-awaited comeback *Pathaan* broke box office records and earned a whopping ₹1,050.30 crore worldwide. Khan had a dream run at the box office, and his other two releases in the subsequent months of 2023 — *Jawan* and *Dunki* — too shattered box office records. *Jawaan* was the second highest-grossing Hindi-language film of all time as it earned an impressive ₹1,148.32 crore at the global box office.

Not just SRK, but Ranbir Kapoor and Sunny Deol too created an impact with their films *Animal* and *Gadar 2* respectively. With many films and audiences back in the theatres in full force, Hindi films made a strong statement that it isn't easy to write Bollywood off in the age of OTT platforms.

A DIVIDED AUDIENCE

If there was any film that divided its audience, it would easily be filmmaker Sandeep Reddy Vanga's *Animal*. The film featured Ranbir Kapoor, Anil Kapoor, Rashmika Mandanna, Bobby Deol, and Tripti Dimri in lead roles, and narrated a story of the troubled relationship between a father and son. Seeped with misogyny and brutal violence, the movie received backlash from the critics but was loved by the masses as it broke box office records and became one of the highest-grossing Hindi films of 2023. Some watched the film out of curiosity, while others loved the dark, problematic Ranvijay (Ranbir Kapoor) and his problematic love for his father (Anil Kapoor). Whatever may have been the reason, the film's success was also a testament to the fact that the Indian audience had a complex mindset that seemed fine with the brutality shown on screen.

SMALL FILMS, BIG IMPACT

Simple and effective. That's how one would describe films like *12th Fail* and *Laapataa Ladies*. Both were made on a small budget with no big A-list star in the cast and told heartwarming stories of regular people who fought odds and won in life. With incredible stories, both these films won at the box office as well.

12th Fail, directed by Vidhu Vinod Chopra, and featuring Vikrant Massey in the lead narrated the real-life story of IPS officer Manoj Sharma, who fought poverty and worked hard to crack the civil service exams. Sharma's journey, brilliantly played by Vikrant Massey, was heartwarming, realistic, and inspirational. The film was a surprise hit and worked mostly due to word-of-mouth publicity, becoming one of the best films of 2023.

Following the footsteps of *12th Fail*, filmmaker Kiran Rao and producer Aamir Khan released *Laapataa Ladies* in March 2024. The film focussed on a curious case of two missing brides and highlighted many pertinent issues, from women empowerment to female friendships to the importance of education. Yet none felt like a jargon as the treatment was light and funny. Featuring rank newcomers, *Laapataa Ladies* tugged at the heartstrings and was received well by critics and masses alike.

INDIA AT CANNES 2024

After years of simply sashaying down the red carpet and making noise style and not cinema, India created an impact at the Cannes Film Festival 2024 with incredible films. The festival also highlighted that the Film and Television Institute of India is a force to reckon with when it comes to cinema. FTII's ex-alumni Payal Kapadia created history as her film *All We Imagine as Light* won the Grand Prix. It was the first Indian film to win the prestigious honour in the history of the festival. Meanwhile, Chidananda S. Naik's FTII certificate film *Sunflowers Were the First Ones to Know...* bagged the La Cinef first prize, only the second Indian film to do so. That's not all, Indian actress Anasuya Sengupta clinched the best actress prize in the Un Certain Regard sidebar for her performance in Konstantin Bojanov's India-set drama *The Shameless*. Indian cinematographer Santosh Sivan was awarded the prestigious Pierre Angenieux ExcelLens in Cinematography honour. India truly shined at the festival which has for all these years hosted a bevy of Indian actors on the red carpet dressed in their designer best. Indian cinema's incredible performance in 2024 will go down in the pages of history when Indian films and artists beyond Bollywood fetched coveted prizes at the festival.

THE RISE OF THE DEOLS

Dharmendra, at eighty-eight, played a key role in Karan Johar's film that was headlined by Ranveer Singh and Alia Bhatt. Not just the senior actor, but his sons, Sunny Deol and Bobby Deol, made remarkable comebacks the same year. Sunny's *Gadar 2*, smashed box office records and became one of the highest-grossing Hindi films of the year. Bobby's act in *Animal* drew fear and awe amongst his fans in equal measures. For those who had written off the three actors due to their absence from the big screen for a long gap, the Deols quite shut them up with their remarkable performances in 2023, reaffirming that they belong in Bollywood and will remain here for a long time.

SAG-AFTRA, WRITERS STRIKE

It was a year when the world was compelled to notice the work of those who work behind the scenes in the business of cinema. The Screen Actors American Federation of Television and Radio Artists, which represents practically the entire Hollywood, put the film industry on a standstill from July to November 2023 and led to a loss of jobs and an overall slumped economy. The longest strike in SAG-AFTRA history, along with the Writers Guild of America Strike, led to the halting of shoots and thereby delaying major film releases by months. Actors — all part of the SAG-AFTRA union — were not allowed to promote their upcoming releases or speak to the press due to the clauses within the strike. The members primarily went on strike to fight the growing use of AI in all mediums of moviemaking by studio bosses, especially for replicating the extras for other scenes and paying wages for only a day's work. The strike was called off in November, and by December the union and the studio bosses came to an understanding and changed clauses in contracts of hundreds of workers.

LOVE: AN AGENT OF CHANGE

Bollywood is used to stories where a boy meets a girl, falls in love, and marries. However, filmmaker Karan Johar showed that love is timeless and doesn't see age. In his directorial venture *Rocky Aur Rani Kii Prem Kahani*, Johar showed two over-the-hill characters rekindling their romance years after separation. Facilitated by the grandchildren, the two revived their clandestine romance much to the discomfort of others. The film also parodied the set gender roles prevalent in Indian households and flipped the narrative where the women ran the household while the men pursued their passion in the field of arts. The film also served a cinematic moment when the leading man Ranveer Singh performed kathak with his onscreen father-in-law, played by Tota Roy Chowdhury, much to the discomfort of his conservative and conventional Punjabi family.

Amid chest-thumping patriotism and alpha heroes, Bollywood also subtlety served stories that challenged set rules of society. Much like Johar, filmmaker Shirsha Guha Thakurta's *Do Aur Do Pyaar* talked of giving love a second, third, and fourth chance. Starring Pratik Gandhi and Vidya Balan as a married couple who find love again in each other even as their marriage is falling apart, the movie takes a very real approach to fidelity and modern marriages in an imperfect world.

THE ARCHIES COMES TO BOLLYWOOD

The iconic comic book series *The Archies* came to Bollywood. Filmmaker Zoya Akhtar's Netflix film launched six newcomers, including Shah Rukh Khan's daughter Suhana, Sridevi's daughter Khushi Kapoor, and Amitabh Bachchan's grandson Agastya Nanda. Akhtar shifted the very American story to 1960s India, where (in a fictional town) Archie and his gang fight the authorities to save their favourite park from being turned into a commercial space. The film was high on aesthetics but low on performances from the leads. While Akhtar flipped the narrative to make Betty and Veronica ditch Archie together, the film still was not able to create an impact on the audience and was mostly panned.

MONKEY MAN GIVES INDIA A MISS?

Slumdog Millionaire star and Indian-origin actor Dev Patel made a remarkable debut as a director in 2024 with *Monkey Man*. The story was set in Mumbai, India and consisted of mostly Indian actors. While the film was released overseas to rave reviews and packed theatres, becoming one of the surprise hits in the first half of the year, *Monkey Man* did not make it to Indian cinemas. The censor board did not clear the film, anticipating controversy around the contents of the film, which reportedly showed a certain religious group in shades of grey. While Patel's team was willing to change and modify certain scenes to suit the palate of the Indian audience, the censor board simply avoided clearing the film lest it create communal tension. The verdict is still out on this one.

By **SHOMINI SEN**

WHAT'S HEATING UP THE BOOKSHELVES?

If the industry buzz is anything to go by, publishing agents spent the year swooning over five sizzling genres. Drumroll, please, for romance, fantasy, contemporary fiction, romantasy, and young adult fiction. Romance and fantasy have always been like that secret crush you just can't shake off. Now, they have fused into the delightful romantasy, a hot trend on 'BookTok' and 'Bookstagram'. While the term is new, the concept is not. Romantasies have been enchanting readers for ages. Ali Hazelwood's *Bride* was flagged as a standout in this rising trend. As if blending fantasy with romance wasn't enough, there was also a growing interest in multigenerational love stories that transcend time and space. This trend was exemplified by hits like Kaliane Bradley's *Ministry of Time* and Lotte Jeff's *This Love*.

Contemporary fiction, set in the present day, also gained traction, contrasting with last year's preferences. Meanwhile, young adult fiction maintained a solid presence, albeit slightly lower in ranking. Adding to the literary landscape was a rise in genre-defying books, illustrated by Asako Yukuzi's *Butter: A Novel of Food and Murder*, which resonated with both writers and readers eager to explore beyond traditional boundaries. Literature also seemed to be delving into themes of wealth disparity and societal critique. Kiley Reid's *Come and Get It* and Bri Lee's *The Work* intertwined love and power dynamics, while Carrie Sun's memoir *Private Equity* offered a stark portrayal of life in finance. 'Eat the rich' motifs spanned genres from literary to crime fiction.

Finally, going back to the readers' response, a quick scan of popular sites like Goodreads revealed a fascinating trend: books featuring strong female protagonists dominated the charts. Among the top ten most beloved books of the year, nine spotlighted fierce female leads, and one proudly showcased a non-binary protagonist. Clearly, stories led by powerful, diverse characters resonated deeply with the readers.

LITERATURE TAKES ON GLOBAL ISSUES

Pressing social issues were central themes in the publishing industry. The London Book Fair in March underscored this trend, where prominent discussions ranged from war to neurodiversity to sustainability. Raja Shehadeh's June 2024 release, *What Does*

Israel Fear from Palestine? notably contributed to discussions on conflict and Palestine, a testament to this trend. Issues of neurodiversity have been gaining momentum in literature for some time, evident in a variety of genres including fiction, memoirs, and children's books. Fern Brady's award-winning *Strong Female Character* (published in 2023), which poignantly portrayed growing up autistic, further propelled this trend, highlighting the growing celebration of diverse voices. Sustainability also remained a critical focus, with a host of new and forthcoming titles addressing environmental issues. Standouts include *Ocean* by David Attenborough and Colin Butfield, slated for release in 2025, and *Coastlines: A Four-Billion Year Journey Along the World's Seashores* by Ben Wilson, scheduled for 2026—both under Hachette imprints.

RISE OF SELF-PUBLISHING MAVERICKS

Gone are the days when self-publishing played second fiddle to traditional routes! Self-publishing was seen as asserting dominance in the evolving 2024-25 publishing landscape. According to a report by Forbes, the industry experienced explosive growth, with self-published books soaring by 264 per cent in five years, thanks to platforms like Amazon Kindle Direct Publishing (KDP). The reason behind this could be how these platforms give creators complete control, from content creation to global distribution. Take KDP, for example—it lets authors release ebooks and paperbacks worldwide in just forty-eight hours, offering royalties from

amazon kindle | direct publishing

35 per cent to 70 per cent, a sharp contrast to traditional rates. Apart from book sales, self-publishing also opens doors to workshops, consulting gigs, and speaking engagements. Successful authors can establish themselves as industry experts, leveraging their visibility and credibility. Resultantly, with digital platforms continuing to evolve, it seems like self-publishing is here to stay providing a dynamic and profitable pathway in the publishing landscape, shaping its future beyond 2024.

PUBLISHING IN INDIA

The Indian publishing scene burst with creativity and dynamism, driven by tech-savvy strides, evolving reader tastes, and a bustling literary vibe. The year saw a grand celebration of India's multilingual splendour, as publishers dove headfirst into regional literature in translations, bringing forth treasures like Sandhya Mary's *Maria, Just Maria* (translated by Jayasree Kalathil), Ismail Darbesh's *Talashnama* (translated by V. Ramaswamy), and *The Thief: The True Story of Manianpillai's Life* by Manianpillai and G.R. Indugopan (translated by Nandakumar K)—all clearly reflecting a burgeoning interest in minority lives and concerns. A glance at the publishing lists confirms that indeed, this was the year of the underdog, with standout releases such as Neha Dixit's *The Many Lives of Syeda X* and Anjali Kajal's *Ma is Scared*, which vividly portrayed the voices of Muslim and Dalit women, respectively. The year also saw much-anticipated releases like Salman Rushdie's *Knife*, where he chose to respond to violence with art, and Kanan Gill's *Acts of God*, hailed as a significant evolution of one of India's finest comedic voices.

Non-fiction also made a significant impact with works such as Sam Pitroda's *The Idea of Democracy* and *Artificial Intelligence and National Security* by Amit Sinha and Vijay Khare, which addressed issues of privacy and data sovereignty. Conflict-driven narratives captured attention too, with books like Siddhartha Gigoo's *A Long Season of Ashes*, Romesh Bhattacharji's *Travels in Paradise on Earth*, and Vishal Pandey's *Israel War Diary*. Meanwhile, Neha Bhat's *Unashamed: Notes from the Diary of a Sex Therapist* broke new ground in the self-help genre, offering insightful explorations of mental health and sexuality.

NOTABLE LITERARY PRIZE WINNERS

- Caine Prize for African Writing 2023: Senegalese writing duo Mame Bougouma Diene and Woppa Diallo for their story *A Soul of Small Places*
- International Dublin Literary Award 2024 (Prize: €100,000): Romanian author Mircea Cărtărescu and American translator Sean Cotter for the novel *Solenoid*
- International Prize for Arabic Fiction 2024 (Prize: $50,000): Imprisoned Palestinian writer Basim Khandaqji for his fourth novel *A Mask, the Color of the Sky*
- JCB Prize for Literature 2023 (Prize: ₹ 25 lakhs): Perumal Murugan for his novel *Fire Bird*, an English translation of his Tamil novel *Aalanda Patchi*
- Booker Prize 2023 (Prize: £50,000): Irish author Paul Lynch for his novel *Prophet Song*
- International Booker Prize 2024 (Prize: £50,000, shared equally between author and translator): Jenny Erpenbeck's novel *Kairos*, translated by Michael Hofmann from German
- Stella Prize 2024 (AU$ 50,000): Alexis Wright for *Praiseworthy*
- Windham-Campbell Literature Prize 2024 ($165,000 each):
  1. Non-fiction: Christina Sharpe (Canada/United States) and Hanif Abdurraqib (United States)
  2. Drama: Christopher Chen (United States) and Sonya Kelly (Ireland)
  3. Fiction: Deirdre Madden (Ireland) and Kathryn Scanlan (United States)
  4. Poetry: Jen Hadfield (Canada/United Kingdom) and M. NourbeSe Philip (Canada/Trinidad and Tobago)
- Yoto Carnegie Medal 2023: Manon Steffan Ross for writing and translating *The Blue Book of Nebo*
- Yoto Carnegie Medal for Illustration 2023: Jeet Zdung for illustrating the graphic novel *Saving Sorya: Chang and the Sun Bear*, by wildlife activist and scientist Trang Nguyen

SELECT AWARD WINNING CHILDREN'S BOOKS FROM 2023-24

- *The Eyes and the Impossible* by Dave Eggers winner of the 2024 John Newbery Medal for the most outstanding contribution to children's literature
- *An American Story* by Kwame Alexander and illustrated by Dare Coulter, winner of the Coretta Scott King Awards recognising an African American author and illustrator of outstanding books for children and young adults (for illustration)
- *Nigeria Jones* by Ibi Zoboi, winner of the Coretta Scott King Awards recognising an African American author and illustrator of outstanding books for children and young adults (for text)
- *Fox Has a Problem* by Corey R. Tabor, winner of the Theodor Seuss Geisel Award for Beginning Readers
- *Mexikid: A Graphic Memoir* by Pedro Martin, winner of Pura Belpré Medal for Latinx Literature
- *The Blue Horse and Other Amazing Animal Stories from Indian History* by Nandini Sengupta, winner of the Sahitya Akademi Bal Sahitya Puraskar in English

NOTABLE LITERARY DEATHS

- Jayanta Mahapatra (27 August 2023), first Indian poet to win the Sahitya Akademi award for English poetry
- Robert Klane (29 August 2023), American comic novelist and screenwriter who wrote the screenplay for *Weekend at Bernie's*
- Khaled Khalifa (30 September 2023), Syrian novelist, screenwriter and poet
- Eve Bunting (1 October 2023), Northern Irish-born American children's writer and winner of Caldecott Medal
- Louise Glück (13 October 2023), American poet and essayist who won the Nobel Prize in Literature in 2020
- Henri Lopes (2 November 2023), Congolese writer known for his novel *Le Pleurer-Rire* (*The Laughing Cry*)
- A.S. Byatt (16 November 2023), English critic, novelist, poet and short story writer and Booker Prize winner
- Benjamin Zephaniah (7 December 2023), British writer and poet and winner of BBC Young Playwrights Festival Award
- Refaat Alareer (6 December 2023), Palestinian writer and poet
- Hinako Ashihara (29 January 2024), Japanese manga artist known for her manga series *Sand Chronicles*
- Alice Munro (13 May 2024), Canadian short story writer who won the Nobel Prize in Literature in 2013
- Caleb Carr (23 May 2024), American author known for his dark thriller *The Alienist*

By Anurima Chanda

RECORD BREAKING SALES

'The Story Teller', a painting by artist Amrita Sher-Gil, became the most expensive work of an Indian artist ever. In September 2023, the piece sold for ₹ 61.8 crores at Saffronart's *Evening Sale: Modern Art* in New Delhi. Sayed Haider Raza's painting 'Gestation', also an oil-on-canvas painting, became the second highest, selling at ₹ 51.75 crore in Pundole Auction House in Mumbai in August 2023. Expressionist Tyeb Mehta's bronze sculpture 'Two Heads' sold at ₹ 14.95 crores, making it the world auction record for a modern Indian sculpture.

RETROSPECTIVES GALORE

An important retrospective exhibition by DAG, *Flower of Fire: The Life & Art of Gopal Ghose*, was held in New Delhi between December 2023 and January 2024. An extraordinary painter and one of the founding members of India's first artistic collectives, the Calcutta Group, Ghose had an illustrious career that spanned from the 1930s to 1980. This retrospective showcased paintings, sketches, notebooks, and journals of the artist along with his signature lush landscape paintings. Many of his unseen works and his overall massive talent with watercolours were on display.

Another significant exhibition, *One Hundred Years and Counting: Re-Scripting KG Subramanyan*, curated by Nancy Adajania, was held between April and June 2024 to mark the birth centenary of KG Subramanyam at Emami Art, Kolkata. One of India's biggest artists, Subramanyam's career spanned seven decades and included several forms – reverse paintings on acrylic, pen on paper, drawings, and toys. This retrospective celebrated over 200 of his works, including archival material not many know of, such as handcrafted mock-ups of children's books, preparatory sketches for murals, and the maquettes for iconic 'The War of the Relics' (2013).

Art aficionados also got a taste of the wonderful albeit lesser-known works of the Karnataka-born artist Rumale Chennabasaviah in 'Varna Mythri' in April 2024. 'India's Vincent Van Gogh' or Rumale as he was fondly known by the artist community, donned many hats, that of an artist, a freedom fighter and an editor among others. Through this retrospective show at the National Gallery of Modern Art, Mumbai, eighty of his best artworks were showcased, focusing on landscapes, cityscapes, and spirituality—his favoured subjects. KS Srinivasa Murthy of Bengaluru's Rumale Art House and Shruti Das, deputy curator of NGMA Mumbai, curated the exhibition, in a bid to broaden the audience base for this exceptional artist. If the gorgeous blooms of Bengaluru fascinate you, knowing Rumale's works is a must.

SOME INTERESTING EXHIBITIONS

Presented by Chhatrapati Shivaji Maharaj Vastu Sangrahalaya and the Jehangir Nicholson Art Foundation in collaboration with the Alkazi Foundation for the Arts, cinema lovers were treated to a unique exhibition, *A Cinematic Imagination* at Jehangir Nicholson Art Foundation, Mumbai, in April 2024. Early Indian cinema was defined by Bombay Talkies as the first-of-its-kind production studio in India in the 1930s. A collaboration between Europe and India, Bombay Talkies set the ball rolling for the Indian film industry as we know it. This exhibition lent a peek into that nascent, cross-cultural world with a wide range of photographs of the yesteryear cast, crew, and sets, along with plenty of behind-the-scenes stuff from the archives.

In the early nineteenth century, Calcutta had two distinct behaviours and appearances. As the British capital, the city flourished, as did the babus—the nouveau-rich, educated 'bhadralok'—who looked down on popular culture. The masses, on the other hand, found the babus oblivious to real-world problems. Kalighat pat, or the famous watercolour paintings made by the artists that lined the area next to the Kalighat temple, portrayed this divided, interesting world very well. As local prints came up, so did expensive commissioned oil paintings by the uber-rich. DAG's collection of over 200 such gorgeous artworks from that era made it to Ahmedabad for the first time under the exhibition, *The Babu and the Bazaar: Art from the 19th and early 20th century Bengal.* Interestingly, the Kasturbhai Lalbhai Museum, where the exhibition, curated by Professor Aditi Nath Sarker, was on display (from October to December 2023), called it a return to its roots since the KL Museum acquired its permanent collection from the Tagore family in the 1940s.

Everybody is fascinated by the goddess Kali, her symbolism of power and destruction wowing most. In March 2024, an exhibition by DAG in New Delhi, *Kali: Reverence & Rebellion* covered an entire gamut of the goddess' earliest representations to some of the most famous contemporary works. Curated by Gayatri Sinha, the exhibition featured paintings, prints, and figurines of the Hindu deity across decades and countries, and featured works of artists like Satish Gujral and G R Santosh.

No matter what age, Panchatantra has a home in all our hearts. Imagine taking that love and amalgamating it with one's talent. Artist Debjani Bhardwaj created layered tunnel books taking inspiration from the beloved animal characters of the Panchatantra and creatures of Arabian folklore for 'Immortal Tales,

Fantastical Fables' at Delhi's Threshold Art Gallery in the spring of 2024. Installations included a shadow puppet film on ancient yoga poses. Most of the works comprised of vivid imagery and magical worlds that had the power to shift perspectives and teach lessons from ancient wisdom, layer by layer.

POLITICALLY YOURS

2024: Notes from a Generation, a multi-media collaboration between photographer Prarthna Singh and writer Snigdha Poonam, was displayed from March to May 2024 at Tarq, Mumbai. This project was kicked off in 2019 and in the next five years, travelled to small cities of India, where the duo interviewed and tried to understand the youth's voice of today's India. Through a series of portraits accompanied by powerful soundscapes, the exhibition, curated by Skye Arundhati Thomas, hopes to convey an important message from the younger generation of this nation.

ORIGINALS OR NOT?

Controversy stirred in May 2024 when several artists claimed that over thirty artworks displayed in the exhibition *Nandalal's Mahabharat* were not originals. Art historian Debdutta Gupta, who states his familiarity with Nandalal Bose's Mahabharat series, claimed that the positioning of the seal of the artist seemed wrong in some of the pieces at the Kolkata gallery where the exhibition was held.

Previously, in February 2024, another exhibition, also in Kolkata, had met with the ire of several artists for allegedly displaying fake artworks of the celebrated artist Jamini Roy.

INDIA'S POWER MOVE IN FULL DISPLAY

The fifteenth edition of the India Art Fair (IAF), held in February 2024, was its largest yet, with many firsts. The iconic Carpenters Workshop Gallery with works like Karl Lagerfeld's water fountain and Maarten Baas' single-edition coloured clocks, made its entry to India. A design section was added to the fair for the first time, highlighting the blurring lines between the various disciplines.

India's Northeast found great representation too; the photography and film of Tripura-based collective, Egaro Photo Festival, poignant photographic captures by Sikkim's Kunga Tashi, and performative art from Ziro's Millo Ankha made a solid mark at the fair.

AI AND ART

Artists Madhuban Mitra and Manas Bhattacharya met with grand success at the IAF's PhotoInk booth with 'People Who Do Not Exist', a large-scale work that featured 1,000 portraits of people who 'do not exist'. The AI-generated portraits looked very real and emotive, raising questions about the future of photography and the impact of AI in the field, things that the artists themselves pondered over a ChatGPT-generated message along with the piece.

Protest art also found its way to the IAF, with artist Vikrant Bhise's *Rise of Protest and Request for Justice* series at display by the Delhi-based Anant Art Gallery. His latest artwork, 'We Still Resit (Gaza)' is an ode to the thousands of Palestinian lives lost in the recent conflict.

TEARFUL GOODBYES

November 2023 saw the passing of art historian and critic B. N. Goswamy—a goliath in his field—shortly after the release of his book *The Indian Cat: Stories, Paintings, Poetry, and Proverbs.*

Padma Bhushan awardee A. Ramachandran passed away in February 2024. A prolific painter and master of Indian aesthetics and classical art, Ramachandran was eighty-nine when he died.

By RUNA MUKHERJEE PARIKH

STAR-STUDDED SPECTACLE

The theatre scene sparkled with a lineup that felt like a reunion of the film world's finest. It was a year where names you'd expect on the marquee of cinematic masterpieces took centre stage. Kicking off with a bang, we saw Sarah Jessica Parker, our forever Carrie Bradshaw, team up with the *Godzilla* star Matthew Broderick in Neil Simon's romantic comedy *Plaza Suite*. Movie star Rachel McAdams made her Broadway debut with *Mary Jane*. Meanwhile, the award-winning Sarah Snook, famous for her role in HBO's *Succession*, wowed audiences with a solo performance in a fresh, imaginative adaptation of Oscar Wilde's *The Picture of Dorian Gray*. And let's not forget Dominic West, who has become a household name thanks to his role in Netflix's *The Crown*. He delivered a gripping portrayal in Arthur Miller's *A View from the Bridge*, bringing 1950s Brooklyn to vivid life.

The spotlight also turned to the UK's National Health Services (NHS), with not one but two plays celebrating its legacy. Keeley Hawes, known for her work in the TV spy drama *Spooks*, joined forces with Jack Davenport in *The Human Body*, a poignant postwar romance that delved into the creation of the NHS. Meanwhile, Michael Sheen, who captured hearts as Aro in the *Twilight* series, took on the titular role in *Nye*, portraying the father of the NHS.

REEL-TO-STAGE

2024 also witnessed a wave of films making their way to the stage, predominantly as vibrant musical adaptations. Studio Ghibli's beloved *Spirited Away* made its London debut, featuring a live orchestra and captivating puppets, after enchanting audiences in Japan. Another standout was *The Devil Wears Prada*, which took on a new life as a musical with compositions by none other than Elton John, adding a fresh twist to the iconic tale of high fashion. Stanley Kubrick's celebrated film, *Dr. Strangelove*, made its stage debut—marking the first theatre adaptation of Kubrick—reviving Cold War tensions in a bold new theatrical rendition. Often hailed as a cult classic, *Mean Girls*, originally a book and then a hit film and then a hit Broadway musical, returned with a fresh spin to the West End stage. Joining the lineup of film-inspired transformations was *Starter for Ten*, jumping from David Nicholls's debut novel to the big screen and now lighting up the stage with its vibrant storytelling.

INDIAN THEATRE SCENE

The Indian theatre scene dazzled with productions fearlessly confronting societal challenges. *Raghunath*, an Assamese standout at the Mahindra Excellence in Theatre Awards (META) 2024, brought back the discussion to the poor state of rural India by showcasing a villager's ethical struggle as he is forced to fabricate a story about an ancient deity statue to bring attention and development to his flood-prone Assam village. The story was no different at the National School of Drama's annual theatre festival, Bharat Rang Mahotsav, which marked its twenty-fifth anniversary this year. The twenty-one-day festival began with *Mai Ri Main Ka se Kahoon*, based on Vijaydan Detha's *Duvidha*, which vividly portrays a woman's journey from her parental home to the crematorium, highlighting the oppressive societal expectations she faces at every stage of life. Another notable play from the META scene was *Agnisuta Draupadi*, the story of Draupadi, the daughter of the mighty King Drupad from the Mahabharata, that unfolds through her eyes to question the many paradoxes and ironies of her life. Her quest is the key narrative around which the play revolves.

Among other standout productions, Bengaluru's theatre scene was thrilled by the Bangalore Little Theatre's (BLT) *Arsenic and Old Lace*. This fantastical dark comedy, directed by Kanchan Pandhare, Naimunniusa Khan, and Munavar Syed, captivated young audiences with its sharp wit and humor. Written by Joseph Kesselring in 1939 and popularized by its 1944 film adaptation, the play blends satire with murder.

WORLD THEATRE DAY 2024 CELEBRATIONS

Amidst ongoing discussions about the evolving relevance of theatre, the global community came together to reaffirm its enduring significance on 27 March, known as the World Theatre Day. This annual celebration was marked by theatre enthusiasts, professionals, and institutions worldwide, emphasizing the profound cultural and social impact of this art form. The theme this year, 'Theatre and a Culture of Peace,' resonated deeply, highlighting theatre's role in fostering understanding, dialogue, and harmony across diverse communities. It served as a poignant reminder of theatre's power to transcend boundaries, advocate for social justice, and promote a culture of inclusivity and reconciliation. As performances, workshops, and discussions unfolded across stages and digital platforms, World Theatre Day 2024 underscored the ongoing vitality and relevance of theatre in shaping our shared global narrative.

PUSHING BOUNDARIES AND INNOVATIONS

The theatre landscape has in general been undergoing a transformative shift towards innovation and inclusivity. Predictions suggest that interactive performances will continue to push boundaries by blending audiences and actors through sensory experiences and intimate theatre-in-the-round setups. Future productions may follow the lead of Bridge Command, which immerses audiences in a spaceship mission, or Monopoly Lifesized—a gigantic Monopoly game in the heart of London that brings the board game to life. Virtual reality has also emerged as a game-changer, transporting viewers into immersive worlds via VR headsets and revolutionizing the global theatre experience. Recently, the play *Smile*, based on legendary football manager Jim McLean, was staged at the Dundee Repertory Theatre, where audiences were provided with VR headsets to fully immerse themselves in the world of the play.

In addition to these innovations, 3D projection mapping has redefined set design, allowing for dynamic backgrounds at the touch of a button in productions like *Anastasia* and *The Lion King*. Sustainability has also gained prominence, with theatres embracing eco-friendly practices such as using recycled materials, implementing energy-efficient lighting and sound equipment, and applying biodegradable paints. Subscription plans and customizable tickets, combined with a shift towards paperless operations, have enhanced accessibility. Such changes reflect a broader trend of theatres embracing technology and sustainability to craft memorable global experiences. This is just the beginning, and such innovations are set to become the hallmark of theatre in the future.

By **Anurima Chanda**

NEW DELHI CELEBRATES DIVERSITY AT THE 9TH INDIA INTERNATIONAL DANCE AND MUSIC FESTIVAL

The ninth India International Dance and Music Festival, organized by the Indian Council for Cultural Relations (ICCR), was held in New Delhi on 20 October 2023. This three-day event was a celebration of the harmonious convergence of diverse cultures and traditions. It brought together talented artists from various countries, showcasing the rich cultural tapestry of India and the world. Notable performances included the euphonious music of Elisa Troetsch from Panama and the traditional sword dance Kumpanija from Croatia. The festival promoted cultural interaction and sent a message of peace, providing a platform for artists to share their extraordinary talents.

VAIBHAVA DANCE SCHOOL SHOWCASES CULTURAL HERITAGE WITH 13TH BHARATANATYAM RECITAL

The Vaibhava Dance School, based in Bedford, presented its thirteenth annual Bharatanatyam dance recital, 'Rasa Vaibhava 2024,' on 8 June 2024. The event took place at the John Glenn Middle School in Bedford. The recital was open to the public and free of charge. The theme, *Endearing Traditions of Bharatanatyam,* promised a mesmerizing journey into the essence of Bharatanatyam, a classical Indian dance form known for its expressive hand gestures (mudras), intricate footwork, and captivating storytelling.

The performance was based on the Tamil god Murugan, a Hindu deity revered for his wisdom, bravery, and victory over evil. The recital showcased the growth, progression, dedication, and hard work of the students, with a special segment featuring rhythmic patterns from simple to complex and intricate footwork. This segment highlighted the beautiful interaction between the dancer, percussionist, and conductor, demonstrating years of nurturing, guidance, and hard work from their guru (teacher). The recital was a culmination of the students' year-long learnings, reflecting their unique artistic voices within the framework of Bharatanatyam.

CLASSICAL MUSIC LOSES A GEM: PRABHA ATRE PASSES AWAY

Renowned classical singer and Padma Vibhushan recipient, Prabha Atre, considered the doyenne of the Kirana Gharana, passed away on 13 January 2024 in Pune at ninety-two. She suffered a cardiac arrest in her sleep at her residence. Atre played a significant role in popularizing classical music across the globe during her illustrious career spanning seven decades. Born in September 1932 in Pune, she received her training in classical music from the renowned Sureshbabu Mane, a prominent exponent of the Kirana Gharana. Atre was known for her versatility and innovative approach to Indian classical music. She was equally proficient in different classical genres, be it khyal, tarana, thumri, dadra, ghazal, or bhajan. Her demise is a great loss to the world of Indian classical music.

USHA UTHUP: A BEACON OF JOY AND BROTHERHOOD RECEIVES PADMA BHUSHAN

Veteran singer Usha Uthup, known for her unique voice and captivating performances, expressed immense joy upon receiving the prestigious Padma Bhushan award on 23 April 2024. She described it as the biggest moment of her life, a recognition and appreciation by her country and government. Uthup, who has enthralled audiences with hit songs such as 'Ramba Ho Ho', 'Hari Om Hari', and 'Koi Yahan Aha', among others, remarked on the significance of the award. She stated that while it's natural for classical artists to receive such honours, it's a huge thing for 'ordinary people' like her to be chosen.

Uthup, who believes in peace, brotherhood, and unity, aims to make people smile through her music. Uthup's award is a testament to her significant contribution to the music industry.

PADMA SUBRAHMANYAM: A LIFETIME OF DANCE HONOURED WITH PADMA VIBHUSHAN

Renowned Bharatanatyam dancer Padma Subrahmanyam was conferred with the prestigious Padma Vibhushan award on 26 January 2024. Known for her significant contributions to the field of dance, Subrahmanyam has dedicated her life to the art form, reviving many forgotten elements of Bharatanatyam, including ancient temple dance forms. Born in Chennai in 1943, she started teaching dance at the age of fourteen and has since trained numerous students. Her research into the dance form led to the

discovery that karanas, often considered stationary, had movement and were not just static postures. This revelation transformed the understanding and practice of Bharatanatyam globally. The award is a recognition of her lifelong commitment to dance and her efforts to bring the rich cultural heritage of India to the global stage.

LOLLAPALOOZA INDIA 2024: A GRAND CELEBRATION OF MUSIC AND DIVERSITY

On 27 and 28 January 2024, Mumbai hosted the second edition of Lollapalooza, one of the world's biggest music festivals. The event, held at Mahalaxmi Racecourse, featured an impressive lineup of nearly forty artists performing across four stages. The festival was headlined by the Jonas Brothers, marking their first-ever performance in India, and the legendary musician Sting, who last performed in India in 1980. Other international acts included Lauv, Halsey, OneRepublic, and the Korean indie-rock band The Rose. Indian acts such as When Chai Met Toast, The Raghu Dixit Project, Jatayu, Skrat, Kamakshi Khanna, and JBABE also graced the stage. The festival offered more than just music, with art installations, a Ferris wheel, and a food park featuring over fifty F&B outlets. The event was a testament to the power of music in bringing people together.

By **Namit Hans**

STREAM ON!

With AI (Artificial Intelligence) powered apps dominating the news over the last year, it was no surprise that it would soon make inroads into the music industry as well. We already have AI-generated music creator software, much like AI art generators. Music industry insiders are on both sides of the fence regarding the use of AI in music, with some claiming it will advance creativity while others are concerned about copyright issues. Recently, Canadian rapper Drake released a song, 'Taylor Made Freestyle', that features AI-generated vocals of Tupac Shakur and Snoop Dogg. The song was later taken down following a threat of legal action from Shakur's estate.

A little less cerebral, but probably more practical and newsworthy has been the integration of AI into Spotify and Amazon Music user experiences by generating playlists based on text prompts, which could be anything from genre to mood. Something similar and non-AI driven already exists as users can finetune their listening experience based on their likes and previous streams, not to mention search inputs, so it remains to be seen how different this really will be.

AI or no AI, music streaming services have hit it big. According to the International Federation of the Phonographic Industry (IFPI), streaming subscriptions grew by 11.2 per cent across the world, totalling to more than 500 million subscribers. Music streaming services provided 84 per cent of the recorded music revenues in the US in 2023 and nearly half of the global recorded music revenues. Perhaps deriving inspiration from such figures, Spotify decided to hike their premium subscription rates twice in one year! Music streaming services have also provided independent artists with easy accessibility to a fan base, and they accounted for half the revenue payouts on Spotify.

Amidst all this news about surging music streaming revenues, traditional audio formats, such as vinyl (gramophone records), compact discs (CD), and even the much-hated cassettes are slowly but surely making a comeback with greater sales over the year. Partly driven by nostalgia and partly due to the assurance of having a physical copy of a record, music lovers may find these formats preferable over a playlist on a smartphone that is prone to disappear at any moment.

HITS AND BITS

Two big album releases of 2024 are by the leading female singers of the present day: Taylor Swift's *The Tortured Poets Department* and Beyoncé's *Cowboy Carter*. Other major albums of the year include Dua Lipa's *Radical Optimism* and also releases from veterans Lenny Kravitz and Sheryl Crow. Some of the biggest hits of the year were 'I Had Some Help' by Post Malone featuring Morgan Wallen, 'Not Like Us' by Kendrick Lamar, 'We Can't Be Friends (Wait for Your Love)' by Ariana Grande and 'Carnival' by Kanye West and Ty Dolla $ign.

K-pop continues making it big as the latest *Now That's What I Call Music K-Pop* debuted at number 1 on three Billboard charts. BTS's RM debuted on the Billboard rap album charts at number 1 with *Right Place, Wrong Person*. *Circle* by SHINee's ONEW ranked number 1 on Billboard's top 25 K-pop albums of 2023 in December.

Contemporary classical music is rarely popular but is richly rewarding for its few diehard listeners. New music in this genre includes recordings in the post-minimalism field by Kali Malone and Kelly Moran, a new solo album from the master of minimalism Philip Glass, and recordings from Nils Frahm and Ludovico Einaudi.

In contemporary jazz, one of the best-selling albums has been *Compassion* by Vijay Iyer, Linda May Han Oh, and Tyshawn Sorey. There were also albums by Norah Jones, Matthew Shipp, and Joel Ross.

MUSIC AND EVOLUTION

Scientists at the Max Planck Institute for Psycholinguistics have found strong evidence of 'cross-cultural regularities' in rhythm and melody, in comparison to speech, in an experiment that included well-known songs such as 'Scarborough Fair' and

'Bella Ciao'. It is believed that songs are more predictable because they facilitate social bonding and group singing. Analysing samples of audio excerpts in over fifty languages, it was found that melodies and songs were slower than regular speech while the pitch in music was higher. Scientists believe this will help shed further light on the relationship between the cultural and biological evolution of language and music.

GRAMMY AWARDS

The 2024 Grammy Awards were dominated by female artists. The Record of the Year and Best Pop Solo categories were won by Miley Cyrus for 'Flowers', Taylor Swift won the Album of the Year and Best Pop Vocal Album awards for *Midnights*, Billie Eilish won the Song of the Year award for 'What Was I Made For?' while the Best New Artist Award went to Victoria Monét. Boygenius won the Best Rock Song award for 'Not Strong Enough'.

CAMP AND KITSCH IN EUROPE

For the last few decades, the 'Eurovision Song Contest' has been considered more of a spectacle than a singing competition, and it has had its politics as well, with the Ukraine war and Israel's war on Gaza. The 2024 edition was won by Switzerland for the song 'The Code' by Nemo, although the highlight of the competition was the spectacular performance by Ireland's Bambie Thug and her remarks on Israel.

Those who have passed

- Robbie Robertson (5 July 1943 – 9 August 2023) Member of The Band.
- Goa Gil (11 October 1951 – 26 October 2023) DJ and one of the founders of the Goa trance genre.
- Shane MacGowan (25 December 1957 – 30 November 2023) Irish singer, lead vocalist of The Pogues.
- Frank Farian (18 July 1941 – 23 January 2024) Music producer, founded the disco band Boney M.
- Melanie (3 February 1947 – 23 January 2024) American singer-songwriter.
- Toby Keith (8 July 1961 – 5 February 2024) US country singer.
- Eric Carmen (11 August 1949 – 11 March 2024) Singer-songwriter.
- Steve Albini (22 July 1962 – 7 May 2024) American music producer.

By **Sourav Dutta**

TV LIST (2023–2024)

A great year for television ensued, with all kinds of interesting content getting greenlit by the head honchos of various production companies. Storytelling remained at the forefront along with some amazing acting, sets and overall production quality. With the pandemic well behind us, the audience got a taste of how grand and gorgeous human imagination can be when captured on our television sets (or, ahem, mobile phones).

JAPANESE EPIC BECOMES A RUNAWAY HIT

Away from the typical American setting came a historical drama with a 99 per cent Rotten Tomatoes rating this year. *Shogun*, a Disney+ Hotstar series adapted from the famous James Clavell novel of the same name, shows a feudal Japan of the 1600s, with the dreaded Lord Yoshii Toranaga as the central character. The plot unfurls in an atmospheric setting, with political unrest, enmity, and mayhem at the core of its measured storytelling. Fans of the show fell head over heels with the brilliant dialogues and settings, which were reminiscent of true Japanese culture. A treat to the eyes, *Shogun* was rewarded with two new seasons for its massive success.

FANTASY AHOY!

Fantasy remained a favourite with the Indian youth as a brand-new television series, *Percy Jackson and the Olympians,* made its debut on Disney+ Hotstar in December 2023. Talented young actors donned the role of Percy and his two loyal demi-god companions on the journey to return something valuable to a very angry Greek god residing in Olympia. Just the right amount of mystery and thrills made it a series worth waiting for every week.

In a similar vein, Netflix's *Sweet Tooth* returned to our screens for a third season. Gus, the human-deer hybrid boy, and his comrades set off on an adventure to Alaska. Much like *Percy Jackson*, this lot also faced several villains, with Gus realizing that his purpose in saving the world was much bigger than he thought.

TELEVISION

Now, the fantasy genre is never complete without the presence of author George R.R. Martin, eh? The second season of his Targaryen epic, *House of the Dragon* (HOTD), premiered on HBO in June 2024, appeasing millions of fans after a wait of two years. A prequel to the much-loved series, *Game of Thrones*, HOTD lived up to its name and cult, with each episode setting up the complex characters of Rhaenyra Targaryen and Daemon Targaryen for thunderous action.

UNIQUE AND OH SO FRESH

Amazon Prime presented us with the most unique prank show, *Jury Duty*, where the whole cast and crew were actors and in on a fake legal case except one Ronald Gladden. The unassuming 30-year-old was the star of this reality hoax show, where he was called in for jury duty in a made-up case. Everything that ensued in the proceedings was fake and absolutely hilarious. The fact that a famous actor like James Marsden was part of this jury, along with what one could only define as a wide range of strange, dysfunctional characters, only added to the viral hit show's appeal.

In Hindi, Netflix had its own hit legal comedy series, *Maamla Legal Hai*. The Ravi Kishan-starrer was a series of episodes that threw light on bizarre cases, weird loopholes, and funny legalities of the Indian judicial system. While the cases kept us hooked, the show ran under the able performances of some great comedians and actors who played dysfunctional, envious, and funny lawyers to a tee.

KOREAN DRAMAS, A BALM TO OUR SOULS

Year after year, the makers of Korean dramas prove their mettle by reigning in our hearts with lovely stories that are slice-of-life yet magical. This year too, the audience found a winner in *Twinkling Watermelon*, a story about a young boy with a deep passion for music and a superpower of travelling through time. *Queen of Tears* on Netflix also made for a great watch, depicting a rich wife and a middle-class husband who find their love fading after marriage and later rekindle their romance in the quirky and sweet style of Korean dramas, complete with typical memory losses and mind-blowing cliffhangers in every episode.

BHANSALI'S DIAMONDS SHINE

Hear, hear! Ace Indian filmmaker Sanjay Leela Bhansali made his OTT debut in 2024 with the web series *Heeramandi: The Diamond Bazaar*. Known for his elaborate and opulent sets and attention to detail, Bhansali mounted a historical world of rich nawabs, tawaifs, and English soldiers with a part-real part-fictitious story that evoked equal amounts of passion and nostalgia in its viewers.

The funny man of Indian telly, Kapil Sharma, also made his OTT debut with *The Great Indian Kapil Show* on Netflix. The comedy show, led by him and several star comedians through skits, celebrity interviews, and some stand-up, trended on the global Netflix lists for weeks after its debut. His flavour of fun found takers in other countries too, and guests like Ed Sheeran made it to his popular TV couch!

CRIME AND WEDDINGS ALL THE WAY

Hindi content captivated audiences with a fab combination of storytelling and casting. After the success of *Scam 1992 – The Harshad Mehta Story* in the year 2020, Sony LIV and Hansal Mehta brought us a thrilling peek into the life of yet another scamster in *Scam 2003 – The Telgi Story.* Mehta captured on screen the journey of Abdul Karim Telgi, a fruit seller who became the mastermind behind the infamous Stamp Paper Scam of the 90s, which involved eighteen states of India and led to the arrests of over fifty people, including some very high-ranking officials. With his portrayal of this mammoth scam, Mehta hit it out of the park yet again.

Some of the most interesting stories came out of the crime genre – JioCinema's *Murder in Mahim*, Zee5's *Duranga 2*, Disney+ Hotstar's *Bad Cop*, and the quirky *Guns and Gulaabs* from Netflix, to name a few. The stories were tautly written and had nail-biting thrills, along with brilliant performances by some big names from the Indian film industry, like Rajkummar Rao, Anurag Kashyap, and Ashutosh Rana. Interestingly, actor Gulshan Devaiah starred in *Duranga 2*, *Bad Cop* and *Guns and Gulaabs*, proving his prowess in a myriad of acting roles.

And finally, the much-awaited Amazon Prime series on Indian weddings, *Made in Heaven*, released its second season in August 2023. A story about two friends who start a wedding planning agency in Delhi and, through its many ceremonies, expose the uncomfortable truth about the society we live in, was lapped up by the audience in its debut season in 2019. The second instalment took its own sweet time to be made. However, it met with glowing reviews for its very real take on subjects like caste, gender, fashion, and class.

IT'S A LOVE STORY!

The young adult genre had a roaring success with several massive hits. Adaptions from YA novels ruled the roost with Jenny Han's *The Summer I Turned Pretty* (season 2 adapted from the book *It's Not Summer Without You*), Ali Novak's *My Life with the Walter Boys*, and Holly Smale's *Geek Girl*—all being turned into shows by Amazon

Prime and Netflix. *Geek Girl*, with its beloved protagonist Harriet Manners, gave us all the things we love – high school, fashion, and a story of self-discovery.

And the super cute heartthrobs of TSITP, *XO Kitty*, and *My Life with the Walter Boys* didn't disappoint either. These boy-meets-girl stories were swoon-worthy, and the novelty didn't wear off even when we had to witness love triangles one too many!

Fans of the *Bridgerton* series on Netflix (also adapted from the book series by the same name) got to see the love story of the scribe Lady Whistledown play out this year. As most of us already knew, Penelope Featherington, neighbour and childhood friend to both Eloise and Colin Bridgerton, turned out to be the face behind the gossip journalist in the last season of the show. Even then, our hearts were not ready for the scandal that broke out when Penelope's love match clashed with her professional identity. Made in true Shonda Rhimes style, this series truly keeps getting better!

DOCUMENTARIES THAT TUGGED AT THE HEART

It rained special documentaries this year, leading with Vinay Shukla's *While We Watched*. It was released in India on MUBI and captivated people with its realness. Following the work and life of the Ramon Magsaysay Award-winning Indian journalist Ravish Kumar, the documentary simultaneously showed how the fourth estate of the nation found itself in the throes of radical change. This documentary went on to win the Peabody Award for Best Documentary in 2024.

In sports, the original G.O.A.T of tennis, Roger Federer, made a tear-jerker of a documentary titled *Federer: Twelve Final Days*. Readying for his last tournament, the 2022 Laver Cup, the Swiss great's heartfelt documentary on Amazon Prime has been termed subtle, sad, and beautiful in equal measure by reviewers. It offered fans many unknown nuggets, about how Federer hurt his right knee, when he decided to retire, and some heartfelt bytes from his wife Mirka, competing greats Rafael Nadal and Novak Djokovic, among others. An absolute must-watch.

Another documentary about another sports legend, *Shooting Stars* captures the life of basketball icon LeBron James and his buddies Lil Dru, Willie McGee, and Sian Cotton. The biographical drama covers the highs and lows of the 'Fab Four', who discover the value of true friendship through life's many challenges. The story gives a glimpse into the life of a young LeBron, which is special on its own accord.

By **Runa Mukherjee Parikh**

SPORTS

It was a year of more hits than misses in global sports. From remarkable performances in the Asian Games by an enthusiastic Indian contingent to a heartbreaking end to the much-fancied ICC ODI World Cup, from a remarkable turnaround for a famed franchise in the Women's Premier League to a yet another EPL trophy for Pep Guardiola's Manchester City—the world of sports had everything to offer to its ardent viewers.

CRICKET: MEN'S

ASIA CUP

India were consistent and clinical in the 2023 Asia Cup. While the high-octane India-Pakistan was marred by rain on the scheduled fixture, the reserve day served everything a die-hard fan could have asked for. India progressed to the finals after decimating all its opponents, and the stage was set for a 10-wicket drubbing of Sri Lanka in which Mohammed Siraj ripped through the line-up to register his career best figure of 6/21, in the process also becoming the first Indian to take 4 wickets in an over.

ICC ODI WC

The stage was set for an encore of the 2011 edition of the marquee event in the world of cricket. India capitalized on the home advantage, as the No. 1 ODI side in the world stomped its way into the knockout stage through all-round performances on the field. While skipper Rohit Sharma and Virat Kohli ensured the batting department was solid, Mohammed Shami and Jasprit Bumrah kept opponents in their dugouts. However, the fairytale ended in a heartbreak after Australia outclassed the star-studded Indian team in front of a packed stadium in Ahmedabad.

ICC T20I WC

India's long wait of eleven years for an ICC trophy finally ended with a clinical victory in the T20 World Cup held in the US and West Indies. A redemption of sorts for skipper Rohit Sharma, the Men in Blue ticked all boxes to decimate all opposition teams. This trophy also draws the curtains on a stellar career for Rohit Sharma, Virat Kohli and Ravindra Jadega - the backbone of the Indian team - in the 20-over format. Head coach Rahul Dravid also signed off his national duties with a much-awaited ICC crown.

IND VS ENGLAND TEST SERIES

The Barmy Army came with the reputation of Bazball—a fearless brand of cricket perpetuated by England men's coach Brendon McCullum. However, the spotlight quickly shifted from a star-studded English line-up led by Ben Stokes and Joe Root to India's young guns Yashasvi Jaiswal and Sarfaraz Khan. And with Jasprit Bumrah in the team, India handed out a drubbing to the visiting side, winning the five match Test series by a thumping 4-1 margin.

RANJI TROPHY

The 2023-24 domestic season—the 89th Ranji Trophy—began with Saurashtra as the defending champions. However, as the tournament progressed, the tenacity and class of record winners Mumbai came to the fore. Led by Ajinkya Rahane, the iconic team lifted its 42nd title, backed by impactful performances by Shardul Thakur in the semis and Musheer Khan in the final.

WTC 2023-25

The 2023–25 ICC World Test Championship began with The Ashes [between England and Australia] in June 2023 and will conclude with the final at the Lord's stadium in England in June 2025. As per the current standings, India is the No. 1 Test side in the world, sitting comfortably at the top with 68.52 per cent of wins, ahead of Australia with 62.50 per cent. Yashasvi Jaiswal has scored the most runs in the current cycle, with a staggering 1,028 runs at an average of 68.53, powered by two double centuries against England in 2024.

IPL 2024

The stage was set for a historic clash of titans at the biggest cricketing league in the world as bidding at record prices, never heard before in the history of the sport, brought some of the biggest names in world cricket to India. While the return of Hardik Pandya to Mumbai Indians, replacing national captain Rohit Sharma, was rejected by the fans, the return of Gautam Gambhir to the Kolkata Knight Riders flipped a switch for Shah Rukh Khan's two-time champion team. With clinical performances in all three departments—batting, bowling, fielding—KKR raided the den of every opponent and held fort bravely at the Eden Gardens. Led by a firing Sunil Narine and with the injection of Aussie spearhead Mitchell Starc, KKR lifted its third IPL title in front of a packed Chepauk crowd in Chennai.

CRICKET: WOMEN'S

WPL 2024

The second edition of the Women's Premier League drew a larger crowd than in 2023, with new players added by the five franchises. National women's captain Harmanpreet Kaur had a less-than-stellar campaign as the Mumbai Indians lost some close matches. However, national women's vice-captain Smriti Mandhana led her team to the finals with excellent captaincy, supported by Aussie all-rounder Ellyse Perry. The final saw Mandhana's team face veteran Australian captain Meg Lanning. Mandhana's leadership and Perry's skills helped the Royal Challengers Bengaluru win their maiden WPL title.

IND-W VS SA-W: ONE-OFF TEST

India and South Africa faced-off for a solitary Test match in Chepauk Stadium in Chennai on 28 June in what was expected to be a cracker of an encounter, especially with star player Smriti Mandhana in prime form. India won the toss and batted first, as openers Shafali Verma and Mandhana stitched together a record partnership. Both went on to score centuries, with Shafali scoring her maiden century and that too a double ton. India posted a mammoth total of 603/6 before declaring the innings and putting SA to chase a never-before-achieve target. It was now the turn of ace off-spinner Sneh Rana to bamboozle the South African line-up, picking up a 10-wicket haul, as India routed its opponent to take home a 10-wicket victory.

FOOTBALL

EURO 2024

The Spanish dominance in world football is back! The tiki-taka glory days seemed forgotten as Spain struggled in recent Euros and World Cups. With star retirements and administrative changes, a young team under coach Luis de la Fuente excelled in possession football, forcing opponents into errors. Despite a strong challenge from England in the final in Berlin, Spain triumphed, reigniting their passion for the game. This Spanish team is poised to be a dominant force for the next decade. Special mention to Cristiano Ronaldo and Luka Modrić, who likely played their last major tournament.

ENGLISH PREMIER LEAGUE

The 2023-24 Premier League season saw Manchester City being crowned champions for a record fourth consecutive time. While the title race went down to the wire, City scraped towards the end and finished just two points ahead of a raging Arsenal. City's Erling Haaland won the 'Golden Boot', while his teammate Phil Foden won the 'Player of the Year' award. Cole Palmer of Chelsea took home the 'Young Player of the Year' award in his impressive debut season. Arsenal and

Manchester City dominated the 'Team of the Season', while Chelsea had a rollercoaster season, managing to secure a Europa Conference League spot with a late surge.

LA LIGA

Real Madrid dominated the 2023-24 La Liga season, clinching their 36th league title with as many as four matches to spare.

Real Madrid finished the season as champions with a comfortable lead over their rivals, while Jude Bellingham scripted an iconic debut campaign for Real Madrid. Overall, it was a season that saw Real Madrid's dominance continue, while several young talents emerged and made their mark on the league.

SERIE A

Inter Milan clinched their 20th league title with five matches to spare, finishing the season with 94 points, 17 clear of arch rivals AC Milan. Inter's Lautaro Martínez was the league's top goal scorer with 24 goals, while Spanish national goalkeeper Unai Simón of Athletic Bilbao had the cleanest sheets with 17 saves.

BUNDESLIGA

Bayer Leverkusen had a dream run in the last Bundesliga season, becoming the champions unbeaten and ending the campaign with twenty-eight wins (a record) and six draws under the guidance of coach Xabi Alonso. In the process, they also set a club-record of ten consecutive Bundesliga wins. Veteran footballer Thomas Müller became the first league player to score in fifteen different Bundesliga seasons for Bayern Munich.

FA CUP

Manchester City and Manchester United set up a classic derby clash in the 2024 FA Cup final at the Wembley Stadium in London. After a hard-fought contest, Manchester United emerged winners, securing their 13th FA Cup title with a final score of 2-1, thanks to goals from Alejandro Garnacho and Kobbie Mainoo.

LAWN TENNIS

US OPEN 2023

The 2023 US Open began on 28 August and concluded on 10 September. Local girl Coco Gauff stormed her way into the finals and beat the big serving Belarusian Aryna Sabalenka 2–6, 6–3, 6–2 to become the women's singles champion. Modern day legend and Serbian juggernaut Novak Djokovic defeated Daniil Medvedev 6–3, 7–6(7–5), 6–3 to pick up his fourth title at the US Open.

AUSTRALIAN OPEN 2024

The 2024 Australian Open was a marquee moment for all Indians after our very own Rohan Bopanna and his partner Matthew Ebden won their first Grand Slam together in Men's Doubles. Bopanna became the oldest player in the Open Era to win a Grand Slam and also the oldest to become No. 1 in Doubles rankings. Jannik Sinner of Italy was the winner in the Men's Singles category while Belarusian Aryna Sabalenka won the Women's Singles title.

FRENCH OPEN 2024

Young tennis sensation from Spain Carlos Alcaraz Garfia won the clay court Slam in the Men's Singles category, beating Alexander Zverev of Germany 6-3, 2-6, 5-7, 6-1, 6-2. In the Women's Singles category, World No. 1 Iga Świátek of Poland beat Italian Jasmine Paolini in straight sets (6-2, 6-1) to bag her fourth title at Roland Garros. This could have also well been the final appearance of Spanish legend of clay court Rafael Nadal, though he has not officially announced his retirement from tennis!

WIMBLEDON 2024

The world of men's tennis may have witnessed a change of guard as Carlos Alcaraz successfully defended his title becoming the youngest player in the Open Era to defend his Rolland Garros and Wimbledon titles. The final was a clear indicator of how fast this game as evolved, as a twenty-one-year-old Alcaraz decimated twenty-four-time Grand Slam winner Novak Djokovic in straight sets, winning the encounter 6-2, 6-2, 7-6. In the women's tie, Czech player Barbora Krejčiková defeated Italian sensation Jasmine Paolini 6-2, 2-6, 6-4 to lift her second Grand Slam title.

ATHLETICS

ASIAN GAMES 2023

Indian athletes put up a stupendous performance in the 19th Asian Games, held in Hangzhou, China, with a record haul of 107 medals—28 gold, 38 silver, and 41 bronze, crossing the three-figure mark for the first time in the Asian Games history. With this, the Indian contingent bettered its previous best tally of 70 medals, including 16 gold, at the 2018 Asian Games in Jakarta, Indonesia. Our athletes excelled in almost all disciplines, especially in the track and field categories.

PAAVO NURMI GAMES 2024

India's golden boy and ace javelin thrower Neeraj Chopra proved his mettle at the

Paavo Nurmi Games 2024 in Turku, Finland by bagging yet another gold medal with a throw of 85.97 mts in his third attempt. This victory was crucial as he came back from a brief precautionary break in preparation for his Gold Medal defence at the Paris Olympics 2024.

ASIAN GYMNASTICS CHAMPIONSHIPS

Dipa Karmakar created history at the Asian Gymnastics Championships in May 2024, held in Uzbekistan's Tashkent, winning the Gold Medal, becoming the first Indian gymnast to achieve this feat at the Asian championships. Earlier, gymnasts from India had won four bronze medals in the championships, but the 30-year-old's historic win has broken grounds for more focus on India's gymnastics arena.

ASIAN PARA GAMES

The Asian Para Games 2023, held in October in Hangzhou, China, saw the Indian contingent perform tremendously well, bagging a medal tally of 111 (best ever), including 29 gold, 31 silver, and 51 bronze medals. This performance surpassed our previous record of 72 medals (15 gold) at the 2018 Games.

YOUTH WORLD WEIGHTLIFTING CHAMPIONSHIPS

Child weightlifting sensation Priteesmita Bhoi set a youth world record at the Youth World Weightlifting Championships in Lima, Peru in May 2024 by lifting 76 kg in the Clean-and-Jerk category. She became the first Indian weightlifter to win a Gold medal and title in this discipline, creating history and setting the future secure for our every child who aspires to be a sportsperson.

MIXED MARTIAL ARTS

Puja Tomar, nicknamed 'The Cyclone', is a strawweight MMA fighter who became the first woman from India to win the Ultimate Fighting Championship, defeating Rayanne dos Santos of Brazil at the UFC Louisville in June. She has an impressive professional record of 9 wins against 4 losses, and has lately made significant progress in her professional career.

PARIS OLYMPICS 2024 (JULY UPDATES)

The 2024 Summer Olympics, held in Paris from 24 July till 11 August 2024, marked the 100th anniversary of the games being hosted by the French capital city. Indian athletes such as 'boy with the golden arm' Neeraj Chopra (javelin), star shooter Manu Bhaker (10-metre air pistol), ace pugilist Lovlina

Borgohain (women's middleweight boxing), PV Sindhu, Lakshya Sen, Chirag Shetty and Satwiksairaj Rankireddy (all badminton), Deepika Kumari (archery), Manika Batra (table tennis), and Vinesh Phogat (wrestling) are some of the sporting icons who have brought glory to our nation for several years and we will continue to root for them for many more Olympic games.

BADMINTON

THAILAND OPEN 2024

Power packed Indian shuttle pair Chirag Shetty and Satwiksairaj Rankireddy yet again proved why they are the best by winning the Thailand Open 2024 in the Men's Doubles category, decimating the attacking Chinese pair Chen Bo Yang and Liu Yi in just 46 minutes with a scoreline of 21-15, 21-15. This was their second title of the 2024 season after remaining unbeaten in the BWF Super 500 finals. They are currently the No. 1 ranked men's pair in World Badminton.

CHESS

Indian chess prodigy Rameshbabu Praggnanandhaa beat world champion Magnus Carlsen at the Norway Chess 2024 to secure his first ever classical 'over the board' victory against the Norwegian. The Indian grandmaster made it even more special as this was his first victory against Carlsen after three draws and one defeat in the run up to this competition.

Dommaraju Gukesh became the youngest contender for the World Chess Champion title after winning the 2024 Candidates Tournament in April. He was in searing form, winning five games, and losing only one, barring eight draws. His consistent performances took him to a career-high ranking of World No. 6 in May this year, and he is just 18-years-old!

HOCKEY

WOMEN'S HOCKEY – PARIS OLYMPICS QUALIFIER

The 2024 Women's FIH Olympic Qualifiers ended on a disappointing note as our valiant Indian contingent went down fighting to Japan 0-1 in Ranchi in front of a packed home crowd. The qualifiers were held in Spain's Valencia, other than Ranchi, from January 13-20. Belgium, Germany, Spain, Japan, the United States and Great Britain are the six teams that sealed their spots for the main draw.

By MURUKESH KRISHNAN

ABOUT THE CONTRIBUTORS

Thirumoy Banerjee is a journalist with over thirteen years of experience. He has worked with leading media houses in the country, including The Times of India, Business Standard, Press Trust of India, The Indian Express, and The Telegraph. He has translated a book (*Yamraaj 5003*) from Odia to English, and has been a visiting faculty at premier institutes, including the Indian Institute of Mass Communication, several DU colleges, and Bharatiya Vidya Bhavan (Kolkata), among others. He has been contributing to the Scholastic Yearbook since 2019 and can be reached on X (formerly Twitter) and Instagram at @thiru_the_moy.

Dr Anurima Chanda is currently an Assistant Professor in the Department of English of Birsa Munda College, University of North Bengal. She completed her PhD in Indian English Children's Literature from Jawaharlal Nehru University. She was a pre-doctoral DAAD fellow at the University of Würzburg, Germany, and a SUSI 2023 Fellow at the University of Montana. She is also a literary translator and a children's author.

Namit Hans is an academic researcher and writer. He has worked as a journalist with organizations like Indian Express and has taught Mass Communication at University of Delhi. He continues to write for various organizations.

Murukesh Krishnan is a journalist with over twelve years of experience in reporting and editing on politics, current affairs, foreign affairs, business, and sports, across various vibrant newsrooms such as Hindustan Times, Times Now, and India Today. A polyglot, he spends his spare time learning new Indian languages as he believes there lies the fabric of our nation. You can reach him at: *krishnanmurukesh@gmail.com*.

Runa Mukherjee Parikh is an independent journalist with over fifteen years of experience in writing on education, art and pop culture for both national and foreign publications. She has reported for media mammoths like Times of India and India Today. Runa has also authored a collection of six short stories on new age relationships titled *Your Truth, My Truth* in 2017 and made a documentary about the economic after-effects of the pandemic on the idol makers of Kolkata titled *Mother will Arrive* in 2021.

Milan Jacob George is a multimedia storyteller. With an interdisciplinary background, he has collaborated with researchers, filmmakers, artists, and development practitioners to raise awareness and inspire action on climate change, sustainable development, and public health-related issues. He currently works as a Communications Specialist at the Council on Energy, Environment and Water (CEEW), a New Delhi-based policy research institution.

Sandhya Ramesh is a senior editor of science at *ThePrint*. Her work focuses on all kinds of science, especially in the Indian subcontinent. She loves to write and create videos about space and astronomy. She can be reached on X (formerly Twitter) at @ sandygrains.

Vikram Hegde has been practising as a lawyer at the Supreme Court of India. He regularly writes on legal issues for various media outlets.

Shomini Sen has over fourteen years of experience in the media industry. A film critic and journalist at WION currently, she has worked with CNN News18, Zee News, and Times Group in the past.

Sourav Dutta has worked with numerous Indian and international publishing and media houses, including Oxford University Press, Tehelka, Down to Earth, and many others. He is also a writer for graphic novels and comic books.